STREETWISE®

D0520856

BUSINESS VALUATION

Proven Methods to Easily
Determine the True Value of Your Business

HEATHER SMITH LINTON, CERTIFIED VALUATION ANALYST

Adams Media
Avon, Massachusetts

A Streetwise® Publication.
Streetwise® is a registered trademark of F+W Publications, Inc.

Published by Adams Media, an F+W Publications Company
57 Littlefield Street, Avon, MA 02322 U.S.A.
www.adamsmedia.com

ISBN: 1-58062-952-0

Printed in the United States of America.

J I H G F E D C B A

Library of Congress Cataloging-in-Publication Data
Linton, Heather.
Streetwise business valuation / Heather Linton.
p.   cm.
ISBN 1-58062-952-0
1. Business enterprises--Valuation. 2. Small business--Valuation.
I. Title: Business valuation. II. Title.
HF5681.V3L56 2004
658.15--dc22
2003015206

This publication is designed to provide accurate and authoritative information with regard to the subject matter covered. It is sold with the understanding that the publisher is not engaged in rendering legal, accounting, or other professional advice. If legal advice or other expert assistance is required, the services of a competent professional person should be sought.
— From a *Declaration of Principles* jointly adopted by a Committee of the American Bar Association and a Committee of Publishers and Associations

This publication is intended to provide current and prospective business owners with useful information that may assist them in preparing for and obtaining business capital loans and investment funding. This information is general in nature and is not intended to provide specific advice for any individual or business entity. While the information contained herein should be helpful to the reader, appropriate financial, accounting, tax, or legal advice should always be sought from a competent professional engaged for any specific situation regarding your enterprise.

Many of the designations used by manufacturers and sellers to distinguish their products are claimed as trademarks. Where those designations appear in this book and Adams Media was aware of a trademark claim, the designations have been printed in initial capital letters.

Cover illustration by Eric Mueller.

This book is available at quantity discounts for bulk purchases. For information, call 1-800-872-5627.

Contents

Contents

Dedication

This book is dedicated to the memory of my parents,
Ann L. Smith and Hector W. Smith.

Acknowledgments

I thank my friends and family for supporting me through the process of writing this book, or at least not disowning me. I look forward to being the good friend, niece, cousin, and sister you all deserve. I especially appreciate everyone at Linton & Associates, PA, for working hard to get the job done at the office while I was working on the book. Special thanks to my agent, Jessica Faust, of Bookends, LLC, whose encouragement, support, professionalism, and sense of humor got me through this project.

Preface

The working title for this book has been *Streetwise® Business Valuation for the Busy Business Owner.* The alliteration brings to mind the image of business owners working like busy bees *in* their companies rather than *on* them. When we work in our businesses rather than on them, we often get mired in the details and lose sight of the big picture. Most entrepreneurs start companies with the goal of growing their business to either sell it or pass it down to the next generation. However, if we don't focus on increasing the value of our companies and measuring that increase, we may not achieve our ultimate and most important goal. This book is for the business owner who is ready to step away from the daily fray and focus on value creation. This book is also for the business owner who *needs* to know what his or her business is worth for tax, divorce, or other potentially adversarial purposes. You will also learn why you may still want to hire a professional to value your company in some of these situations.

You will learn the basic valuation techniques that the professionals use to value closely held companies, and, perhaps more important, you will discover all the financial and nonfinancial components of value. You can use this information not only to determine what your company is worth today, but also to increase the value of your company going forward. You will also find that your business has different values for different purposes. For example, the value of your company for divorce purposes would not be the same as the asking price in a sale situation.

What about all the complicated formulas and mathematical calculations involved in valuing a business? I started out life as a philosophy and art history major who avoided any books like this with scary mathematical symbols that I didn't understand. Consequently, I have tried to break down all of the calculations to their simplest forms and discuss them in terms of the basic algebra we all studied in high school. If you have a financial calculator, you can make most of the calculations very simply by punching in a few numbers, which will allow you to gloss over all of the algebra. In any case, if I can do it, you can do it.

Since my liberal arts days, I have gotten an M.B.A. and several certifications related to my practice as a C.P.A., including becoming a certified valuation analyst (C.V.A.). I have been working with closely held businesses and their owners for more than twenty years and have had my own company for fifteen years. I confess that I have spent most of those fifteen years working *in* my business rather than *on* it because I enjoy what I do, helping clients realize their personal and business goals. As I have had more opportunities to work with clients valuing their businesses, I have seen the importance of working *on* the business as well as the importance of measuring the value of the business so we can manage our progress toward our big-picture goals. I hope this book will inspire you to focus on the long-term goal of creating value in your business by starting to measure it.

> **Chapter 1**

Overview of Business Valuation

Part One

Part Two

Part Three

Part Four

Part Five

Part Six

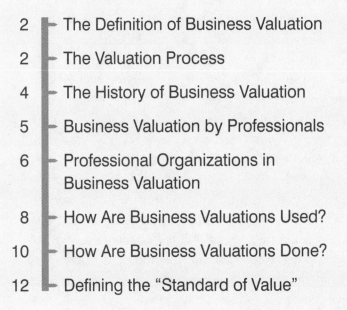

The Definition of Business Valuation

Business valuation is the process that is used to determine the financial worth of a closely held company. For large, widely held companies that sell shares of their stock on an open market such as the New York Stock Exchange (NYSE) or the National Association of Securities Dealers Automated Quotation System (NASDAQ), determining the value of a company is a relatively simple matter. The economics of the free market system and the laws of supply and demand determine the price of the stock. Once you know the price per share, you simply multiply that price by the total outstanding shares of stock to arrive at the value of the company.

If, on the other hand, you are an owner, or prospective owner, of closely held company stock, you do not have the luxury of multiplying one known number by another known number to arrive at the value of your company because the stock price is not listed anywhere. So how do you come up with the value of the business?

The process that you, or a professional business valuator, uses to value closely held businesses is just that—a process. The business valuation process often appears to be more art than science; this is despite the fact that you frequently need to use a number of complicated calculations.

You may be tempted to apply a "rule of thumb" method or just perform a few quick calculations from one of various methodologies to come up with a quick value. However, such a shortcut method may result in short-changing yourself on the true value of your business; it also may provide a figure that will not stand up under IRS scrutiny or possible litigation.

The Valuation Process

The process begins with first understanding the company you are valuing. If you own the company, you know more about it than anyone else, but you still need to go through the basic steps to arrive at a supportable value. The basic steps in valuing a business are:

- Determining the purpose of the business valuation
- Analyzing the company's financial statements
- Analyzing comparative and statistical information

- Analyzing external and internal qualitative factors
- Using business valuation methods to calculate the value
- Determining appropriate discounts and premiums

Part Two of this book discusses many of the purposes for business valuation. You are probably already familiar with the most common ones: buying or selling a business, estate planning and estate tax returns, and divorce situations. Have you thought about strategic planning, buy-sell agreements, insurance planning, and bankruptcy? You will learn about these different reasons to value your business and how the purpose of the valuation actually affects the value itself.

You may look at your company's financial statements everyday, but do you analyze them? Many business owners have one or two numbers that they focus on to let them know how the company is doing. This may work for managing your business on a day-to-day basis, but it is not enough to determine the value of your company. You will need to get out your calculator and crunch some numbers. This process will help you better understand your financial statements and your company. Even if you are not actually selling the business, the information you get from this part of the process can be very helpful in managing the company going forward.

Using Information to Strategic Advantage

After you have learned everything you can from your own financial statements, you will use that information to compare to other companies and to the industry as a whole. It can be an eye-opening experience to discover how you stack up against the competition. In addition to using this information to arrive at a value for your company, you can also learn from it and use it as a management tool to set performance goals for the future.

Once you "know everything" about your company from a financial standpoint, you will have to consider how some

What Is a Closely Held Business?

Closely held businesses are companies that are owned and managed by a relatively small number of individuals or family members. However, a closely held business is not necessarily a "small business." Many closely held companies have billions in sales or assets. For example, the Mars Corporation, makers of M&M's, started in the early 1920s by selling buttercream candies door to door. Mars is now a $14 billion global business with operations in the food, pet care, drinks, vending, and electronics sectors. The organization of a closely held business can run the gamut of sole proprietorship, partnership, limited liability company, S corporation, or C corporation. In addition, the financial and tax situation of the owner or owners is directly influenced by what happens at the company level. The reverse is often also true—the financial health of the individual owners often has an impact on the company's financial health.

qualitative factors might impact your business and, therefore, its value. For instance, what is happening with the economy, nationally and locally? Is the market consolidating, becoming more global, or franchising? Will changing technology and regulations affect your business? What is the competition doing? Are you seeing new entrants into the market? Again, the answers to these questions will not only help you value your company, but will also help with the strategic planning process.

The Five Basic Methods

After you have a thorough knowledge of the business you are valuing and the industry and economic environment in which it operates, you can start calculating the value of the company. In this book, you will learn how to use the five basic valuation methods and how to choose the appropriate method for your situation. The five basic methods and the chapters where you will learn how to apply them are:

- Adjusted Net Assets Method—Chapter 10
- Capitalization of Earnings Method—Chapter 11
- Excess Earnings Method—Chapter 12
- Discounted Cash Flow Method—Chapter 13
- Rule of Thumb Methods—Chapter 14

The History of Business Valuation

Business valuation emerged as a specialized professional service in the 1920s with the advent of Prohibition. The Eighteenth Amendment, enacted in 1919, prohibited the manufacture, distribution, and sale of alcoholic beverages. Businesses such as breweries, distilleries, saloons, and wholesalers and retailers of alcoholic beverages needed to value their businesses so they could calculate their losses for tax purposes.

Since the 1920s, and especially since the latter part of the twentieth century, the need for business valuations has mushroomed and thereby created a demand for valuation professionals. In addition to the reasons for business valuation mentioned above, developments that have fueled the growth of the business valuation profession include: corporate spinoffs, initial public offerings (IPOs), shareholder disputes, compensatory damage cases, employee stock ownership plans (ESOPs), and increases in general litigation. In the current litigious environment, the business valuation professional must not only value a company, but also must be prepared to defend his or her value and methodology in a court of law.

Business Valuation by Professionals

A variety of professionals perform business valuations, but the field is becoming more specialized. Chapter 24 will go into more detail about the different types of professionals who perform business valuations and how to choose the best one for your situation. Historically, business brokers, accountants, lawyers, and bankers have helped their clients by performing valuation services. The services that these professionals can provide with their normal level of education, experience, and training is generally limited to helping to set or negotiate a sales or purchase price for a business.

Business brokers are the most "in-touch" with the market and probably have the best sense of what businesses sell for in certain areas. However, since they make their money by selling and buying businesses, they are rarely trained to perform full valuations that would hold up in court.

Accountants—especially CPAs—have the necessary training to analyze the financial statements and make the calculations necessary to do a business valuation. However, general practitioners often do not have the time or the inclination to do the market research and analysis of the qualitative factors that are an important component of a full valuation report. Many CPAs are starting to specialize in this field and acquire the additional training necessary to serve as a full-service valuation professional.

Commercial bankers usually look at the value of business from the standpoint of whether the company can pay back any loans. They are less concerned with what the present value is than they are with future cash flows. However, bankers are usually experienced with actual sales transactions and have access to a lot of good information that can be very helpful when setting a price for your business or trying make an offer on another. Lawyers have gotten into the business valuation arena mainly through their ability to help their clients negotiate the purchase or sale of a business.

> Historically, business brokers, accountants, lawyers, and bankers have helped their clients by performing valuation services.

Through this experience, they may have a sense of the type of deals that have been made in a particular area. However, lawyers in general do not have the financial skills or training to perform a rigorous valuation.

Professional Organizations in Business Valuation

As the demand for professional valuation services has increased, individuals from these professions and others have sought additional training to become qualified business valuation professionals. Even though more professionals are specializing in business valuation, they each will still have particular areas of expertise and experience that make them more qualified for certain types of business valuation services. Consequently, several professional organizations certify and regulate the business valuation profession. The courts, the business community, and the Internal Revenue Service have significantly increased their reliance on and recognition of these professional organizations and their professional standards over the last ten years. This positive trend of growing professionalism in the business valuation and appraisal industry has been accompanied by a proliferation of different standards, which has produced some confusion. The primary professional organizations in the business valuation field include:

- The Appraisal Foundation
- National Association of Certified Valuation Analysts (NACVA)
- The American Society of Appraisers (ASA)
- The Institute of Business Appraisers (IBA)
- American Institute of CPAs (AICPA)
- Canadian Institute of Chartered Business Valuators (CICBV)

Leading professional appraisal organizations established the Appraisal Foundation in 1987 (in the aftermath of the savings and loan scandals of the early 1980s) in order to implement uniform standards for business appraisers. Substandard and unprofessional appraisals caused many banks and lending institutions to lose a great deal of money during this crisis. The Appraisal Foundation is a nonprofit educational organization comprised of other organizations; it oversees the work of the Appraiser Qualifications Board (AQB) and the Appraisal Standards Board (ASB). The ASB issued the Uniform Standards of Professional Appraisal Practice (USPAP) in 1989. Although these standards are becoming generally accepted, many business valuation professionals feel that they are more appropriate for real estate rather than business valuation engagements.

The **National Association of Certified Valuation Analysts (NACVA)** provides a certification program for business valuation professionals who already possess the CPA certification. Certified valuation analysts (CVAs) must adhere to NACVA's standards for professional practice and report writing as well as take continuing professional education courses to maintain and expand their expertise. CVAs generally specialize in the valuation of closely held businesses.

The **American Society of Appraisers (ASA)** provides certifications for appraisers of real estate, business equipment and machinery, gems and jewelry, and personal property, as well as business valuations. Accredited members (AM) and accredited senior appraisers (ASA) must pass comprehensive examinations, submit appraisal reports for review, and meet experience requirements of two years for accredited members and five years for accredited senior appraisers. In addition, accredited members and accredited senior appraisers must comply with the American Society of Appraisers Business Valuation Standards, which incorporate the Uniform Standards of Professional Appraisal Practice (USPAP).

Members of the **Institute of Business Appraisers (IBA)** specialize in the valuation of small to medium-size businesses. IBA members can become either certified business appraisers (CBA) or business valuation accredited for litigation (BVAL) by passing tests and submitting valuation reports. They must also comply with yet another set of professional standards. The IBA standards include most of the concepts of USPAP, but IBA members are not required to comply with USPAP.

The Uses of USPAP

Professional appraisers use the Uniform Standards of Professional Appraisal Practice (USPAP) to guide them in performing appraisals and business valuations. Federal and state regulatory agencies and the court system also rely on USPAP when they are trying to determine the validity of appraisals or business valuations. These organizations may disregard or discredit an appraisal that did not meet USPAP standards. Although some professional valuation organizations, such as the American Society of Appraisers, have adopted USPAP as part of the professional standards to which their members must adhere, not all valuation organizations have followed suit. This produces a dilemma for valuation professionals who are complying with the standards of their respective organization, which may not be in compliance with USPAP. In addition, USPAP is a continually evolving document with more than seventeen Amendments, ten Statements on Appraisal Standards, and more than twenty-three Advisory Opinions.

The **American Institute of CPAs** is of course the umbrella organization for all CPAs, but the organization also offers a specialty designation in business valuation: accredited in business valuation (ABV). To achieve this status, CPAs must complete more than fifteen days of course work, take a one-day exam, and perform at least ten business valuations.

The **Canadian Institute of Chartered Business Valuators (CICBV)** is the largest professional valuation organization in Canada. The CICBV, established in 1971 to provide professionalism in the business valuation field, offers training and certification to chartered business valuators (CBV) who must also comply with the organization's standards.

Business valuation has come from being an ancillary service provided by another professional to the point where specialized business valuation professionals are held accountable to high professional standards by their own organizations, the court system, the Internal Revenue Service, and parties to any dispute involving a business valuation engagement. Consequently, even though this book will teach you how to value your business, you should employ a certified professional to do the valuation if the purpose of it may involve litigation.

How Are Business Valuations Used?

You can use a business valuation in a variety of ways, depending on its original purpose and how it was prepared, but you need to recognize that a valuation prepared for one purpose may not be suitable for another. For example, let's suppose that you are thinking of selling part of your company to one of your loyal employees. You want to give her a good deal because she is the key to your succession plan and ultimately your retirement. You use the information in Chapter 13 to help you calculate the value using a discounted cash flow method and you come up with a value of $1 million. Then you read Chapter 23 and determine that you should apply both lack of marketability discounts and minority interest discounts totaling 35%, because you are only selling her a 25% share of your business, which is not highly marketable because it is a closely held company. The value of that 25% share becomes $162,500 ($1,000,000 x 25% x 65%) instead of $250,000. Then the two of you agree that this is a fair price and work out favorable payment terms.

A year later you are going through a divorce, and so you are performing the calculations to determine how much you will have to pay your wife to buy out her half of your company. (Even if she does not have any ownership interest in your business, she does have marital rights to half of it, assuming you acquired it during your marriage.) You may think that your recent valuation can be used to extrapolate the value as follows: $1 million − $250,000 − $262,500 = $487,500 / 2 = $243,750. This represents the original $1 million valuation less the 25% sold to your employee less the 35-% discounts for lack of marketability and minority interest; all divided by two to get her half. If you can get your spouse to agree to use this number, good for you! However, if your settlement is litigated rather than mediated, your valuation probably will not hold up in court. First of all, if you are not a valuation professional, you probably did not prepare your valuation report—if you even did one—in accordance with the business valuation standards mentioned above. Secondly, business valuations for divorce often do not use the same standard of value or other assumptions that are part of the calculation of the value of a business for purposes of a sale. For instance, lack of marketability discounts are often not seen in a divorce setting, because you are trying to calculate the value of the business in the hands of the owner who is in fact going to continue to own it.

Thus, two of the primary uses of business valuation are to get an idea of how much a company is worth for use in arm's length negotiations and to use in a litigation setting. You can use your own valuation in the first case, but in the case of litigation, you should hire a professional to perform the valuation and write a report that will stand up under the scrutiny of your adversaries as well as the court. The money you spend on a professional valuation will usually be a good investment.

In divorce and other litigation involving the value of a closely held business, each side usually retains a valuation professional to value the company. If the valuations are reasonably similar, you can often settle the case without going to court. If you do go to court, the opposing attorneys will try to discredit the work and/or the expertise of the respective business valuators. If one party's valuation expert is clearly superior and has done a more professional valuation, then the court may decide in favor of that party. However, this is not usually the case, and the court often ends up "splitting the difference" even if that solution makes no theoretical sense.

Two of the primary uses of business valuation are to get an idea of how much a company is worth for use in arm's length negotiations and to use in a litigation setting.

How Are Business Valuations Done?

Business valuations are done the old-fashioned way—research and number crunching. However, modern technology in the form of computers, software, searchable databases, etc., makes both research and number crunching easier and more efficient. With the advent of business valuation software, you may be tempted to "plug in" your numbers, let the computer run through the standard calculations, and instantaneously see the value of your company. Try to resist this temptation. Instead, go through the full process of analyzing your company from a financial standpoint, making normalizing adjustments, comparing it to other companies and the industry as a whole, and looking at qualitative factors that can influence the value.

The first step in doing a business valuation is to identify the property you are valuing. This may appear obvious, but you need to know whether you are valuing stock or assets. If you are valuing the stock of the company, do you want to know the value of 100% of the company or of a minority ownership share? If you are valuing the assets for a sale, you need to identify the assets and liabilities that will be included. Often cash, accounts receivable, and accounts payable do not transfer in the sale of a small business.

Next, you need to determine the date of the valuation. This is necessary for you to determine the relevant financial data and other information. Depending on the purpose of the valuation, the effective date may be several years in the past. For example, business valuations for divorce purposes usually have an effective date as of the date of separation or date of divorce. Valuations for estate or inheritance tax returns are related to the date of death or an alternate date of six months after the date of death. To the extent that you can have any input into the valuation date, try to pick a date at the end of the fiscal year, which will make getting financial information easier and more reliable.

Finally, you need to be clear about the purpose of the business valuation. As discussed above, the intended use of the valuation will determine whether it is something you can do yourself or whether you need to hire a business valuation professional. In addition, you or the professional appraiser will have to apply different laws, standards of value, valuation

> The first step in doing a business valuation is to identify the property you are valuing. You need to know whether you are valuing stock or assets.

methodologies, etc., to the valuation depending on its intended purposes. For example, if you are valuing your business for gift or estate tax planning purposes, you need to consider all of the factors spelled out in Internal Revenue Service Revenue Ruling 59-60. On the other hand, if you are just interested in coming up with a reasonable sales price for a portion of your business, you do not need to even think about Revenue Rulings.

Factors Considered in Business Valuation

Although Revenue Ruling 59-60 only needs to be incorporated into valuations that involve taxes, it does spell out the major factors that you should consider for any business valuation:

1. The nature and history of the business
2. The economic outlook
3. The financial condition of the business
4. The earnings capacity of the business
5. The dividend paying capacity of the business
6. Whether or not the enterprise has goodwill or other intangible value
7. Prior sales of stock
8. The market price of stocks of corporations engaged in the same or similar lines of business

You can see from this list that valuing your company involves much more than plugging the numbers from your year-end financial statements into a formula that will automatically produce the magical number. If you look closely at the list, you may be surprised to see that only about half of the items can even be determined by analyzing your own financial statements. The other factors involve research about the economy, the industry, comparative sales, prior sales of your own stock, and the history of your company. Understanding these factors will give you the knowledge and background to make good judgments regarding the financial analysis and calculations. Some of the specific judgment calls you will need to make are choosing appropriate capitalization and discount rates.

Business Valuation: Mystical Art or Inexact Science?

In the past, business valuation was more like a mystical art but now it is a profession, which probably classifies it as an inexact science. It is scientific in that it has specific methodologies and standards and it is certainly inexact—rarely would two valuation analysts come up with the same value for a business at the same point in time. These differences do not arise because two professionals cannot make the same mathematical calculations correctly, but rather because two professionals make different judgments about the numbers that go into the calculations. Their professional judgments are based on their own training and experience as well as their assessment of how the economic climate will impact the company—for example, if this company is inherently riskier than other companies in the industry, if the company is poised for growth, etc.

Sometimes, even professionals make mistakes or errors in judgment. Some common errors stem from not fully understanding the company being valued; this is often a result of not obtaining and documenting all of the necessary information for the valuation. In addition, sometimes valuation professionals do not apply the correct standard of value or the most relevant valuation method. Finally, two very common problems involve focusing on the results to the exclusion of the details and not objectively reviewing the conclusion of value. All of these problems are even more common when someone other than a valuation professional takes a turn at valuing a company, so "let the valuer beware!"

> Sometimes, even professionals make mistakes or errors in judgment. Some common errors stem from not fully understanding the company being valued.

Defining the "Standard of Value"

The **standard of value** is the definition of the type of value you are trying to calculate. You may be surprised to learn that fair market value is not the only standard of value that you can or should use to value a business. However, fair market value is the legal standard used for tax and many other valuation situations. **Fair market value** is the price at which a property would change hands between a hypothetical willing buyer and a hypothetical willing seller when neither is acting under compulsion and when both have reasonable knowledge of the relevant facts. In contrast, **investment value** relates to the value of an investment to a particular investor.

Intrinsic value represents what an investor or analyst thinks an investment is "really worth," in other words, its "true value." If you determined that the intrinsic value of an investment is higher than the fair market value or asking price, then you would buy it. Fair value is often the legal standard of value in minority shareholder disputes, and it relates in that situation to the value immediately before the corporation did whatever they did to upset the minority shareholder. Although no clear definition of fair value exists, it is distinguished from fair market value in that usually no discounts are applied when the standard of value is fair value.

The standard of value is not always clear-cut. For example, the family law statutes of many states require a fair market value standard for valuing businesses in a divorce setting; however, the courts often rule in a manner more consistent with a fair value standard by disallowing any discounts. This is why it is not enough for the valuation professional to know the applicable rules and statutes, but they also must be familiar with the case law of the state to know how the courts interpret the laws.

As a business owner wanting to learn the value of your own company, business valuation is more like the magic trick where the magician shows you the secret of being sawed in half. You have a much greater understanding of how it works, you know what specialized tools are required, you can actually do it yourself, but you are probably not ready to go up on stage in front of hundreds of people to perform your new found skill. This book will teach you how to value your own business and, unlike dangerous magic tricks, you are encouraged to "try this at home!" However, you will also learn when to turn the job over to the professionals.

> **Chapter 2**

Papa's Construction Company: A Valuation Case Study

Part One

Part Two

Part Three

Part Four

Part Five

Part Six

PART ONE: INTRODUCTION TO BUSINESS VALUATION

■ CHAPTER 1 Overview of Business Valuation

■ CHAPTER 2 Papa's Construction Company: A Valuation Case Study

Compiling Background Information and Making a Qualitative Analysis

The following case study will give you a real life example of some of the issues, methodologies, and concepts involved in performing a business valuation for a closely held company. You will learn more about the specific techniques and components of the business valuation process in future chapters, but for now you can get an overview of the whole system through a valuation of Papa's Construction Company.

Papa's Construction Company ("the Company") is a closely held business incorporated in 1983 by Owen Duke Jr. The Company, located in Durham, North Carolina, has grown over the years and is still owned entirely by the Duke family. Papa's Construction Company is organized as an S Corporation and has annual sales in excess of $2.5 million. Owen is ready to retire and he wants to completely turn the company over to the two of his three children who work with him in the business, Frank and Tom. Owen has previously gifted about two-thirds of his shares to his children, and now he wants to give them his remaining 24.28% portion of the company. Owen needs to value his company as of December 31, 2002, for gift tax purposes so he can give the rest of his stock to Frank and Tom as of January 1, 2003 and correctly complete and file IRS Form 709, Gift Tax Return.

Gifts and Taxes

A gift is a transfer of property from one person to another where the donor relinquishes all control over the property, i.e., a completed gift.

What is a gift for gift tax purposes? A gift is a transfer of property from one person to another where the donor relinquishes all control over the property, i.e., a completed gift. If the donor retains some elements of control, the transaction is not a completed gift and, therefore, is not subject to tax. The property can be tangible, such as real property, securities, and art, or it can be intangible, such as a patent or copyright. Gifts can also be indirect, such as the forgiveness of debt or the imputed interest on a no-interest or below-market interest loan. When do you need to report and pay tax on gifts? The annual gift exclusion for 2003 is $11,000, which means that you can give $11,000 per person to any number of people each year without reporting or paying gift tax. The IRS will index this amount for inflation in future years. In addition to the annual exclusion, you can make unlimited gifts directly to education institutions for tuition or to health care providers for medical expenses without filing a gift tax return. When you exceed the annual exclusion amount, you must file Form 709, Gift Tax Return, and a state gift tax return, if applicable. If you and your spouse join together to give over $11,000, but less than $22,000 (gift-splitting), you must file the Short Form Gift Tax Return, Form 709-A, even though you won't have to pay gift tax or reduce the amount of the applicable credit against taxes. In addition to this annual exclusion, the applicable credit shields up to $1 million in gifts from gift tax during your lifetime. Thus, if you make gifts over the annual exclusion amount in any year, you will not pay gift tax until you exceed $1 million in cumulative gifts. The applicable credit is reduced each time you make a gift over the annual exclusion amount.

A Company Overview

Papa's Construction Company is in the road building and paving construction industry in the central region of North Carolina. Commercial work represents 25% of the company's revenues, and 75% comes from residential developments. The company has adapted to changing economic and industry trends throughout the years by focusing on profit margin and decreasing its volume of lower margin contracts. Consequently, although sales volume has decreased over the last five years, profit margins have increased. Weather is the primary factor affecting the seasonality of the business. The company is in a capital-intensive industry. The fair market value of total machinery, equipment, and vehicles at the date of valuation is $527,975. The company does not maintain inventories for resale.

Papa's Construction Company has two major local competitors and one large national competitor. Papa's competitive strengths are a reputation for consistent quality, productivity, and experience of key personnel. Owen Duke built strong relationships with the development community during his more than twenty-five years in the industry. His son Frank has continued to solidify these relationships with the best developers. Therefore, developers continue to choose Papa's Construction to build their roads because they do a quality job in a timely manner—even though they are often not the lowest bidder on the job.

In addition, unlike the other competitors, Papa's Construction Company is debt free, so it has a lower overhead. Papa's also keeps overhead low by renting low-cost space in a no-frills environment as well as by employing fewer, more experienced workers year-round who work overtime when the seasonality demands it.

Owen has previously transferred the management responsibilities to his children. Frank has been the president and chief operating officer since 1995. He has a bachelor of science degree in engineering and a master's degree in geotechnical engineering. He has been with Papa's Construction Company for over fifteen years.

Tom Duke has been the treasurer and chief financial officer since 1995. He has a bachelor of science degree in accounting and is a certified public accountant. He has been with Papa's Construction Company for over twelve years.

Harold Smith, the foreman, worked for many years with Owen Duke at another company. When Owen started Papa's Construction Company in 1983, Harold went to work for Papa's.

Currently, Papa's has twelve other employees, most of whom have been employed for over ten years with the company. The average age of the employees is forty-eight.

The customer base of Papa's Construction Company is concentrated in the North Carolina counties of Durham, Orange, Wake, Chatham, and Granville. This region is known as the Research Triangle Area, in reference to the three research universities in the state (the University of North Carolina at Chapel Hill, North Carolina State University in Raleigh, and Duke University in Durham). The area contains a high concentration of research and technology-related companies, and the rapid growth of these industries over the last ten years has fueled a building boom. Although many developers are working in the area, Papa's Construction Company has a highly concentrated client base because they choose to work with high-end, high-profit developers. Consequently, they do work for about ten developers, but 50% of their business is with one major developer.

National and Regional Economic Trends

The national economy slowed in the fourth quarter of 2002, but the gross national product still grew by more than 2% and is forecast to grow by about 3% in 2003.

However, several negative factors have started to take a toll on the economy: continued lack of confidence in big business in the wake of accounting and corporate malfeasance scandals, decline in equity values, and the uncertain international situation. The Conference Board's consumer confidence index (CCI) declined by more than 9% from the previous year. Consumer spending has kept the economy from falling into recession up to this point, but economists expect consumers to become more conservative as unemployment rises. In addition, part of the consumer spending was due to extraction of home equity in the form of "cash-outs" during refinancing while interest rates have been low. The stock market decline over the last two years has substantially eroded net wealth, which has a negative affect on consumer spending.

> Economists expect consumers to become more conservative as unemployment rises.

The economic outlook in the Southeast has mirrored the national slowdown. However, home sales and housing starts have remained strong nationally and regionally due to historically low interest rates and continued demand for new housing from an expanding population. North Carolina's population is continuing to expand due to an influx of people from other states and a large number of immigrants. North Carolina has the fastest growing Hispanic population in the country. Because North Carolina's economy in general has been dependent on the manufacturing sector, the loss of jobs has been higher than in the rest of the country. The national unemployment rate at the end of 2002 was 5.7%, compared to 6.4% for North Carolina. However, the economy in the Research Triangle Area is faring better than the rest of the state and the country as shown by its unemployment rate of 4.7%.

The industry outlook is tied directly to both the residential and commercial real estate industries, which are heavily influenced by the economy. However, since Papa's is heavily concentrated in the residential real estate sector, the local economic conditions are more important than national trends. The residential real estate market is highly volatile, especially in any individual market. In large markets such as Atlanta, demand for new single-family homes can change by 50% in just two years; in smaller markets the change can be 100%. Low unemployment, low interest rates, and increasing wages created a boom in construction that culminated with a fifteen-year high in 1999. Nationally, total construction spending was up 0.2% from 2001, with residential construction spending up a comparably robust 5.5%. Growth in single-family home building was 5.2% and multifamily construction was up 9.6%. The price index for paving asphalt, a major cost for Papa's Construction Company, was up very slightly from last year. It is not expected to increase substantially unless oil prices skyrocket due to world events.

Financial Statements and Ratio Analysis

The following exhibits show the adjusted balance sheets (**Chart 2-1**) and common size statements (**Chart 2-2**) as of December 31, 1998, through December 31, 2002, and the adjusted income statements (**Chart 2-3**) and related common size statements (**Chart 2-4**) for the fiscal years ended December 31, 1998 through December 31, 2002 of Papa's Construction Company. The last exhibit (**Chart 2-5**) shows selected ratio analysis. Chapter 17 discusses the "normalizing" adjustments that you make to the historical financial statements to arrive at the adjusted statements you will use in calculating the value of the company. Chapters 15 and 16 discuss analyzing the financial statements, and in Chapter 18 you will learn more about common-size statements and ratio analysis.

PAPA'S CONSTRUCTION COMPANY

CHART 2-1

Adjusted Balance Sheets ($000)
As of December 31 Each Year

	2002	2001	2000	1999	1998
ASSETS					
Current assets					
Cash	$298	$459	$387	$256	$238
Trade accounts receivable (net)	444	447	403	666	707
Inventories	—	—	—	—	—
Prepaids and other current assets	36	18	37	28	41
Loans to shareholders	—	—	—	—	—
Total current assets	$778	$924	$827	$950	$986
Fixed assets	$1,551	$1,631	$1,798	$1,755	$1,763
Less: accumulated depreciation	(1,023)	(1,290)	(1,434)	(1,329)	(1,201)
Total fixed assets (net)	528	341	364	426	562
Other assets	—	—	—	—	—
TOTAL ASSETS	$1,306	$1,265	$1,191	$1,376	$1,548
LIABILITIES AND OWNERS' EQUITY					
Current liabilities					
Notes payable (short-term)	$ —	$ —	$ —	$ —	$ —
Accounts payable	101	222	112	239	275
Accrued expenses	70	86	121	123	125
Current portion of long-term debt	—	—	—	—	—
All other current liabilities	19	140	19	66	39
Loans from shareholders					110
Total current liabilities	$190	$448	$252	$428	$549

Chart 2-1 continues ▶

CHART 2-1
(continued)

PAPA'S CONSTRUCTION COMPANY

Adjusted Balance Sheets ($000)
As of December 31 Each Year

	2002	**2001**	**2000**	**1999**	**1998**
Noncurrent liabilities					
Notes payable (long-term)	—	—	—	—	—
Deferred income taxes	—	—	—	—	—
Other noncurrent liabilities	—	—	—	—	—
Total noncurrent liabilities	0	0	0	0	0
Total liabilities	$190	$448	$252	$428	$549
Owners' equity					
Common stock	30	30	30	30	30
Preferred stock	—	—	—	—	—
Additional paid-in capital	290	290	290	290	290
Retained earnings	719	719	767	719	701
Normalized dividends	77	(222)	(148)	(91)	(22)
Total owners' equity	$1,116	$817	$939	$948	$999
TOTAL LIABILITIES AND OWNERS' EQUITY	$1,306	$1,265	$1,191	$1,376	$1,548

PAPA'S CONSTRUCTION COMPANY

CHART 2-2

Common Size Analysis (%)
As of December 31 Each Year

	2002	2001	2000	1999	1998
ASSETS					
Current assets					
Cash	22.8	36.3	32.5	18.6	15.4
Trade accounts receivable (net)	34.0	35.3	33.8	48.4	45.6
Inventories	—	—	—	—	—
Prepaids and other current assets	2.8	1.4	3.1	2.1	2.7
Loans to shareholders	—	—	—	—	—
Total current assets	59.6	73.0	69.4	69.1	63.7
Fixed assets	118.7	128.9	151	127.5	113.9
Less: accumulated depreciation	(78.3)	(101.9)	(120.4)	(96.6)	(77.6)
Total fixed assets (net)	40.4	27.0	30.6	30.9	36.3
Other assets	—	—	—	—	—
TOTAL ASSETS	100.0	100.0	100.0	100.0	100.0
LIABILITIES AND OWNERS' EQUITY					
Current liabilities					
Notes payable (short-term)	—	—	—	—	—
Accounts payable	7.7	17.6	9.4	17.4	17.8
Accrued expenses	5.4	6.8	10.2	8.9	8.1
Current portion of long-term debt	—	—	—	—	—
All other current liabilities	1.5	11.0	1.6	4.8	2.5
Loans from shareholders	—	—	—	—	7.1
Total current liabilities	14.6	35.4	21.2	31.1	35.5

Chart 2-2 continues ➤

CHART 2-2
(continued)

PAPA'S CONSTRUCTION COMPANY

Common Size Analysis (%)
As of December 31 Each Year

	2002	2001	2000	1999	1998
Noncurrent liabilities					
Notes payable (long-term)	—	—	—	—	—
Deferred income taxes	—	—	—	—	—
Other noncurrent liabilities	—	—	—	—	—
Total noncurrent liabilities	0	0	0	0	0
Total liabilities	14.6	35.4	21.2	31.1	35.5
Owners' equity					
Common stock	2.3	2.4	2.5	2.2	1.9
Preferred stock					
Additional paid-in capital	22.2	22.9	24.4	21.1	18.7
Retained earnings	55.0	56.9	64.3	52.2	45.3
Normalized dividends	5.9	(17.6)	(12.4)	(6.6)	(1.4)
Total owners' equity	85.4	64.6	78.8	68.9	64.5
TOTAL LIABILITIES AND OWNERS' EQUITY	100.0	100.0	100.0	100.0	100.0

PAPA'S CONSTRUCTION COMPANY

CHART 2-3

Adjusted Income Statements ($000)
For the Years Ending December 31 Each Year

	2002	2001	2000	1999	1998
Revenue	$2,544	$2,666	$2,829	$3,961	$4,429
Cost of revenue	1,874	2,064	2,225	3,342	3,624
Gross profit	670	602	604	619	805
Operating expenses	731	703	671	719	701
Normalizing adjustments	(333)	(222)	(148)	(91)	(22)
Total operating expenses	398	481	523	628	679
Net operating income	272	121	81	(9)	126
Other income					
Interest income	22	19	14	15	21
Other income	5	6	43	35	27
Total other income	27	25	57	50	48
Income before income taxes	299	146	138	41	174
Provision for income taxes	—	—	—	—	—
Net income	$299	$146	$138	$41	$174

CHART 2-4

PAPA'S CONSTRUCTION COMPANY

Common Size Analysis (%)
For the Years Ending December 31 Each Year

	2002	2001	2000	1999	1998
Revenue	100.0	100.0	100.0	100.0	100.0
Cost of revenue	73.7	77.4	78.7	84.4	81.8
Gross profit	26.3	22.6	21.3	15.6	18.2
Total operating expenses normalized	15.6	18.1	18.5	15.9	15.4
Net operating income	10.7	4.5	2.8	(0.3)	2.8
Other income					
Interest income	0.9	0.7	0.5	0.4	0.5
Other income	0.2	0.2	1.5	0.9	0.6
Total other income	1.1	0.9	2.0	1.3	1.1
Income before income taxes	11.8	5.4	4.8	1.0	3.9
Provision for income taxes	—	—	—	—	—
Net income	11.8	5.4	4.8	1.0	3.9

PAPA'S CONSTRUCTION COMPANY   **CHART 2-5**

Selected Ratio Analysis
For the Years Ending December 31 Each Year

	2002	2001	2000	1999	1998
LIQUIDITY					
Current ratio	4.1	2.1	3.3	2.2	1.8
Quick ratio	4.1	2.1	3.3	2.2	1.8
GROWTH					
Sales growth	(4.6)	(5.8)	(28.6)	(10.6)	
Earnings growth	104.1	5.8	236.6	(76.3)	
EFFICIENCY					
Accounts receivable turnover	5.8	5.1	6.3	5.7	
Inventory turnover (N/A)					
PROFITABILITY					
Return on assets	23.1	11.9	10.8	2.8	
Return on investment	30.8	16.6	14.6	4.2	
RISK					
Debt to assets	14.6	35.4	21.2	31.1	35.5
Debt to equity	17.0	54.8	26.8	45.2	55.0

Financial Statement Analysis

Before you can start analyzing financial statement trends and performing ratio and comparative analyses, you may need to make adjustments to the financial statements to make them comparable to other companies and the industry as a whole. According to industry standards, the owners of Papa's Construction Company have taken compensation in excess of the standard industry compensation by an average of around $188,000 per year. Consequently, the "excess compensation" is added back to income to arrive at the Adjusted Balance Sheet and Adjusted Income Statement shown in the previous exhibits. Chapter 17 discusses all the normalizing adjustments you should consider before using any valuation methods.

> The first step in valuing a company is to analyze the financial statements to see how the company has performed over time.

The first step in valuing a company is to analyze the financial statements to see how the company has performed over time and to get a sense of where it is heading in the future. Starting with the balance sheet (**Chart 2-1**), you can see that total assets decreased from a high of $1.5 million in 1998 to a low of about $1.2 million in 2000 and have been modestly increasing since then. Accounts receivable (also **Chart 2-1**) have followed a similar pattern of a steady and significant decrease from 1998 until 2000 and then a small increase to what looks like a relatively stable number at around $446,000. The most significant feature of the balance sheet of Papa's Construction Company is that the company has no long-term debt. The short-term liabilities are primarily accounts payable, which have been decreasing on average. You can see by looking at the common-size balance sheet (**Chart 2-2**) that liabilities, all current, have decreased from 35.5% in 1998 to 14.6% in 2002. Accounts payable did increase in 2001, which mirrors the increase in receivables, but accounts payable decreased in 2002, rather than stabilizing as did receivables. Owners' equity has been relatively stable for the last five years at around $1 million. However, owners' equity has grown as a percentage of total liabilities and owners' equity, from 64.5% of total to 85.4%, which is a very positive trend.

The Adjusted Income Statements for Papa's Construction Company (**Chart 2-3**) indicate that revenues have been dropping steadily from a high of $4.4 million in 1998 to just over $2.5 million in 2002, and gross profit has decreased from $805,000 in 1998 to $670,000 in 2002. This represents nearly a 43% drop in revenue and a 16% decrease in gross profit over the last five years. Normally you would consider these figures to be a negative trend, but if you look at the related gross profit percentages on the common-size income statement (**Chart 2-4**), you will see that as a percentage of sales, gross profit has actually increased from 18.2% in 1998 to 26.3% in 2002. Even more importantly, net income (shown on **Chart 2-3**) has increased from $174,000 in 1998 to $299,000 in 2002, and as a percentage of sales, net income has increased from 3.9% to 11.8% over this same period (shown on **Chart 2-4**). The strategy adopted by Papa's Construction Company of being "lean and mean," and doing fewer but higher margin projects, has obviously been successful.

Now turn your attention to the Selected Ratio Analysis Exhibit (**Chart 2-5**). (Chapter 18 has a full discussion of ratio analysis and how to calculate some of the most useful ratios.) You can see from looking at the liquidity ratios shown in the Selected Ratio Analysis that Papa's Construction Company is in a good position to meet its current operating needs. The quick ratio and current ratio are the same because Papa's does not carry any inventory. These ratios range from 1.8 in 1998 to 4.1 in 2002, which means that Papa's Construction Company has four dollars of current assets for every dollar of current liabilities in the most recent year.

Growth ratios indicate whether a company is expanding or contracting. Looking at the sales growth ratios (also on **Chart 2-5**), you can see that sales have been declining for the last five years. In contrast, earnings growth has been not only positive, but practically off the charts in two of the last three years. This indicates that the company has become more profitable as it has decreased sales and been able to decrease the overhead associated with those sales. You can also see this growth in profitability by looking at the return on assets and return on investment ratios. Both ratios have grown steadily over the last five years to a 23.1% return on assets and a 30.8% return on shareholders' investment by the end of 2002.

The debt to assets and debt to equity ratios indicate the level of risk inherent in the company. These two ratios are consistently below 50%, and in 2002, debt as a percentage of assets was only 14.6% and debt as a percentage of equity was only 17%. This means that the Company has very little risk exposure because it could satisfy all of its debt by liquidating only 14% of its assets. As you saw previously from the current and quick ratio, the company can satisfy all of its liabilities with its current assets. Consequently, Papa's Construction Company is a very safe investment.

Financial statement and ratio analysis can help you identify trends in the company's financial statements, but it does not help you place the company in the context of other companies or the industry as a whole. The next step is comparative analysis, which you can learn more about in Chapter 19. **Chart 2-6** shows a comparison between selected balance sheet, income statement, and financial ratios of Papa's Construction Company and the industry averages for the year ended December 31, 2002.

CHART 2-6

PAPA'S CONSTRUCTION COMPANY

Comparison with Industry Financial Data

	INDUSTRY	PAPA'S CONSTRUCTION
BALANCE SHEET		
ASSETS		
Current assets		
Cash and equivalents	14.7	22.8
Accounts receivable	34.2	34.0
Inventory	3.3	0
Other current assets	4.8	2.8
Total current assets	57.0	59.6
Noncurrent assets		
Fixed assets (net)	35.2	40.4
Other noncurrent assets	7.2	0
Total noncurrent assets	42.4	40.4
TOTAL ASSETS	99.4	100.0
LIABILITIES		
Current liabilities		
Notes payable (short-term)	6.7	0
Trade payables	18.0	7.7
Accrued expenses	3.1	5.4
Current portion long-term debt	5.9	0
Other current liabilities	16.6	1.5
Total current liabilities	50.3	14.6

PAPA'S CONSTRUCTION COMPANY

Comparison with Industry Financial Data

CHART 2-6

(continued)

	INDUSTRY	PAPA'S CONSTRUCTION
BALANCE SHEET		
Noncurrent liabilities		
Long-term debt	15.9	0
Deferred taxes	0.4	0
Other noncurrent liabilities	3.4	0
Total noncurrent liabilities	19.7	0
Net worth	30.0	85.4
TOTAL LIABILITIES AND NET WORTH	100.0	100.0
INCOME DATA		
Net revenue	100.0	100.0
Gross profit	26.1	26.3
Operating expense	24.1	15.6
Operating income	2.0	10.7
Other income (expenses)	1.0	1.1
Income before taxes	1.1	11.8
RATIOS		
LIQUIDITY		
Current ratio	1.5	4.1
Quick ratio	1.2	4.1
PROFITABILITY		
Gross profit percentage	26.1	26.3
Return on assets	5.6	23.1
Return on investment	18.1	30.8
EFFICIENCY		
Accounts receivable turnover	10.6	5.8
RISK		
Debt to equity	33.3	17.0

Papa's risk and liquidity ratios are much more positive than the industry averages. The company's gross profit percentage is in line with the industry, but Papa's operating profit percentage of 10.7% is much higher than the industry percentage of 2%. The most striking difference between Papa's Construction Company and the industry average is the lack of long-term debt and relatively few current liabilities on Papa's financial statements. The only area where Papa's Construction underperformed the industry averages was in the category of accounts receivable turnover. Papa's turns its accounts receivable over about six times a year, compared to the industry average of about eleven times per year. Overall, Papa's performance was considerably better than the industry average for the year ending December 31, 2002.

Four Approaches to Value

Historically, valuation analysts have used three traditional approaches and a fourth hybrid approach to valuing an interest in a closely held entity such as Papa's Construction Company:

1. The Income Approach
2. The Market Approach
3. The Underlying Asset Approach
4. The Hybrid Approach

The **income approach** establishes value by methods that capitalize future anticipated benefits, such as cash flow, by a discount or capitalization rate that incorporates a market rate of return as well as the risk of the investment. The capitalization of earnings or discounted cash flow methods would be examples of the income approach. The capitalization of earnings method produced a value of $1,328,888 before discounts. (See Chapter 23 for a discussion of discounts.) Because the stock of Papa's Construction Company is closely held rather than traded on a public exchange, you can take a discount for lack of marketability. The theory is that since you can't just sell on the open market, you will have to incur some costs to sell the stock, and this reduces the value of the stock. After applying a 25% discount for lack of marketability, the capitalization of earnings method produced a value of $996,666. Management has not made any projections of future cash

> The capitalization of earnings or discounted cash flow methods would be examples of the income approach.

flow due to the uncertainty of future earnings, so the discounted cash flow method was not calculated. The income method does not take into account any underlying value of the assets.

The **market approach** involves comparisons with companies that are similar to Papa's Construction Company. You can use comparisons to publicly traded guideline companies or actual sales transactions of similar businesses. BizComps, a database of actual sales transactions, showed a sale of a similar company in Colorado in the $800,000–$900,000 range.

The **underlying asset approach,** also known as the **adjusted asset or cost approach,** establishes value by netting the fair market value of assets with the liabilities to determine the net asset value or net worth of the business.

The adjusted asset approach yielded a value of $1,116,000 before discounts. After applying a 25% discount for marketability, the adjusted asset approach produced a value of $837,000. This method does not take into account the value of the future earnings or any intangible value.

The **hybrid approach,** which is called the **excess earnings reasonable rate method,** is a combination of the income and asset approach. The underlying theory behind the excess earnings method is that the total value of the business is the sum of the adjusted net assets and the value of the intangibles determined by capitalizing the "excess" earnings of the business. The "excess" earnings are the earnings in excess of a reasonable rate of return on the adjusted net assets of the business. The capitalization rate is a combination of the risk-free rate of return on twenty-year Treasury bonds at December 31, 2002, and a risk premium that reflects the greater risk inherent in the stock of a closely held company. You calculate the risk premium based on a number of factors, including competition, financial strength, management ability and depth, and profitability and stability of earnings. You divide the excess earnings by the capitalization rate to arrive at the value of the company's intangible assets, which you add to the value of the net tangible assets. The excess earnings method produced a value of $1,993,529 before discounts. Applying the same 25% lack of marketability discount will produce a value of $1,495,147.

After making all of the calculations and reviewing your qualitative and financial analyses of the company, the industry, the economy, etc., you must choose which method you think is the most appropriate. Remember that the purpose of this valuation was to determine the value of the stock for gift tax purposes. In this case you must choose a single value rather than a range of values. On the other hand, if the purpose of this valuation were to help you set a sales price for your business, you could consider the range of values produced, i.e., $800,000 to $1,500,000.

And the answer is . . . ?? You be the judge. Business valuation is as much about using your judgment as it is about making calculations. It is certainly necessary to first learn the science of business valuation—how to analyze financial statements, perform comparative and qualitative analyses, and make both simple and sophisticated valuation calculations. But the art of business valuation comes from applying your judgment and experience to select the appropriate conclusion from all of the scientific output.

Calculations for Each Method

The capitalization of earnings method is based on the theory that the company's ability to produce future earnings is what a potential buyer is really buying, not the assets that produce those earnings. In the case of Papa's Construction Company, assume that the 2002 earnings of $299,000 (**Chart 2-3**) are your best estimate of future earnings. Next you must choose a capitalization rate to apply to these earnings. After considering all of the factors discussed in Chapter 22 about capitalization and discount rates, you choose a capitalization rate of 22.5%, which represents a risk-free rate of 6.2% and a risk premium of 16.3%. You also plan to take a 25% discount for lack of marketability because no ready market for the stock exists. You make the calculation of capitalized earnings as follows:

CHART 2-7

$$\text{Value} = \frac{\text{Expected income}}{\text{Capitalization rate}} = \frac{\$299,000}{22.5\%} = \$1,328,888$$

$$\$1,328,888 - 25\% \text{ discount} = \$996,666$$

In order to properly calculate the adjusted asset method, which is described in Chapter 10, you may need to get appraisals of fixed assets if you do not have the knowledge or experience to properly assess their individual values. Assume an appraiser told you that the value of the machinery and equipment was $333,157 higher than was recorded in the financials.

You would make this adjustment as well as reduce other current assets by $25,000, which represents an investment in another company that would not be sold with the business. Assume that all of the other balance sheet items are reported at fair market value. Compare the results of the adjusted net asset method to the book value on the balance sheet of Papa's Construction Company:

PAPA'S CONSTRUCTION COMPANY

CHART 2-8

Net Adjusted Asset Value Method ($000)
As of December 31, 2002

	BOOK VALUE	ADJUSTED BOOK VALUE
ASSETS		
Current assets		
Cash	$298	$298
Trade accounts receivable (net)	444	444
Inventories	—	—
Prepaids and other current assets	11	36
Loans to shareholders	—	—
Total current assets	$753	$778
Fixed assets	$1,551	$1,551
Less: accumulated depreciation	(1,356)	(1,023)
Total fixed assets (net)	195	528
Other assets		
TOTAL ASSETS	$948	$1,306

Chart 2-8 continues ➤

CHART 2-8
(continued)

PAPA'S CONSTRUCTION COMPANY

Net Adjusted Asset Value Method ($000)
As of December 31, 2002

	BOOK VALUE	ADJUSTED BOOK VALUE
LIABILITIES AND OWNERS' EQUITY		
Current liabilities		
Notes payable (short-term)	$ —	$ —
Accounts payable	101	101
Accrued expenses	70	70
Current portion of long-term debt	—	—
All other current liabilities	19	19
Loans from shareholders		
Total current liabilities	$190	$190
Noncurrent liabilities		
Notes payable (long-term)	—	—
Deferred income taxes	—	—
Other noncurrent liabilities	—	—
Total noncurrent liabilities	0	0
Total liabilities	$190	$190
Net assets	$758	$1,116
Discount for lack of marketability-25%		(279)
Total value using adjusted net asset value		$837,000

You will need to determine several important numerical factors before you can apply the capitalization of excess earnings method. First, look up the risk-free rate of return based on twenty-year Treasury bonds, and then calculate a risk premium, which you will add to the risk-free rate to determine the total rate of return. Then use one of the databases described in Chapter 19 to look up the average rate of return on assets for the industry. Next, multiply this average rate of return to the net assets of the company to get the fair return on net assets in the industry. Finally, subtract the fair return from the adjusted earnings to get the excess earnings. Rather than using the most recent year's financials, you could also use a five-year average or weighted average to estimate earnings. Then, capitalize the net earnings, which produces a value for the intangible assets that you add to the tangible net assets to get a total value for the company. See below for an illustration of the capitalization of excess earnings method for Papa's Construction Company:

1. Risk-free rate of return based on twenty-year Treasury bond = 6.2%
2. Risk premium for small companies based on the build-up summation method = 16.3%
3. Total rate of return (6.2% + 16.3%) = 22.5%
4. Rate of return on assets based on industry average = 9.1%
5. Adjusted net assets at December 31, 2002 = $1,116,000
6. Fair return on net assets = $1,116,000 x 9.1% = $101,556
7. The excess earnings = 2002 earnings of $299,000 – $101,556 = $197,444
8. Value of intangibles = capitalized excess earnings: $197,444 / 22.5% = $877,529
9. Value of the company = the value of the intangibles + the value of the adjusted net tangible assets: $1,116,000 + $877,529 = $1,993,529
10. Apply 25% discount for lack of marketability: $1,993,529 – $428,382 = **$1,495,147**

Choosing the "Best" Value

You can see that the basic methods produce a range of values from around $800,000 to about $1,500,000. You may be tempted to "split the difference" and say that Papa's Construction Company is worth about $1,000,000. You should avoid this temptation because taking an average of several valuation numbers leaves you without a valuation methodology that is supportable. You should instead choose an appropriate method based on the type of business and information that you have. In a case like Papa's Construction Company where you don't have projected future earnings, but both assets and earnings are important, you may want to choose the excess-earnings method. However, you would not be wrong if you chose one of the other methods, as long as you could establish why that method is the most appropriate.

Now that you have a general sense of how the numbers, calculations, and concepts fit together, we will move on in Part Two to learn more about the various reasons that business owners need business valuations.

> **Chapter 3**

Business Reasons for Business Valuation

Part One

Part Two

Part Three

Part Four

Part Five

Part Six

PART TWO: PURPOSES OF BUSINESS VALUATION

■ CHAPTER 3 Business Reasons for Business Valuation ■ CHAPTER 4 Tax Reasons for Business Valuation and Related Issues ■ CHAPTER 5 Business Valuations for Divorce ■ CHAPTER 6 Other Business Valuation Situations

Keeping Score—Are You Making Progress?

Do you know if the value of your business is increasing, decreasing, or staying about the same? Small business owners often have a "gut feel" about the value of their business. This usually means that they wouldn't sell it for less than a certain amount of money if someone approached them unsolicited to buy it. This same "gut feel" would produce a smaller value for the business if they had to give half of the value to their soon-to-be ex-spouse in a divorce property settlement.

Small business owners focus most of their attention on cash on hand—is there enough money to pay the bills and have enough to take home as salary, bonus, or dividends? This is a good starting point for keeping score. If there is cash to do all these things, then progress is usually being made, and you are "winning." However, using cash available to keep score can be misleading. Where did the cash come from? Did it all come from the sale of products and services, or did some of it come from investors or loans? Is any of the cash on hand committed for other uses, such as paying taxes on the company's profits?

The other basic way small business owners keep score is to monitor the "net profit" of the business. The profit, or loss, of a company is determined by subtracting the expenses from the revenues generated over a specific period of time, usually a year. Conveniently, this is also the way the Internal Revenue Service keeps score. The format of business tax returns is a variation of the standard financial statement, the income statement. Many small businesses and their bankers use the annual tax return to keep score. The benefits of this are that a tax return is a simple straightforward format that is consistent from year to year, and it must be produced within a relatively short time after the year-end.

The major problem with this method of keeping score is that there is a big incentive to show as little profit as possible in order to incur less tax. Unlike publicly traded companies whose incentive is to report as much income as possible, maybe even inflate it, closely held companies want to be aggressive with deductible expenses and defer the reporting of income whenever possible. Owners of closely held companies can also create a "win-win" situation by personally taking advantage of benefits that are deductible to the business. Benefits, such as company cars, health insurance, retirement plans, and large bonuses, can reduce the taxable income of the company and thereby make it difficult to determine if the company's financial health is improving.

A third method of keeping score is to keep track of all the assets that are being accumulated over time and subtracting the related liabilities. This equation is reflected on another of the standard financial statements, the balance sheet. You may be familiar with the maxim: "The assets of the company minus the liabilities equal the net worth of the company." The term "net worth" is another way of saying "book value of the company." Although this method makes theoretical sense, it does not take into account the fact that the values of assets on the financial statements may not be reflective of their true values. For example, many companies record depreciation using accelerated tax methods that would reduce the value of depreciable property, such as equipment and furniture, on the balance sheet. Buildings and other real estate holdings frequently are worth much more than the value reflected by their historical costs on the balance sheet. Other valuable assets, such as goodwill or patents, are not even recorded because they are intangible in nature.

Using standard valuation techniques to value the business at regular intervals is the best way to keep score. The business valuation process takes into account the cash flow and net profit over time as well as the fair market value of tangible and intangible assets. Adjustments are made to the standard financial statements or tax return information to account for "excessive" owner compensation and perquisites. Using consistent valuation methods and assumptions to value the business on a periodic basis should give a clear picture of whether the business is becoming more or less valuable over time.

Strategic Planning

Strategic planning is the formal process of setting business goals for the future. Although many of these goals are financial

What Is Cash Flow?

Cash flow is used in a valuation context to refer to the cash that is generated by the operations of the business or specific assets in the business. A separate financial statement, called the *statement of cash flow*, shows the sources of cash and uses of cash in the business for a specific time period. Cash flow from operations would be distinguished from cash from financing activities such as investment of capital or loans. Cash flow is not the same as taxable income. Cash flow is reduced by items such as principal payments on loans and purchases of capital assets that do not reduce taxable income. However, cash flow is not reduced by the depreciation or amortization deductions that reduce taxable income.

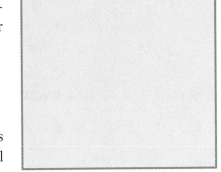

in nature, strategic planning includes aligning the actions of the organization with its vision. The strategic planning process can help clarify the vision and values of the organization and encourage team members to be on "the same page of the play book."

Strategic planning can be useful to an organization in a variety of ways:

1. Defining the purpose of the organization and establishing realistic goals and objectives consistent with that mission
2. Communicating these goals and objectives to responsible and/or interested parties
3. Encouraging team members to "buy in" to the plan for achieving these goals
4. Prioritizing projects and allocating resources
5. Setting up mechanisms to quantify or measure the progress being made

The basic components of the strategic planning process include:

- Review the mission of the organization and incorporate it into the planning process.
- Assess the current and future environment.
- Analyze the situation using SWOT (*strengths, weaknesses, opportunities, and threats*) or other analysis.
- Set goals based on the mission and the SWOT analysis.
- Determine strategies to reach these goals.
- Break goals down into objectives, assign responsibilities to individuals or groups, and set time frames for completion.
- Communicate the plan.
- Determine when the process will be complete and acknowledge progress and success.

SWOT Analysis

Using SWOT analysis is the business equivalent of using the law enforcement SWAT team. It is an efficient and effective method of getting to the target. SWOT is an acronym for Strengths, Weaknesses, Opportunities, and Threats. Each of these concepts is assessed to come up with an overall analysis of the organization and its environment. For example, if you own a hardware store in a small town, your SWOT analysis might include strengths such as employees know your clientele by name, you provide exceptional customer service, your company has a history of being a good community citizen, and you offer quality products. Your weaknesses may be higher prices, lack of parking, normal business hours, and limited inventory compared to warehouse stores like the Home Depot. You may identify opportunities to capitalize on the loyalty of your customers and your hometown reputation. You could provide products and services tailored to the needs and desires of your customers rather than try to compete on the basis of price and seemingly limitless selection. However, you must assess the very real threat of a Home Depot or Wal-Mart opening on the outskirts of town. You would probably lose some business due to their low prices, convenient parking, and long hours. What will this mean for your profitability and, ultimately, for your ability to stay in business? What do you need to do now to counteract this threat?

Strategic Planning and Business Valuation

Business valuation can and should be an important component of the strategic planning process. Knowing the current value of the business is crucial to the goal setting and completion phases of the process. Goals must be specific and measurable in order to be achieved, and just as important, to know if they have been achieved. The primary goal of most businesses is to grow to a desired value or at a desired rate. In order to make this a reasonable goal, you need to know the current value of the organization or operation. Likewise, you need to be able to determine the value of the organization in the future to see if the goal has been achieved.

> The primary goal of most businesses is to grow to a desired value or at a desired rate.

Financing the Business

The money to start or continue a closely held business generally comes from the owner/managers either in the form of capital investments or loans. In an effort to leverage their own funds, business owners look to commercial banks to provide additional funds in the form of loans. The original owners may also look to "outside investors" to buy an interest in the business or to loan the company money.

Types of Investors

Commercial bankers and individual lenders want to know the value of the business so they can assess whether their loans will be paid back. By their very nature, start-up businesses are difficult to value because they do not have an extensive financial history. Therefore, business valuations are more useful in the financing decisions of ongoing companies. A business valuation can help the banker assess the value of any collateral and the quality of the cash flow that could be used to make payments. Bankers protect themselves by securing small business loans with as much collateral as possible as well as the personal guarantee of the owner (and his or her spouse). In addition, they often use the owners' home equity as additional security. Business valuations can aid the business owner by showing the banker that the business is capable of generating the necessary cash and/or has sufficient collateral so that the business owner does not need to pledge personal assets to get a business loan.

Individuals who are willing to lend money to a closely held business often fall into the category of "related parties." These are usually friends, family, or business associates who take a personal interest in the success of the company. Even though these lenders may not base their lending decision on strict financial principles, business valuations can be helpful in convincing them to loan their money to the effort.

Assessing Risk and Return

A major component of the business valuation process is assessing the risk of the company. This risk is incorporated into the discount rate or capitalization rate used in technical business valuation calculations. (Capitalization and discount rates are discussed in detail in Chapter 22.) Assessing the risk of the business is an important component in determining what interest rate to pay individual lenders. These lenders will often require a relatively high rate of interest to compensate them for putting their savings into a risky venture. Although they may have a personal connection to the company,

> Start-up businesses are difficult to value because they do not have an extensive financial history.

these investors are usually looking for a greater rate of return than they can achieve with safer investments such as cash, bonds, or other marketable securities.

The value of the business is even more important to outside investors who are buying shares of stock, partnership interests, or LLC interests. Closely held businesses that need additional cash often seek outside capital infusions when banks or other individuals are not willing to lend them the money due to the uncertainty of being repaid. Some investors are willing to take the risk of putting money into small businesses when they feel that there is a potential for a large return. The greater the chance of losing money (i.e., the riskier the business), the greater the potential return would have to be to invest a given sum. The business valuation is the key to determining what percentage of the business the investor will receive for his or her investment.

The Value of Buy/Sell Agreements

What do closely held businesses do when a partner or shareholder dies? If they don't have a buy/sell agreement, they usually go into a panic trying to determine how they are going to work with their new partners, usually the heirs of their former business partner. Think about it . . . how would you like to work with your business partner's spouse or children? The survivors are often just as panicked wondering how they can get money out of the business to live on, send kids to college, or start another business they know something about.

Having a buy/sell agreement in place doesn't eliminate the emotional or business trauma caused by the death of an owner, but it does set forth a rational method of determining how much money will be transferred in exchange for a deceased owner's share of the business. A well-crafted buy/sell agreement addresses questions such as:

- What situations will cause the agreement to be invoked?
- How would the resultant buyout be funded?
- When will the transaction take place?
- How will the business be valued?

One of the three "D's"—death, disability, or departure—usually triggers the provisions of a buy/sell agreement. Having a buy/sell agreement is always better than not having one in case of a crisis. However, if you don't make provisions for funding the agreement, you may wish you never had it. The common funding mechanisms are insurance, borrowing money, company resources, and personal funds. You can execute the buyout within a few months of the triggering event if the valuation and funding sources are already in place. In situations where a valuation needs to be secured, the process can take from several months to a year to arrive at an agreed upon value. Common valuation methods for buy/sell purposes include flat amounts, formulaic approaches, and formal valuations.

> Common valuation methods for buy/sell purposes include flat amounts, formulaic approaches, and formal valuations.

Methods of Valuation for Buy/Sell Agreements

What are the pros and cons of the common methods of valuing companies for buy/sell agreements? Some companies just agree on a dollar value each year. They may use a professional valuator to help them, or they could just pick a number out of the air. This method works fine as long as yearly meetings are held, the value is agreed upon, and it is written into the updated agreement. The danger with this method is that years may go by without a formal meeting or an agreement on a new value. The good news is that there is a methodology in place and a value to use for buying out the deceased owner's share. The bad news is that the value may no longer even approximate the true value of the company.

Another common method is to use a formulaic approach, such as a percentage of sales or income. The primary benefits of this method are that it is simple and that the value will change automatically as the business grows or contracts, whether or not the owners meet on an annual basis. The negatives are that these formulas don't take into account important issues that affect the true value of the business. For example, if the owners are taking large salaries to reduce taxes, formulas based on net income may not be appropriate. In addition, many business owners will not review this calculation after the initial agreement is signed. Consequently, they may be unhappy if an unexpected value is calculated upon a triggering event.

The third and most accurate method is a formal valuation of the company. In some cases the company has formal valuations performed on a regular basis and the agreement refers to the most recent one. In other cases the buy/sell agreement specifies that a formal valuation will be performed when a death or other value-related situation occurs. The obvious benefit with this method is its conceptual integrity. The downside is that it is the most expensive method, and it can take up to several months if a new valuation is necessary.

Buy/Sell Agreement Scenarios

Buy/sell agreements are important not just when an owner dies. What if you or your business partner wanted to leave the business? What if they wanted you to leave? Buy/sell agreements can help make these transitions easier. When setting the valuation methodology and funding mechanisms you should think about all of the possible eventualities, not just the most likely scenarios at the time. Ideally you should be comfortable with the value produced by the specified method whether you or your family would be on the buying or selling end of the transaction.

Buy/sell agreements are set up in one of two ways. Either the company buys back the stock or ownership interest of the departed owner (or the dearly departed owner's heirs) or the remaining owners purchase the ownership interest. Generally these methods are referred to as the **stock-repurchase** and **cross-purchase** methods. The cross-purchase method is used when there are only a few owners and often is funded by insurance. In the case of two owners, each would personally buy an insurance policy on the other's life in an amount indicated by the valuation method specified in the buy/sell agreement. Upon the death of an owner, the other owner would receive the life insurance proceeds tax-free (if they were paid for individually rather than through the business). He or she would use these funds to purchase the shares from the estate of the deceased owner, as required by the agreement. This allows the heirs to convert what would normally be a not very marketable security into cash in a relatively short period of time with little or no tax consequence.

The cross-purchase method becomes cumbersome when there are many owners. There would need to be provisions for each of them to buy a specified percentage of each other's shares in the event of a departure. Insurance funding would become more complicated also. Usually when there are more than four owners, the stock-repurchase method is more feasible. This method requires the company to buy back the ownership interest of the departed owner. This method often uses a self-funding mechanism because a smaller percentage of the business is being purchased if there are more owners and the company may have greater resources than the individual owners. However, companies should consider funding stock-repurchase agreements with insurance, since using operating resources to buy back stock may affect the ability of the business to meet its strategic goals.

Bringing on New Owners

Why would you want a partner or additional shareholders? Can they bring additional capital or credit worthiness? Do they have specific technical expertise? Do they have proven management skills? Are they rainmakers? Do you trust them?

Whatever the reason for wanting an additional owner or owners, think through the decision carefully. Becoming a business partner is just like getting married—it is a contract with financial and emotional ramifications. Dissolving a business partnership is just like getting divorced—it is usually very painful and costly.

Once you have decided to take the leap to dilute your ownership, coming up with a fair price for both parties is extremely important. In general, the current owner would like to receive more money for a smaller share of the business and the potential new owner would like to pay less for more of the company. An independent professional valuation can help both parties feel comfortable with the price ultimately paid. The comfort level of both parties in this situation is more important than if the entire business were being sold since the owners will be working together after the deal is struck.

Mergers and Acquisitions

"Mergers and acquisitions," also known as "M&A," is the term used for buying and selling businesses at the corporate level. **Mergers** are the financial combination of two companies with only one of them surviving as a legal entity. **Acquisitions** involve one company purchasing or taking over another company. Acquisitions can be friendly, in situations where there are agreed upon benefits to both companies. Often the benefits to the acquired company include cash and stock of the new company and an exit strategy for owners. The new company benefits by acquiring already developed resources such as personnel, technology, patents, equipment, etc., which might otherwise take years and many dollars to develop. Acquisitions can also be unfriendly when the management team and directors of the company are not interested in selling. These situations are called "hostile takeovers."

Business valuations are the cornerstone of all merger and acquisition activity. Buyers are trying to "buy low" and sellers are trying to "sell high." The best way to get a good deal is to know the value of your company, or the value of the company you want to buy. Companies or investors who are paying a lot of money are expecting to not only get back their investment but also receive a good return on that investment. The valuation of the business is the mechanism used to determine the likelihood of this outcome.

> The best way to get a good deal is to know the value of your company, or the value of the company you want to buy.

For tax purposes, corporations may elect to treat some stock purchases as asset purchases. Generally these are situations where the acquiring company exchanges its stock for the stock of the target company. In these cases and in straightforward asset purchases, you can use the business valuation to determine a fair price and to allocate the purchase price among the various assets acquired. The IRS requires that the purchase price of any business acquisition be allocated on Form 8594. Since both the buyer and seller of the business must file this form, it is important to agree on the valuation and the allocation.

Insurance Issues

How do you decide how much and what kind of insurance to buy? How much and what type of insurance is your insurance agent trying to sell you? What do you really need? Life insurance to fund a buy/sell agreement has already been discussed. Most companies have property and casualty insurance to cover tangible property such as equipment and buildings. What about liability insurance to cover "errors and omissions" or lawsuits for personal injuries? What about business continuation insurance to help the company pay the bills if a key person is lost?

Making decisions about insurance is a difficult task. The insurance company scenarios often show that you need millions of dollars of insurance to adequately protect your company and yourself from potential liabilities. They are probably right; however, this coverage costs money. How much money do you want to reallocate from funds you are using to grow your business to protecting it? Having a business valuation can help with this decision-making process. Knowing how much your business is worth gives you a better sense of what it is you are trying to protect. For example, the tangible assets reflected on your financial statements are depreciated according to accounting or tax conventions. In fact, your assets may be completely depreciated on your books. However, these assets still have value to your business and need to be insured. This value is reflected in the business valuation.

> Knowing how much your business is worth gives you a better sense of what it is you are trying to protect.

Having adequate insurance coverage is a factor in the business valuation itself. Think about two companies that are identical, except that one of them is adequately insured and the other is not. Which one is more valuable? Since insurance has reduced the financial risk of loss, the well-insured company would be the more valuable.

Taking a Company Public

Why would you want to "take your company public"? It sounds exciting, and it sounds as though you have made it to the big leagues. Certainly it is a measure of the growth of your business, but at its essence, taking a company public is just another way of raising capital to finance the growth of the business. Other advantages include increased liquidity for the shareholders when they can sell their stock on the open market instead of just to a limited number of potential shareholders. The cash infusion will also increase the value of the company, which may make it easier to acquire additional financing or investment. If your company has not previously offered its stock for sale to the general public, this process is called an initial public offering, or IPO.

How an IPO Works

First, you will need to hire an investment bank. The investment bankers do the actual work of raising the capital by "underwriting" the offering. Underwriting a security is similar to underwriting in the insurance industry. It means that the investment bank is assuming the risk of buying the new security and selling it to the public. Of course, the underwriters are compensated for taking this risk by earning a profit on the difference between the amount they pay your company for the stock and the amount for which they can sell it to the public.

Secondly, you—or more accurately, the investment bankers—must determine how to price the initial public offering. This process is a type of business valuation and can be more art than science. The usual starting point is the amount of money the company needs for expansion, debt payments, etc. Next, you need to compare your company with similar companies in your industry. A good business valuation would have already provided this analysis.

You then determine how the infusion of anticipated cash will change the fundamentals of your business. Compare these projected changes to companies with these new characteristics. If you can find a "comparable company," you can use its value to determine the value of your own business.

However, it is not easy to find truly comparable companies, so you will likely need to evaluate your financial and management strength using other information. This "other information" is what business valuators use to value closely held companies. It includes all aspects of financial information, projections, history of the company, industry outlook, relative position in the industry, economic trends, and so on. Consequently, valuing your business before undertaking an initial public offering can be a very useful tool for managing your expectations and providing some of the information and analysis your investment bankers will require. In addition to all of the considerations involved in valuing your company, factors outside the company such as the investment climate, the economy, industry trends, etc., will influence the ultimate asking price and timing of the offering.

IPO Costs

How much does it cost to launch an IPO? Michael Colo, an attorney with Poyner & Spruill, LLP, reports on the firm's Web site (⬦ *http://ps-nc-law.com/infocenter/Merger_Acquisitions/IPOArticle_May_2000.asp*) that the underwriting costs usually are 6–7% of the total offering price. In addition, accountants, attorneys, financial analysts, and other professionals will have hefty fees for many hours of complicated work before the IPO takes place, and the stock exchange or automatic quotation system will assess their standard fees. This can all add up to over $1 million. Even in small IPOs, the fees before the 6–7% underwriting fee can exceed $250,000, which is a lot of money for most small businesses. You can look at the Hoover's Online quarterly IPO Scorecard on the Web at ✍ *www.boovers.com/ipo/scorecard/* to see how recent IPOs have fared. In the fourth quarter of 2002, one IPO Scorecard showed that twenty-one companies had gone public. The offering prices totaled $3.7 billion with an average of $175.1 million. Of the twenty-one businesses, the price of ten of them increased by more than 8% on the first day and five of them decreased in price on the first day. The IPO Scorecard also shows the "money left on the table." This is the difference between the first trade valuation and the original pricing valuation. Underwriters generally set the initial price a little low so that the initial investors have some gain when they sell their stock on the open market. The money left on the table in these fourth quarter 2002 transactions ranged from a high of $75.1 million to just less than $2 million.

➤ **Chapter 4**

Tax Reasons for Business Valuation and Related Issues

Part One

Part Two

Part Three

Part Four

Part Five

Part Six

Estate and Gift Planning

I s your business one of your most valuable assets? If you died suddenly, would the business have to be sold or liquidated to pay the estate tax? Would your spouse or children be able to continue running it if they inherited your ownership interest? Estate planning is often avoided because contemplating one's mortality is never fun. Also the process brings up difficult questions for which there are no good answers. However, this is exactly why it is important for everyone, and especially business owners, to start planning now.

Deciding on Asset Division

The most important aspect of estate planning is determining how you want your assets to be divided among your heirs. This is important whether or not there will be any estate tax consequences. Even if you don't have a will, you may have already done a lot of estate planning by naming beneficiaries for your retirement plans, IRAs, and insurance policies. Much of your real estate and many investments may be held jointly with rights of survivorship, meaning that those assets will automatically pass to the person with whom you owned the property.

Your business is different. You will need to specify in your will how you want this ownership interest to pass. If you don't have a will, your business interest will pass according to the **laws of intestacy** in your state. The laws of intestacy are the provisions each state uses to distribute the assets of people who die without a will. Although each state has different rules, the decedent's assets are distributed to family members. However, the state will not necessarily allocate your assets to the same people and in the same proportion as you would have desired. Did you know that in some states, if you die without a will and without children, your estate would be split between your spouse and your parents? Would your spouse be comfortable sharing ownership of assets, such as your business, with your parents? What if your spouse owns part of the business, would you enjoy having your spouse's parents as co-owners?

> The laws of intestacy are the provisions each state uses to distribute the assets of people who die without a will.

Wills and Buy/Sell Agreements

If you have other business partners, having a will does not take the place of executing a buy/sell agreement. Most closely held business owners do not want to continue in business with the spouse or children of their former business partners. The buy/sell agreement provides a mechanism for paying a deceased owner's heirs for their share of the company. This creates a win-win situation where the heirs get needed cash and the other business partner or partners retain exclusive ownership of the company. Conversely, having a buy/sell agreement does not preclude the need for a will. These documents work together, not in place of each other.

Minimizing Estate and Gift Taxes

The second most important aspect of estate planning is structuring the estate plan to minimize or eliminate estate taxes, thereby having more of your assets pass to your heirs. You should seek the advice of a CPA or estate planning attorney to help structure your plan to incorporate the current estate tax regulations. However, you will need to know the value of your closely held business no matter which planning strategies you pursue. The IRS has specified that "fair market value" must be the standard of value used for estate, gift, and inheritance tax purposes. "Fair market value," as defined by the IRS, "is the price at which the property would change hands between a willing buyer and a willing seller, neither being under any compulsion to buy or to sell and both having reasonable knowledge of relevant facts."

The Gift Tax Exclusion

Gifting the business to your spouse or other heirs is a good way to get one of the more valuable assets out of your estate before your death. You may make unlimited gifts to your spouse without paying any gift tax. You can make gifts of company stock over time using the annual gift tax exclusion, which is currently $11,000 ($22,000 per couple). Under this provision you can give shares of stock worth up to $11,000 per year to any number of individuals without paying gift tax or filing a gift tax return. If you are married you can "gift-split" with your spouse to give up to $22,000 per year even if the property is titled in only one of your names. Although no tax is due on gifts under

$22,000 per couple, a gift tax return should be filed. Please check with your tax advisor to verify the exclusion amount in effect at the time of your gift.

Each person is also eligible for a lifetime gift tax exclusion of $1 million. Instead of giving small percentages of your company stock over the years, you could make a large gift of up to $1 million. You would not owe gift tax on this amount, but you would need to file a gift tax return to report the amount of the gift over the annual exclusion amount of $11,000 ($22,000 per couple). However, the lifetime gift tax exclusion of $1 million is tied to the estate tax exclusion. If you use all or part of your $1 million exclusion during your lifetime, you will reduce the amount of the estate tax exclusion by the same amount. Consult your tax advisor to make sure you are utilizing the current regulations. States may have different gift tax laws than the federal government, and these exclusion amounts may not be operable in all states.

Filing Gift Tax Returns

You should file federal and state gift tax returns even if you do not owe tax, if you are making a gift of closely held stock. Attach the business valuation documentation to each of these returns to show the government how you have determined the fair market value of your gifts. Filing these returns starts the "statute of limitations." The statute of limitations is the law that limits the period of time available to make changes or file an enforcement action. For tax purposes, the statute of limitations is generally three years. This means that the IRS or state revenue department has three years to review your returns and assess additional tax, and you have three years to file amended returns to make any changes that have come to your attention.

You may ask, "Why would I want to file a tax return that is not specifically required and give the IRS the opportunity to audit me?" You do run the risk that the IRS can question the valuation of your business and any discounts you may have taken. However, the potential cost of any IRS changes at this point is very minimal. For example, if the IRS determined that a gift should be valued at greater than $11,000, any additional tax would usually be offset by the $1 million gift exclusion. If you have already used your $1 million gift exclusion, any tax on what you originally thought was an $11,000 gift would be relatively minimal. The most important benefit of filing the returns is that the IRS only has three years to challenge the returns.

The biggest tax risk you and your heirs face with a gifting program for the family business appears when you die. When your executor files your estate tax return, all the gifts made throughout your life must be added to your gross estate, estate tax is calculated on the total, and then deductions and credits are taken for gift taxes paid and estate tax exclusions. Huge negative tax consequences can result if the IRS determines at this point, or within three years, that the valuation and the discounts were incorrect. Your best defense is to file annual gift tax returns to establish the value of the business with appropriate discounts. Although the statute of limitations does not preclude the IRS from auditing "open years" or the estate tax return, you could argue that the IRS has already agreed with your numbers because they did not change them in the years that are now protected.

Who Gives a FliP?—Family Limited Partnerships and "Discounts"

A **family limited partnership,** also known as an FLP or FLiP, is a sophisticated gift and estate planning mechanism used to shift assets to other family members to reduce estate taxation. FliPs are the same as other limited partnerships except that the partners are family members. All limited partnerships have two types of partners: general partners and limited partners. General partners control the operations of the entity and have unlimited liability in contrast to limited partners who have little control but whose liability is limited to the amount they invested.

You may want to consider setting up a FliP if you anticipate that your estate would still be subject to substantial estate taxes even after using your annual gift tax exclusions and executing the basic tax saving and estate planning documents. Also you may be uncomfortable with making outright gifts of your company's stock to your children or other family members because you don't want them to have any control over the business at this time.

To get started, you would hire an experienced estate-planning attorney to draft the documents and advise you. Secondly you would put some or all of your company stock in the FliP. You would retain a small general partnership interest, but you would also retain total control over the business and the partnership. Next you would give limited partnership interests to your children or other family members. They would end up with most of the equity but none of

> All limited partnerships have two types of partners: general partners and limited partners.

the control. You can make these gifts utilizing the annual gift exclusions over time or use your lifetime gift exclusion to make substantial gifts all at once. The principal benefits of the FliP are the ability to keep assets in the family, reduce estate taxes, and retain management control. What could be better than that? FliP gifts with discounts are better because they leverage the amount of the gift.

What are discounts and how do they leverage your gifts? Discounts are just what they sound like—a reduction in the fair market value of an asset. Limited partnership interests are subject to substantial discounts because of the lack of control that the limited partners have over the underlying assets. Assume that you transferred your business valued at $5 million to a FliP. You retain a 10% general partnership interest and give the other 90% in limited partnership interests to various family members. In this scenario it may appear that a 10% limited partner would have a share representing $500,000 of underlying business assets. However, the limited partner has no title to these assets, no right to receive them, and can't even control how his or her share of the assets is managed. You, as the general partner, continue to make all of the operating decisions for the company. Under these circumstances would anyone pay $500,000 for this 10-percent limited partnership interest? The easy answer to this is no. Therefore, the value of the limited partnership interest is discounted to reflect this inherent lack of control.

Discounts for FliPs usually run in the 20 to 50% range. (See Chapter 23 for a more detailed discussion of discounts and how to calculate them.) These discounts create the magic of leveraging. If you apply a 35% discount to each 10% limited partnership interest in the above example, you will be able to transfer $500,000 in underlying assets while reporting a gift of only $325,000. Discounting also leverages the amount of assets that can be transferred annually without incurring any gift tax. Using the above example of FliP interests with a 35% discount, each $11,000 annual exclusion gift would represent $16,923 ($11,000/ .65) of underlying assets. Gift-splitting with your spouse would yield an annual transfer of $33,846 ($22,000/.65) of underlying assets to each family member with no gift tax.

Charitable Giving Strategies

What happens if you want to contribute stock of your closely held corporation to charity? The first step is to make sure that the intended charitable recipient wants to receive your gift. All charitable organizations want to receive donations, but sometimes the strings attached or the related administrative complexities are not worth it to them. What can the charity do with your stock? Will they receive dividends if they hold it? Are you intending to have an IPO? Can they sell it to someone else to get cash? Assuming that the charity graciously wants to accept your gift, the next step is to have a business valuation performed to determine how much of a charitable contribution you can claim. A copy of the valuation report should accompany the Form 8283, Noncash Charitable Contributions, which should be attached to your tax return in the year you are claiming the deduction.

This sounds like a pretty good deal, especially if you have a lot of closely held business stock. So you may ask, "What is the catch? Are there any limitations?" There are several limitations, some of which apply to all charitable contributions and some that are related to gifts of appreciated securities. Your charitable deduction can be limited to 20, 30, or 50% of your adjusted gross income (AGI). The general rule is that all of your charitable contributions cannot exceed 50% of your AGI if your gift is to a "50% organization." How do you know what organizations are 50% organizations? The easiest method is to ask someone at the organization. If they don't know, you may want to consider a different charity. Beyond that, you can consult IRS Publication 78 for an extensive listing. Most of the organizations you think of as being charities are 50% organizations. For example, the IRS lists churches and religious organizations; educational organizations; hospitals and nonprofit health or medical research facilities; federal or state governments; and publicly supported organizations that further scientific, literary, artistic, or amateur athletic activities in this category. In addition, private operating foundations and private nonoperating foundations that make qualifying distributions of 100% of contributions qualify as 50% organizations.

> All charitable organizations want to receive donations, but sometimes the strings attached or the related administrative complexities are not worth it to them.

Establishing Tax Basis in Purchase

Tax basis is the accounting term for the amount you pay for an asset and any additional costs of putting it into service. For example, you buy a piece of equipment for $5,000 and have to pay $2,000 to have it delivered and installed in your place of business. Your basis in this property is $7,000. Basis is reduced by depreciation, which is an allowance for the exhaustion of the

What Is a Private Foundation?

In typical IRS parlance, every organization that is qualified to be tax-exempt is a private foundation unless it isn't. Generally a tax-exempt organization is not a private foundation if it has broad public support, is organized for traditional charitable purposes, and notifies the IRS that it is not a private foundation. Although families or corporations set up private foundations for charitable purposes, they cannot qualify for tax-exemption because they do not enjoy broad public support. The consequences of having private foundation status as opposed to tax-exempt status are excise taxes on investment income, strict requirements relating to annual charitable contributions and other expenditures, limitations on holdings of closely held companies, and restrictions on related party transactions. With all of these limitations, why would anyone start a private foundation? The benefit is that families or corporations can consolidate and manage their charitable giving to achieve a greater impact.

property over time. Depreciation rates and amounts are often different for tax purposes and financial statement purposes. For tax purposes, you generally want to take advantage of accelerated depreciation schedules and opportunities to elect to expense certain depreciable business assets (Section 179 Expense). The IRS wants to know the tax basis in the property because it is used to calculate the gain or loss on the sale of the asset, and it is the starting point for calculating depreciation.

When you purchase a single asset or small group of assets, it is easy to properly allocate the purchase price to the asset or assets. What happens when you purchase an entire business? For tax purposes, the IRS requires that the purchase price of a business be allocated to assets in proportion to their fair market value in the following order:

1. Certificates of deposit, U.S. government securities, foreign currency, and actively traded securities
2. Assets marked to market at least annually and debt instruments, including accounts receivable
3. Stock in trade, inventory, and property held primarily for sale to customers
4. All other assets except "section 197 intangibles," goodwill and going concern value
5. Section 197 intangibles except goodwill and going concern value
6. Goodwill and going concern value whether or not they are section 197 intangibles

Marked to market assets refer to securities held for sale by dealers as opposed to securities held by investors. The IRS's mark to market requirements specify how to record these assets at fair market value instead of the historical cost basis used for other assets. Securities held for sale by dealers are generally treated as inventory and must be valued at their fair market price. Other securities held by dealers that are not considered inventory or investments are treated as being sold at the end of the year with gain or loss recognized as part of the dealer's taxable income.

Section 197 intangibles include purchased goodwill and most other acquired intangible assets such as covenants not to compete, patents, copyrights, trademarks, client lists, databases, and formulas. These assets can be amortized over a fifteen-year period starting in the month of acquisition. This provision of the IRS Code was enacted on August 10, 1993, and it applies primarily to intangibles acquired after that date. Prior to this legislation, the cost of many intangible assets, such as goodwill, could not be amortized. Also, determining the appropriate amortization period for the intangibles that could be amortized was a challenge because of a myriad of definitions and related "useful lives." Thus, the creation of Section 197 intangibles represents a true example of tax simplification.

Asset Allocation Requirements for Transactions

The buyer and seller of the business must both attach Form 8594 (Asset Allocation Statement) to their income tax returns for the year in which the transaction occurred. Consequently, you should agree in writing how the purchase price will be allocated. This can be an important part of the negotiations because all dollars paid for assets are not the same in the eyes of the tax law.

Why aren't all dollars the same? The first big difference is in the character of the gain to the seller. Sellers want as much of the transaction as possible to qualify for capital gain treatment. Capital gains are taxed at a lower rate than ordinary income on individual income tax returns. When a business owner sells stock rather than assets, that sale qualifies for capital gain treatment just like the sale of any publicly traded stock held for over one year. In addition, sellers of businesses that are "flow-through" entities such as S corporations, LLCs, and partnerships get the benefit of capital gain treatment on the portion of the sales price allocated to capital assets.

Assets and Capital Gains

What kinds of business assets produce "capital gains" when they are sold? "Capital assets," naturally. What are "capital assets"? Don't go to the IRS for the definition; they will only tell you what is not a capital asset.

Things that are not capital assets include inventory, property held for resale, property used in a trade or business, and certain copyrights. Generally, capital assets are assets with a useful life greater than one year. This includes real estate, tangible personal property (as opposed to real property), and intangible property such as patents and goodwill.

Based on this definition, or the IRS's definitive nondefinition, you may ask: "What business asset could you possibly sell that would qualify for capital gains treatment?" Certainly goodwill and patents would qualify, but what about all of the furniture, fixtures, equipment, and real property that make up the core of the business? Although the IRS specifically states that property used in a trade or business is not a capital asset, such property can qualify for capital gains treatment if it is "Code Section 1231" property. Code Section 1231 property is the best of all possible classifications. Why? Gains on the sale of Code Section 1231 property are eligible for lower capital gains tax treatment, but losses are treated as "ordinary" and, therefore, offset other ordinary income from any source.

IRS Code Section 1231 lists several types of property that will qualify for this "best of both worlds" treatment. The types of Code Section 1231 property you are most likely to encounter are real and depreciable property used in a trade or business; i.e., the furniture, fixtures, and real estate you use to run the business. Other types of Code Section 1231 property include property that was condemned or destroyed suddenly by an act of nature, crops sold with the land, certain livestock, timber, domestic iron ore, and coal under special circumstances.

Asset Allocation and Depreciation

The second reason all purchase dollars are not created or treated equally is related to depreciation. Depreciation is an allowance to provide for the loss in value of an asset due to wear and tear or age. Taxpayers can deduct this allowance on an annual basis from their ordinary income. Therefore, buyers of assets want to have the purchase price allocated preferentially to assets with shorter depreciable lives so they can recover their investment in a shorter time. Depreciable lives are relatively arbitrary for tax purposes, so you can refer to the following list to help you determine over what period to depreciate various assets.

1. Land is not depreciable at all.
2. "Three-year property" includes racehorses over two years old, breeding hogs, and highway trucks designed to tow trailers.
3. "Five-year property" includes cars, light and heavy general-purpose trucks, computers, office machinery (e.g., typewriters and calculators), breeding and dairy cattle, and assets used in construction.
4. "Seven-year property" includes office furniture, fixtures and equipment (e.g., desks, files, cell phones, overhead projectors, and fax machines), certain livestock, and assets used in agricultural activities.
5. "Ten-year property" includes vessels, barges, tugboats not used in construction or fishing, trees or vines bearing fruit or nuts, and single purpose agricultural or horticultural structures.
6. "Fifteen-year property" includes municipal wastewater treatment plants and telephone distribution plants, retail motor fuel outlets not including convenience stores, car wash facilities, billboards, and depreciable land improvements not specifically included in any other asset class. Examples of depreciable land improvements are sidewalks, roads, driveways, parking lots, docks, bridges, nonagricultural fences, and landscaping if it is close to a building.
7. "Twenty-year property" includes farm buildings such as barns and sheds.
8. "Twenty-seven and one-half-year property" includes residential buildings.
9. "Thirty-nine and one-half-year property" includes commercial buildings.

Once you determine the useful life of the assets for depreciation purposes, you must select a depreciation method and the applicable convention. The Modified

The Double-Edged Sword of Capital Gains Treatment

Capital gains treatment is advantageous for long-term gains because they are taxed at a lower rate. However, this rate differential may make you a candidate for a punitive flat tax called the Alternative Minimum Tax (AMT). Congress enacted this tax to prevent high-income taxpayers from avoiding taxes with "loopholes." What if you have a loss on the sale of a capital asset? For individual taxpayers, all capital gains and losses are netted, and losses are only deductible to the extent of gains plus $3,000. Any unused capital losses are carried forward indefinitely to offset capital gains plus $3,000 per year of ordinary income. C corporations must completely offset capital losses with capital gains. C corporate capital losses may be carried back three years and forward five years to offset capital gains. Any unused capital losses are lost.

Accelerated Cost Recovery System (MACRS) is required for most property put in service after 1986. You may use the 200-percent declining balance method for properties in the three- to ten-year classes with a half-year convention and a switch to the straight-line method when it becomes more advantageous. The appropriate method for 15- and 20-year property is the 150-percent declining balance method using a half-year convention with a switch to the straight-line method. Real property is depreciated using the straight-line method over its useful life with a mid-month convention.

What are these conventions and how do they affect the depreciation calculation? The half-year convention is an assumption that the property was put in service in the middle of the year, thus only half a year's worth of depreciation is taken in the first year. Similarly, the mid-month convention assumes that real property was put in service in the middle of the month. This means that depreciation is taken for the remaining months plus half a month for the first month.

A Declining Balance Depreciation Example

Assume you have purchased a computer for $2,000. First you divide the number one by the appropriate useful life to get the rate. For example, the rate for a computer that is five-year property would be $1/5$ or 20%. Then you multiply this number by either 2 (for 200 percent) or 1.5 (for 150 percent) to determine the appropriate declining balance rate. The rate for your hypothetical computer would be 20% x 2 or 40% for the 200% declining balance method. Multiply this number by the adjusted basis of the property and the half-year convention to get the first year's depreciation deduction. The first year calculation would be: (40% x 2,000 x $1/2$ = 400). For the second year, subtract the first year depreciation from your basis and multiply the adjusted basis by the same rate (40% in the computer example.) The second year calculation would be: 1,600 x 40% = 640. You continue on in this manner until dividing the basis by the remaining life yields a larger number than you get by multiplying the remaining basis by 40%. This is when you switch to the straight-line method. The switch occurs only after you have depreciated the property for more than half of its useful life.

Tax-Related Business Structure

One of the most important business decisions you will make is the form of organization you choose for your company. Fortunately, this is not an irrevocable decision—you can change your form of organization. However, it is generally easier and less costly to start with a simpler form of organization and move up the hierarchy to more complex forms. What are the basic forms of business organization and their identifying characteristics?

> It is generally easier and less costly to start with a simpler form of organization and move up the hierarchy to more complex forms.

Sole Proprietorship—As the sole owner, you report the company's income or loss on your individual return, pay self-employment and estimated taxes, and have unlimited personal liability for company activities.

General Partnership—A "GP" is a separate entity with two or more owners. The income or loss flows through to the owner's individual tax returns, the owners pay self-employment and estimated taxes, and they have unlimited personal liability for company activities.

Limited Partnership—An "LP" is a separate entity with two or more owners, and at least one owner must be a general partner. The income or loss flows through to the owner's individual tax returns, the general partners pay self-employment and estimated taxes and have unlimited liability, and the limited partners have limited liability and may be limited in their ability to deduct losses as passive investors.

Limited Liability Company or Partnership—An "LLC" or "LLP" is an entity that is structured like a general partnership for tax purposes, but the owners have the same liability protection as corporate shareholders. Single- member LLCs are treated as sole proprietors for tax purposes.

C Corporation—C corporations are the basic corporate form where business income is taxed separately and can be taxed twice if it is distributed to shareholders as dividends or in liquidation. Shareholders are not individually liable for the actions of the business.

S Corporation—S corporations have the same liability protection as C corporations, but the company income or loss flows through to the individual shareholder's tax return. Thus, there is only a single level of tax imposed. S corporations are somewhat limited in numbers and types of shareholders.

As you can see from this list, an important aspect of your choice of entity decision is the liability protection you will receive. However, you should still insure all of your insurable liabilities—no form of organization takes the place of adequate insurance. Other important considerations are the tax consequences of your form of organization as well as the complexity and, therefore, the cost of administering the entity.

Sole Proprietorships

The simplest form of organization is the sole proprietorship because it is not a separate entity. Consequently, if you just start running your business, you will automatically be considered a sole proprietor. This can make sense if you are starting a venture without a lot of capital, without any inherent liability issues, and without a good sense of its chances for long-term success. Under these circumstances it is reasonable to not spend money on legal and accounting fees to set up a more sophisticated entity. However, it is still important to run your business in a professional manner and to keep your business activities separate from your personal finances. You need to do this for tax and business management purposes as well as to have a basis for valuing your business as it grows.

> The simplest form of organization is the sole proprietorship because it is not a separate entity.

Limited Liability Companies and Partnerships

With the single-member LLC, you can retain the simplicity and cost effectiveness of the sole proprietorship while gaining the liability protection of a separate entity. If you have some inherent liability risks or if you are dedicating yourself to the long-term success of the company, you should consider making the initial $500–$1,000 investment to create a single-member LLC. This is a one-time legal expenditure and separate tax returns will not need to be filed. Some states do assess annual fees for LLCs, so you will also need to factor in these costs before making your decision.

The liability protection afforded by LLCs and LLPs has made them much more user friendly than either the general or limited partnership forms that were prevalent in the past. Consequently, most new businesses operating in a partnership format organize as LLCs or LLPs. If your business is currently organized as a partnership, you may want to investigate changing to an LLC or LLP to reduce the liability exposure of the general partners. Again, you would have the upfront legal costs to set up the LLC or LLP and any state fees applicable to LLCs, but you would continue to file the same partnership tax returns.

Since the liability differences between the partnership form and the corporate form of organization have virtually been erased by the creation of the LLC, what is the big difference between the two types of entities? Believe it or not, it comes down to mundane payroll and taxes. Partners and LLC members are not considered employees of their business. Consequently, they must calculate and pay estimated taxes during the year to cover their anticipated income and self-employment tax liability. They are taxed on all of the taxable income of the business, whether they receive it or not. Conversely, if the business reports a loss, they will be able to deduct it against their other personal income if they have basis. They will have basis to the extent that they have contributed or loaned funds to the business or reported income in excess of prior year's losses or distributions taken.

Corporate shareholders working in their businesses are considered employees. They receive W-2s and have all payroll taxes withheld, just like other employees. This can provide a tax planning advantage since income tax is considered withheld ratably throughout the year no matter when it is actually withheld from compensation. You can pay a bonus near the end of the year with enough federal and state income tax withholding to cover anticipated liabilities and avoid underpayment of estimated tax penalties. In contrast to sole proprietors and LLCs, corporate income is calculated after the owners' salaries have been deducted. S corporation income, after the deduction for owners' salaries, does flow through to the owners' individual returns where they will be taxed on it personally. Of course, they will also be taxed on their compensation, which is reported on a W-2.

C and S Corporations

If you do decide to incorporate, how do you decide between the C and S corporation? You should consult your tax advisor to discuss the benefits, drawbacks, and requirements of each entity. However, it is usually advantageous to start a closely held business as an S corporation. This is partly because you will be able to personally deduct losses that may be incurred in the initial stages of a new business, but more importantly you will only pay a single level of tax on the income. This is especially important if you sell your business. In contrast, if a C corporation sells its assets, tax will be paid at the corporate level and again at the individual shareholder level when the owner receives a liquidating dividend distribution. Although it is possible to convert a C corporation to an S corporation, the single level of tax benefit can only be fully realized after ten years. In the meantime a complicated built-in gains tax must be paid when assets are sold. On the other hand, it is very easy to change from S status to C status—you simply "unelect S status" and start reporting and paying tax as a C corporation. As you probably know, tax laws are made to be changed. Always consult your tax and legal advisers to determine if any tax law changes might alter this strategy.

Finding the Most Appropriate Entity for You

Based on all these factors, the streamlined hierarchy of business entities is from simple to complex: sole proprietor, LLC, S corporation, and C corporation. As the value of your company increases, you should reevaluate your form of organization to make sure you have the most appropriate entity for your situation. As your business grows and you think about bringing on new owners or you need additional financing, you will probably want to move up the hierarchy to facilitate these changes.

Tax laws drive the business valuation process in a number of situations, and the tax laws relating to form of organization and depreciation affect the value of the entity. You will learn more in Chapter 8 about how the tax laws and tax purposes for business valuation influence the value.

> **Chapter 5**

Business Valuations for Divorce

Part One

Part Two

Part Three

Part Four

Part Five

Part Six

PART TWO: PURPOSES OF BUSINESS VALUATION

■ CHAPTER 3 Business Reasons for Business Valuation ■ CHAPTER 4 Tax Reasons for Business Valuation and Related Issues ■ CHAPTER 5 Business Valuations for Divorce ■ CHAPTER 6 Other Business Valuation Situations

What Is "Equitable Distribution"—and Is It Equitable?

Equitable distribution is a term of art used to describe how the courts in most states divide the property of a divorcing couple to achieve "fairness." Some of the factors the courts consider in equitable distribution cases are the total amount of assets owned by the couple, the type of assets owned, the respective earning potential of each party, and the length of the marriage. In this sense, equitable distribution is "equitable." However, "equitable" is not necessarily or even usually "equal." Why wouldn't it be fair to always split the assets in a marital estate 50/50?

The first reason that an equal division is not always fair relates to how the property was acquired. Property is classified as either separate property or marital property. Separate property includes property either owned before the marriage, inherited during the marriage, received as a gift during the marriage, or excluded by a contract such as a prenuptial agreement. Marital property includes all other property acquired during the marriage regardless of who owns it. Some states also consider the appreciation of separate property during a marriage to be marital property. Why is the distinction of separate versus marital property so important? Basically, if you own separate property, you will get to keep it in the event of a divorce. Consequently, it is very important to document the separate nature of any property you receive or owned before the marriage. In addition, do not convert separate property to marital property if you are concerned about the potential financial consequences of a divorce.

Let's say, for example, that you inherit $100,000 from your parents. If you put it in a separate investment account in your name only, it will retain the character of separate property. However, if you decide to put it in a joint investment account with your spouse or pay down the mortgage of your jointly owned residence, you will have converted separate property to marital property. As such, it will be subject to division in the divorce proceedings. In some states if you can "trace" the proceeds of separate property to the purchase of another asset, you may still consider it to be separate property. Consult your attorney to make sure you are treating property correctly according to the laws in your state.

> Property is classified as either separate property or marital property.

Community Property and Equitable Distribution

In addition to being able to distinguish between separate and marital property, you need to know whether you live, or have lived, in a community property state or an equitable distribution state. California is the most famous community property state, probably because a number of high-profile celebrities with high-profile divorces live there. The lower-profile community property states are: Arizona, Idaho, Louisiana, Nevada, New Mexico, Texas, Washington, and Wisconsin. In community property states, each party retains their separate property and then everything else is split 50/50. The theory behind community property is that all of a couple's income is treated as if it were earned 50% by each spouse. Therefore, all marital property is split in half by the courts unless the couple negotiates a different settlement between themselves. (See Chapter 6 for a discussion of prenuptial and postnuptial agreements that can be used to change the nature of separate and marital property by contract.) Remember too, once community property, always community property. If you acquire assets in a community property state and later move to an equitable distribution state, the community property assets will still be subject to a 50/50 division in a divorce.

Separate property is also important in equitable distribution states. You will retain your separate property in the event of a divorce in an equitable distribution state, but your marital property will not necessarily be divided in half. For example, assume your business is worth $5 million and it is your separate property. If you and your spouse own another $5 million in real estate and invested assets, the courts may award your spouse over $2.5 million of these assets in an equitable distribution state. Why? Even though your business is not subject to division because it is separate property, it is subject to being included in the consideration of what is a "fair" division of marital assets. Assuming the business provides you with a good income, the courts may decide that you need fewer other assets to provide income or security for the future. This would be particularly likely if your spouse has less earning potential than you.

Types of Assets

Another reason it is not always equitable to split marital assets 50/50 relates to the type of assets involved. All assets are not created equal when it comes to income producing ability, tax consequences, projected growth, liquidity, etc. These are all factors that can and should be taken into consideration in equitable distribution cases. The stereotypical example involves a couple whose primary assets are the marital residence and a retirement plan. Assuming the fair market value of each of these assets is about the same, the dependent spouse usually gets the house and the more highly employed spouse usually gets the retirement plan. If the values really are about the same, what is wrong with this scenario? The problem may not be apparent at the time of the property division, but it can develop shortly thereafter. Often the dependent spouse wants to continue to live in the house to maintain a current lifestyle as well as to provide a measure of stability for any minor children. These are reasonable considerations in a divorce; however, the house generally consumes income rather than producing it, and the only ways to tap into the appreciation of the property are to borrow against it or sell it. Furthermore, the dependent spouse is usually not able to save or make significant retirement contributions. Conversely, the nondependent spouse's retirement plan continues to grow at a relatively rapid rate since additional contributions are being made and the income is not taxed until it is taken out of the plan. Consequently, this stereotypical example often produces a situation where the dependent spouse has a negative net worth in the future, while the other spouse's net worth is very substantial.

Coming Up with an Equitable Distribution

This is what equitable distribution is all about—taking into account all the factors that impact fairness, not just on the date of separation, but in the future. Sometimes you need to think "outside the box" to come up with solutions that will work for both parties. Potential solutions can involve uneven distribution of assets, selling the marital residence with both parties scaling down, increasing or decreasing maintenance (alimony), both parties continuing to own some property jointly, etc. Mediation, as opposed to divorce court, is a good way to start a dialogue aimed at crafting a negotiated settlement that is equitable and less costly both in terms of financial and emotional capital. In this way, equitable distribution can be more equitable than if you rely on the courts and two lawyers going for the jugular to decide what is equitable.

Using a Mediator

The *American Heritage Dictionary* defines mediation as "An attempt to bring about a peaceful settlement or compromise between disputants through the objective intervention of a neutral party." In a divorce situation, the husband and wife are the disputants, the mediator is the neutral party, and the goal is to come up with a favorable result for both parties. The neutrality of the mediator is central to the process. Although the mediator is often an attorney, the mediator cannot give legal advice, only legal information, so it is wise for each party to have their own lawyer to advise them. The mediator works with both parties and their attorneys (and financial advisors such as certified public accountants, certified financial planners, and certified divorce financial analysts) to craft a settlement that will work for both of them. The mediator's role is to facilitate the process of identifying the critical success factors for both spouses and helping them negotiate an agreement that they both feel is fair, or at least that they can live with. The primary benefit of mediation is that "fairer" settlements can be achieved because both parties' priorities are incorporated in the process and the tax, financial, and emotional ramifications of different scenarios are considered. Secondly, mediated settlements usually cost less than divorce court litigation so the parties have a bigger asset base to divide. Protracted divorce litigation can cost from $10,000 to over $100,000 and take months or years to settle. Most of this money goes to attorneys and expert witnesses on both sides. Expenses for a mediated settlement including the mediator's fee and professional fees for attorneys and other financial advisors can mount up, but generally they would be closer to $10,000 than $100,000. If you have a closely held business you may also need to pay for a professional valuation in either a litigated or mediated case. This specialized professional service can add from $5,000 to $20,000 depending on the business and other case-specific information.

> Although the mediator is often an attorney, the mediator cannot give legal advice, only legal information.

Collaborative Divorce

Collaborative divorce is an extension of the mediation process whereby the divorcing spouses and their attorneys commit to resolving all of their issues by negotiation. The aspect of collaborative divorce that backs up this commitment from the attorneys' standpoint is that they must agree to not represent their clients in court if the collaborative process fails. This is an important factor in the process as well, because it encourages everyone to "put all their cards on the table," since information will not be able to be used against them by the opposing attorney in court. In addition, a collaborative law environment reduces the leverage some divorcing spouses and their attorneys like to wield by trying to get the other party to agree to something by threatening litigation. The Collaborative Divorce Lawyers Association of Connecticut, on the Web at *http://collaborative-divorce.com*, describes the process as using "informal methods such as voluntary production of financial documents, four-way conferences, negotiation, and where needed, outside professionals such as accountants, financial planners, and family counselors. . . . Collaborative resolutions are reached through a process in which clients have more control and settlements have been designed to meet each party's needs. These agreements are designed to be more sustainable over longer periods of time."

Dividing the Family Business

When you look at the number of small businesses in America and the divorce rate, you can see that the problem of dividing the family business is more widespread than you might have thought. The Small Business Administration's Office of Advocacy estimates that there are about 22.4 million small businesses. Their definition of small business is one with fewer than 500 employees. According to U.S. Health and Human Services statistics, the American divorce rate is 49%. This means that almost half of all marriages in the United States will end in divorce. To the extent that small business owners are married, this is a sobering statistic.

What are your choices when dividing the family business? The most common solution is for one person to retain the business. This works well when one spouse primarily owns and operates the company. This solution is often mandated by the terms of a company buy-sell agreement when there are multiple owners or when the company is a professional service firm where there are licensure requirements for owners. If you own the business yourself or with outside partners or shareholders, you exchange other assets from the marital estate for the ownership of the business. Of course the first step in this process is determining the value of your business. Generally in a divorce situation you should pay a professional business valuator to appraise the business. This improves your chances of coming up with a "fair" settlement and also one that could hold up in court if the process goes that far.

What do you do when both spouses work in the business and each one wants the business or wants to continue working there? Believe it or not, some couples who can't get along on the home front make good business partners. If communications are good and you and your spouse do work well together, or at least complement each other's talents, you should consider continuing to own the business jointly. If you choose this route, you should treat it like any other business relationship and issue stock or partnership interests, institute a buy-sell agreement, and formalize any other documents such as operating agreements, job descriptions, and employee benefit plans.

The final option is to sell the business and divide the profits. The benefit of this method is that the value will be a true fair market value—what a willing buyer pays a willing seller. This strategy creates flexibility for both parties. They each have the option of using the proceeds to start or buy another businesses or perhaps invest the money and live off the income. The negatives of this option include losing the intangible value of owning a business and having a job. In addition, the process of selling a business can take a very long time. During this period someone needs to run the business and agreements need to be reached about who that will be, how income will be divided, and how management decisions will be made. This can be very complicated and fraught with emotion when a couple is divorcing. In addition, the actual price received may be lower than the asking price if there is pressure to complete the transaction rapidly.

> Generally in a divorce situation you should pay a professional business valuator to appraise the business.

Fair Market Value and Divorce Cases

Most experts state in their valuation reports and in court that the standard of value they used to value a business is "fair market value." As we discussed earlier, this is the IRS-approved definition meaning "the price at which the property would change hands between a willing buyer and willing seller, neither being under any compulsion to buy or sell, and both having reasonable knowledge of the facts." What is wrong with this picture? Generally, the business is not going to be sold subsequent to a divorce, so there aren't any willing buyers or sellers. Consequently, businesses valued for divorce purposes aren't really valued at "fair market value." What are some of the differences between fair market value and the value for divorce purposes? First, discounts for lack of marketability are not often taken since the business is not being sold. Secondly, values for cash and investments are included in the valuation for divorce. Usually these liquid assets would not be included with the assets of a business that was being sold. The critical difference, though, is one of purpose. The purpose of a valuation for equitable distribution is just that—to determine what is a fair or equitable value for both parties in a divorce proceeding. Many state courts use different standards of value in divorce cases, e.g., fair value, going concern value, and equitable distribution value. **Fair value** is an amount that will compensate an owner who is being deprived of the benefit of an asset when there is not a willing buyer or seller. **Going concern value** is the value a company has as a continuing operating business utilizing the assets currently in place. **Equitable distribution value** is similar to fair value with an emphasis on the value to the spouse who does not own the business. Even though there is not an agreed upon standard of value for divorce valuations, you should be aware that the standard definition of fair market value may not be appropriate. Consequently, you should consult your attorney and review the state statutes and case law for guidance on the appropriate standard of value to use in a divorce case in your jurisdiction.

Professional or Personal Goodwill Versus Practice Goodwill

The term "goodwill" in a business valuation context refers to the intangible part of the fair market value of a company that is in excess of the value attributable to the hard assets and the specifically identifiable intangible assets. Specifically identifiable intangible assets include client or patient lists, trademarks, patents, copyrights, licenses, computer software programs, and franchise rights. For example, if you are selling a manufacturing company for $5 million with hard assets appraised at $3 million and a patent valued at $1 million, the remaining $1 million portion of the purchase price would be classified as goodwill. Goodwill is a catchall for the intangible factors that enable a company to be more profitable than its competitors. The presence of goodwill is why someone would pay more than the sum of the values of the identifiable assets for a company. Some of the characteristics that can generate goodwill include:

- Good customer and vendor relationships
- The ability to generate new business
- Experienced and loyal workforce
- Superior internal systems
- Location, location, location

> Goodwill is a catchall for the intangible factors that enable a company to be more profitable than its competitors.

The goodwill component of professional practices such as those owned by health care professionals, accountants, lawyers, architects, and engineers is valued differently than that of other companies. The difficulty with valuing the goodwill in these practices is that professional goodwill is tied to the individual and is based on their education, skills, personality, reputation, and other factors that have made them successful. Professional or personal goodwill is, therefore, not easily transferable. In contrast, practice goodwill relates to the practice's ability to maintain and build the business separate from an individual professional. Practice goodwill, if it exists, could be transferred just like goodwill in other companies. Of course there are constraints on this transfer since most professions are regulated and have restrictions on ownership by persons who are not licensed. The critical issue in determining practice goodwill is how many clients or patients would stay with the practice if the professional left.

In general, the larger the practice, the more potential for retaining clients/patients if one professional left. In smaller firms, practice goodwill exists when the firm treats clients or patients as clients or patients of the firm, not of the individual professional. This situation exists most often when professionals work together on client matters or substitute for each other so clients or patients can receive a consistent level of service. You can determine that there is practice goodwill if patients or clients call the firm and are guided to the appropriate professional. Professional goodwill exists when people call the firm and ask for a specific professional. Many practices receive both types of referrals so they would have both types of goodwill. Even if you know that you have both professional and practice goodwill, it is very difficult to separate the two and value them.

How do the courts handle this difficult issue? It depends on where you live. Most courts consider professional goodwill to be a marital asset even though it is not transferable. Some states treat only practice goodwill as marital property subject for division. In some jurisdictions, noncompete agreements and the value of professional licenses are factored into the mix of professional goodwill. Consequently, it is very important to work with your attorney to determine how professional goodwill is handled in your state. Since the treatment of goodwill is based on case law rather than statute, this is a constantly evolving area of divorce practice.

Alimony and Child Support

Alimony, also known as spousal maintenance, and child support are the two types of continuing payments that arise from divorce. Child support is self-explanatory—it is related to the support of minor children. Every state has structured guidelines regarding how much child support a noncustodial spouse should pay the custodial spouse for the care of the children. The amount of time the children spend with each spouse is factored into this calculation. If you are in an upper income bracket, the guidelines may not apply. In these cases, an agreement about child support is reached or the court awards an amount based on relevant facts about income, lifestyle, and needs. Child support payments end when the children reach the age of majority, which is age eighteen in most states. You cannot deduct child support payments for tax purposes, and the recipient does not declare them as taxable income.

Alimony is not so straightforward. Alimony is the financial support that a higher-earning person pays to a dependent former spouse. Alimony payments are tax-deductible to the payer and taxable to the recipient if they meet the following strict IRS requirements:

1. Payment is received under a divorce or separation agreement.
2. Payments must be made in cash or check to the recipient or a third-party.

> Alimony is the financial support that a higher-earning person pays to a dependent former spouse.

3. The agreement does not designate the payment as *not* being alimony.
4. The spouses cannot be members of the same household or file joint tax returns.
5. There is no liability to make payments after the recipient's death.
6. Payments cannot be construed to be child support.
7. Payments cannot be made to maintain property owned by the payer.

Payments that don't meet these guidelines won't be deductible for tax purposes, even if the couple has mutually agreed that they will. For example, you and your spouse agree that alimony will be reduced when the children graduate from high school because the dependent spouse would then have the opportunity to pursue full-time employment. Reductions in alimony related to child contingencies or children attaining the age of majority can cause alimony to be recharacterized as child support. In this case, the difference between the alimony paid before and after a child turned eighteen could be treated as nondeductible child support by the IRS. This is another trap for the unwary, so please check with your attorney before agreeing to pay any alimony to make sure that you will not be subject to "alimony recapture."

Avoiding Alimony Recapture

"Alimony recapture" refers to the penalty the IRS assesses when they decide that a divorced couple is trying to make a nondeductible transfer deductible by calling it alimony. The penalty is a stiff one—the person who paid alimony must reclassify the excess amount to a nondeductible payment, file amended returns, and pay the related tax. The spouse who received the excess alimony can then file amended returns and claim a refund for the tax on the excess amount. Strictly speaking, alimony recapture only refers to the "front-loading" of alimony, which the IRS considers to be a disguised property settlement. Alimony recapture is an issue if the person paying spousal support reduces it by more than $15,000 from the previous year in the first three years. Although the IRS instituted this rule to prevent couples from deducting otherwise nondeductible property settlements, it can catch an honest spouse trying to help his or her spouse more at the beginning of the divorce.

Alimony Recapture, Part Two

Alimony payments that are reduced at a time period related to a child contingency are an even bigger trap for the unwary and can cause "alimony recapture, part two." If you reduce alimony payments at a time related to a child turning eighteen or twenty-one, graduating from school, moving out of the house, or any other child-related contingency, the IRS can recharacterize your previously deductible alimony payments as nondeductible child support. You can certainly avoid putting any provisions in your agreement that mention these milestones, but you need to also make sure that you don't accidentally reduce or terminate alimony within six months before or after your child's eighteenth or twenty-first birthday. I have seen many cases where the spouse paying alimony wants to reduce it at the time the dependent spouse could go back to work after taking care of children for years or after a specific number of years—e.g., half the years of the duration of the marriage. Many times these proposed reduction or cessation dates inadvertently coincide with the six-month period on either side of the child's eighteenth of twenty-first birthday. You should create a spreadsheet or use some other method to help you determine what I call the "blackout" period. Once you have determined the dates of six months before or after a crucial birthday and any overlap between children, you can make sure to not reduce alimony during these "blackout" periods.

Factors That Determine Alimony

"Alimony" comes with some emotional baggage because in the past it was always associated with "fault." Most states have done away with fault-based alimony and now consider other factors including:

- Net income after taxes of both parties
- Standard of living during the marriage
- Length of the marriage
- Income earning capacity
- Amount of property received in property settlement
- Age and health of both spouses

These factors are aimed at determining need, ability to pay, and whether one spouse "deserves" maintenance from the other. The duration of alimony is also a consideration. The rule of thumb in most states is that alimony is generally paid for a period of time equal to half the number of years the couple was married. Courts award permanent alimony in some cases and rehabilitative alimony in others. Rehabilitative alimony is temporary support that can be used for education and/or reentry into the workforce until a dependent spouse can be self-supporting. Alimony payments stop upon the death of either party and usually if the recipient remarries.

> Rehabilitative alimony is temporary support that can be used for education and/or reentry into the workforce until a dependent spouse can be self-supporting.

Avoiding "Double-dipping" Alimony

What is "double-dipping" alimony? Double-dipping is a term that is used to describe certain situations when an individual wants alimony based on their spouse's income from a closely held business, and they want a property settlement based on the fair market value of the business. One of the first things a business valuator will do when analyzing the financial statements of a company is make adjustments for reasonable salary. For example, salary studies or industry guidelines may indicate that a manager with post-graduate education and ten years of experience earns about $200,000. If you are running your own business and making $1 million per year, the business valuator may adjust your compensation to $200,000 and add $800,000 of annual income back to the company's bottom line. The theory is that the "excess" compensation you are taking represents the value of the company, not a fair wage for the amount or type of work you are doing. Adding the "excess" compensation into the calculation of the value of the business increases the value. Consequently, it is considered "double-dipping" for a spouse to receive a property settlement based on this higher value and alimony based on your $1 million salary. You can avoid "double-dipping" by understanding this relationship and making sure that proposed alimony payments are adjusted for any "excess" compensation factored into the valuation of your company.

Financing the Settlement

If the value of your other assets is sufficient to offset the value of the business, this trade-off is usually pretty straightforward. But, what happens when you don't have enough other assets to give your soon-to-be ex-spouse? One option is selling business assets to generate cash. If you have unproductive business assets, this can be a good solution. However, selling productive business assets to pay a personal liability can undermine the health of the business. This has an obvious negative affect on you as the business owner but could also affect your spouse if he or she plans to receive alimony or child support payments based on your income from the business.

Fortunately, there is a viable solution to this dilemma—the property settlement note. A property settlement note is a legal agreement stating that one party will transfer a certain amount of property to his or her spouse as a nontaxable property settlement incident to the divorce. However, the transferring party will pay off this obligation over a set period of time with interest. In this way a business owner can fund the property settlement from the profits of the business and the spouse will not have to pay tax on these receipts except to the extent of any interest received. Generally the issuer of the property settlement note secures the note with some collateral to protect the recipient spouse in the event that the note is not paid as promised.

When your spouse owns shares of stock in the business, you should carefully structure the repurchase of these shares. If the company buys back your spouse's stock, he or she will have to pay capital gains tax if the stock has appreciated. If on the other hand, you buy your ex-spouse's shares as part of the property settlement of your divorce, neither of you would have any income tax consequences at the time of this transfer. You would retain your spouse's basis and income tax would be due if you sold these shares in the future for a profit. Although this transaction appears to be structured as a sale, IRS Code Section 1041 treats it as a tax-free transfer incident to divorce.

What constitutes "incident to divorce? For IRS purposes, incident to divorce includes transfers made within one year after a divorce or legal separation or those related to the marital dissolution. Transfers are related to marital dissolutions if the divorce decree or legal separation document requires them and if the transfers take place within six years after the divorce or legal separation.

The tax-free treatment afforded by Code Section 1041 is generally beneficial to divorcing couples, but it can also be a trap for the unwary. For example, assume you are recently divorced and your spouse wants to sell some property worth $10,000 to raise cash. You decide to buy it because you believe it is a great investment property and you think you can sell it in a year or so for $15,000. Even if your spouse received the property as a gift with a basis of $5,000, he or she won't pay any income tax on the sale if it is completed within one year after your divorce. The catch is, you will have a carryover basis in the property of $5,000 even though you paid $10,000 for it. This means that if you sell it for $15,000 you will have to pay capital gains tax on a $10,000 gain, not just the $5,000 of appreciation since you bought it. You could have avoided this negative result with a different allocation of tangible assets and cash in the property settlement if your spouse's cash flow needs could have been anticipated earlier in the process. The moral of the story is to consider the needs of both parties for the foreseeable future, not just what looks like a fair split of assets at the date of separation. Also be aware that there are many special tax rules related to all aspects of a divorce settlement.

Many of the tax and emotional issues that surround a divorce influence the value of the business. In an effort to come up with a settlement, the parties may agree on a value for the business that is an average of several estimates of value or they may even pick an arbitrary number just to move forward. You should strive to come up with the most realistic value of your company using the relevant legal statutes and precedents for divorce valuations in your area. Then, if you want to negotiate, you can do that with some knowledge of how the other divorce provisions of the law relate to the value of the company. Remember that valuing your company is the first step in the process, and you can use the wealth of information you gather in that process to aid you with the second step, which is negotiating the various components of the divorce settlement, i.e., the property settlement, alimony, and child support.

> Many of the tax and emotional issues that surround a divorce influence the value of the business.

> # Chapter 6

Other Business Valuation Situations

Part One

Part Two

Part Three

Part Four

Part Five

Part Six

PART TWO: PURPOSES OF BUSINESS VALUATION

■ CHAPTER 3 Business Reasons for Business Valuation ■ CHAPTER 4 Tax Reasons for Business Valuation and Related Issues ■ CHAPTER 5 Business Valuations for Divorce ■ CHAPTER 6 **Other Business Valuation Situations**

Prenuptial Agreements: Not Just for Millionaires Anymore

"Is not marriage an open question, when it is alleged, from the beginning of the world, that such as are in the institution wish to get out, and such as are out wish to get in?" Although Ralph Waldo Emerson wrote this in *The Skeptic* during the mid-1800s, it is still true today. Nobody goes into a marriage expecting to get divorced, but the statistics should not be overlooked—1.2 million people get divorced each year in the United States. Those 1.2 million people translate into a divorce rate of 50%

The term "prenuptial agreement" conjures up images of an older, wealthier, more powerful man coercing his young, beautiful bride-to-be to "sign here" on the back page of a lot of legal mumbo-jumbo. This type of prenuptial agreement only works in the movies. In reality, it would not be valid in most states because one of the parties was coerced and was not represented by legal counsel. So, if you can't just take away your soon-to-be spouse's property rights without his or her knowing the full extent of what you have done, what good is a prenuptial agreement?

The Value of Prenuptial Agreements

Even though it does not initially sound very romantic, a prenuptial agreement can help marriages succeed, and, of course, it can help make the divorce process go more smoothly if the marriage does fail. What exactly is a prenuptial agreement? A prenuptial agreement is a legal contract that prospective spouses enter into prior to their marriage that will specify their rights and responsibilities if they divorce. Sometimes prospective spouses use prenuptial agreements just to identify the separate property that they are bringing into the marriage. This is often the case when family businesses and inherited property are part of the mix. Beyond simply documenting separate property, prenuptial agreements allow you and your soon-to-be spouse to decide how you want to divide your property, rather than being bound by the state laws discussed in Chapter 5 regarding separate property, marital property, and community property acquired before and during the marriage. In addition, you can use a prenuptial agreement to waive a right to receive alimony or an interest in property such as an inheritance or pension, and you can specify how you will handle tax returns and their related liabilities.

This sounds like a great help for planning a divorce, but you might still be asking yourself "how can this help a marriage succeed?" Most experts agree that good communication between spouses is one of the requirements of a successful marriage. Experts also acknowledge that communication about financial issues is one of the biggest problems facing couples today. Two critical elements of a good prenuptial agreement are full-disclosure about financial resources and open discussion of financial issues before the marriage. Consequently, the process of learning about and discussing the financial issues inherent in a prenuptial agreement can foster better communication about a difficult subject and thereby strengthen the relationship and the marriage. In addition, the prenuptial agreement can include provisions about what will happen when someone dies, such as lifetime use of a vacation home that ultimately will pass to the children of a first marriage. Because prenups are primarily agreements about property division, they often contain, either directly or indirectly, some estate planning provisions that you should coordinate with the rest of your estate plan. Prenuptial agreements can also include nonfinancial provisions such as household responsibilities, child rearing guidelines, and religious traditions.

> The prenuptial agreement can include provisions about what will happen when someone dies, such as lifetime use of a vacation home that ultimately will pass to the children of a first marriage.

What to Watch Out For

Can prenuptial agreements lead to divorce? Certainly if your fiancée springs the idea of a prenuptial agreement on you at a time that you consider to be the "last minute," you are not going to be happy about it. The act of "springing" anything on anybody usually creates resentment, if not mistrust, both of which can lead to divorce. Prenuptial agreements also may cause some people to not get married in the first place. Many people think that the concept "what is mine is yours and what is yours is mine" is the perfect formula for marital finances and property division. Others think that if you bring up the idea of a prenuptial agreement, it indicates that you are not committed to the marriage and are already planning for the divorce. In these situations, even discussing the idea of a prenuptial agreement can "poison the well" by creating so much tension and mistrust that one of the parties calls off the wedding. Since the potential downside of initiating the idea of a prenuptial agreement can be so devastating, you should be clear about what you are hoping to achieve and very careful about how and when you introduce the idea.

When should you consider a prenuptial agreement? Susan K. Smith, a Connecticut divorce attorney, mentions several important benefits on her Web site, *http://smith-lawfirm.com*:

- Avoiding protracted proceedings if the marriage fails after a short period of time
- Protecting the financial autonomy that individuals have developed in their careers or because they are marrying late in life
- Providing assurance to families contributing money to a new couple that family money will stay in the family
- Protecting inheritances
- Protecting family or premarital businesses and avoiding the protracted and intrusive litigation concerning the value of business interests that can occur during divorce
- Providing for and protecting children of first marriages (This also serves to ease the entry of a step-parent into the family picture when there are adult-aged children)
- Clarifying respective financial responsibilities when one or more of the spouses has been married

Prenups and Businesses

If you own your own business or are part of a family business, you may want to take the risk of having the potentially painful "prenup discussion" before you are married. You would probably be even smarter to have it before you got engaged. Closely held businesses and especially family businesses are much more than a job or an investment—they are a way of life with emotional as well as financial implications. You would be doing a disservice to your betrothed, as well as yourself and your family (or other business partners), if you do not have a frank discussion with him or her about the business and your expectations for it. You need to be clear in your own mind about what your objectives are and what affect this will have on your soon-to-be partner.

In addition, you should consider having a professional value your company so that you can establish the value at the beginning of the marriage. This is important whether you sign a prenuptial agreement or not. If you do not have a prenuptial agreement and you do get divorced, you will need to know the value of your business right before your marriage so that the appreciation during the marriage can be calculated correctly. Some states consider this type of appreciation on a separate property to be marital and subject to division.

The Legal Aspects of Prenups

Susan K. Smith's Web site *(http://smith-lawfirm.com)* also lists the important legal characteristics of prenuptial agreements. Although her list refers to Connecticut law, the concepts are fairly universal, especially in the states that have adopted the Uniform Premarital Agreement Act (UPMAA). About half the states have adopted this act, and the others have laws that are similar in most cases. You can find some major exceptions, such as some states do not permit prenuptial agreements to alter the right of a spouse to receive court-ordered alimony. You should definitely seek legal advice when considering a prenuptial agreement, not only to be in compliance with state laws, but also to insure that your prenuptial agreement is valid. To paraphrase John Phillips Marquand—who wrote in 1937, "marriage . . . is a damnably serious business, particularly around Boston"—prenuptial agreements are a damnably serious business, particularly in America. The basic legal components of prenuptial agreements are:

- Agreements must be in writing and signed.
- Agreements must be preceded by full financial disclosure by both parties.
- Parties must have adequate time to review the agreement and obtain legal advice "from independent counsel" before signing.
- Agreements must be entered into voluntarily.
- Agreements cannot be "unconscionable."
- Prenups apply to most property and assets, and to spousal support with some restriction.
- Agreements do not apply to agreements concerning children (custody, visitation, and child support).

You should definitely seek legal advice when considering a prenuptial agreement, not only to be in compliance with state laws, but also to insure that your prenuptial agreement is valid.

If you own a business, full financial disclosure would include sharing with your spouse, and his or her attorney, the value of your business. Although you will learn how to value your own business in this book, you may not want to rely on your own calculations for purposes of a prenuptial agreement. A court could invalidate your agreement if your spouse were later able to prove that your business valuation did not constitute full disclosure. You can view hiring a qualified professional business valuator like an insurance policy. It will cost more up front, but it should go a long way to preventing a future attack on the value and it will be your primary defense in the event that your spouse does attack your valuation.

Postnuptial Property Agreements

Just as everyone is getting used to the idea of prenuptial agreements, along come postnuptial agreements to stir up trouble. Some state courts do not even recognize them, and many other states enforce them under statutes that are different from the laws regulating prenuptial agreements. Postnuptial agreements, also known as marriage contracts, have many of the same purposes and goals as prenuptial agreements, with the main difference being that they are entered into after the marriage. Although the provisions of the Uniform Premarital Agreement Act (UPMAA) do not extend to postnuptial agreements, you would be wise to apply the same standards of full financial disclosure and separate legal representation if you want your agreement to be binding.

Just as with prenuptial agreements, opponents contend that they are unfair and coercive to the dependent spouse who has less leverage now that they are married. Consequently, the courts do appear to hold postnups to a higher standard of fairness and full disclosure. This means that you will need to disclose the true fair market value of your business if that is part of the agreement. As with prenups, you should consider hiring an expert rather than trying to do it yourself to avoid or better defend any future litigation about the value of your business.

Why consider a postnuptial agreement? In many cases the spouses were too insecure to bring up the idea before marriage, but the need to define property issues in cases involving businesses and inheritances still remains. Sometimes changing financial circumstances create a need to spell out who gets what in the event of death or divorce. Other times a marriage contract arises out of someone's need for additional security or the desire to "start over with a clean slate" after marital difficulties. If you were too scared to discuss a prenuptial agreement, how are you going to broach the subject of a postnuptial agreement? The Equity in Marriage Institute has a very informative Web site at *⊘www.equalityinmarriage.org* that gives some very practical advice on the subject. They even have a guidebook called *The Commitment Conversation* that gives some suggested conversation starters such as "Now that I have inherited the family business, I'm concerned about what would happen in the case of death or even divorce. I need to be confident that the business stays in the family."

Equity-Based Employee Compensation

Many companies seek to increase their employee's productivity and loyalty by rewarding them with ownership or rights to ownership in the company in the form of stock options, restricted shares, phantom stock, and stock appreciation rights. Equity-based compensation makes up a large part of the compensation package of CEOs and other top executives of large, publicly traded companies. One criticism of equity-based compensation plans is that they work too well as an incentive for creating short-term financial results to the detriment of the long-term health of the company. One could even make an argument that the lure of the big bucks in equity-based compensation created the climate that encouraged the illegal manipulation of financial and accounting information to keep stock prices artificially high in the late 1990s.

Equity-based compensation plans are relatively straightforward to set up in a publicly traded company because the key piece of information you need, the value of the company, is right there in the form of the stock price. These plans are no less viable in a closely held company, but you do have to take the extra step of valuing the company before you do anything else. This is another situation where you should hire a professional business valuator to perform the valuation of your company. Even though you may be able to choose an appropriate method and work through the calculations yourself, you will want to have an independent opinion to prevent future litigation.

> One criticism of equity-based compensation plans is that they work too well as an incentive for creating short-term financial results to the detriment of the long-term health of the company.

Many closely held business owners do not even consider equity-based compensation for their employees because they think it is too complicated or just for big companies. However, these plans may serve as an even more appropriate incentive in a small company because individual managers or other employees may actually have more control over processes and outcomes than employees of large firms. Also, private companies have the "luxury" of setting goals for the long-term, not just the next quarter when public company earnings will be scrutinized by the analysts. Once you have a reliable business valuation, you can consider whether any of the following equity-based compensation plans would be a good fit for your company, your goals, and your employees:

1. Incentive Stock Options (ISOs)
2. Nonqualified Stock Options
3. Restricted Stock
4. Phantom Stock
5. Stock Appreciation Rights (SARs)

Incentive stock options (ISOs) provide an opportunity for an employee to benefit from the increase in value of the company by granting them the right to purchase stock at a set price within a certain time frame. The incentive aspect of the ISO is embedded in the vesting policy, which usually stipulates that employees must reach certain thresholds of employment or the company must meet specified performance goals. The IRS does not tax the employee on the receipt of the options at the grant date, nor does the employee have to pay income tax when he or she exercises the options—i.e., convert them into stock. Long-term or short-term capital gains tax is due if and when the employee sells the stock. However, if the employee does not sell the stock, he or she may have to pay alternative minimum tax at the date of exercise on the differential between the fair market value and the exercise price. This is a particularly onerous tax because it goes against the usual IRS tax policy of levying a tax when the taxpayer has the funds to pay it. In this case, the taxpayer not only has not received funds, he or she has paid money to exercise the options.

Nonqualified stock options operate much the same way as incentive stock options except for the tax ramifications. The IRS taxes nonqualified options at the grant date if they have a readily ascertainable value and at the exercise date if they don't have an ascertainable fair market value. Since the nonqualified options of closely held companies are not publicly traded, they generally would not have an ascertainable fair market value. Consequently, the employee reports ordinary income to the extent of the fair market value of the stock minus the purchase price of the stock or the option at the exercise date. When the employee sells the stock, he or she would pay capital gains tax on the difference between the sales price and their basis, which is made up of the fair market value of the option on which the employee paid tax and the amount he or she paid for the stock. Employers treat nonqualified options like additional compensation and report the taxable income in the employee's W-2. Thus you can use a nonqualified option as a way to reward an employee by giving him or her stock instead of cash.

Under a **restricted stock plan,** a company can sell stock to its employees at a much lower price than the value of the company would warrant. This allows employees to have an ownership interest without spending a lot of money. The hoped-for benefit to the company is that employees will stay longer and work harder to achieve common goals, thereby increasing the value of the company. The "restrictive" aspect of the plan is the requirement that the employee can't sell the stock to the public, rather he or she must sell it back to the company, usually at the original discounted price. These restrictions apply for a set period of time, called a vesting period, which usually lasts five years.

A **phantom stock plan** is an equity-based deferred compensation plan that fluctuates in value with underlying employer securities that are called phantom stock. Generally, the company puts a certain amount of company stock in an account for an employee's benefit, and at maturity the company pays the employee cash compensation in an amount equal to the value of the underlying phantom stock. The employee never receives the actual stock. With this type of

Readily Ascertainable Value

Readily ascertainable value is one of those IRS terms with a very specific meaning. It means that the option meets the following criteria: the option must be transferable; the option must be exercisable immediately upon grant; there can be no restriction that would affect its market value; and the fair market value of the option privilege must be readily ascertainable. Options that are not actively traded rarely meet these conditions, but if you have an option that does, you report income in the amount of the fair market value less anything you paid for the option at the time you received the grant. You would not be taxed when you exercised the option and bought the stock. However, you would pay capital gains tax on the sales price of the stock less your basis, which would be the fair market value of the option on which you already paid tax and the cost of the stock.

plan you would need to value your company stock each year to determine the value of the deferred compensation you are paying and to correctly report the transaction according to Generally Accepted Accounting Principles (GAAP) on your financial statements.

Stock appreciation rights (SARs) give an employee the ability to receive cash compensation in the amount of the appreciation of a certain number of shares of company stock. As with phantom stock plans, the employee does not purchase the underlying stock but does benefit from its appreciation.

Phantom stock plans and stock appreciation rights are an ideal way to provide employees incentive compensation based on the increase in the company's value without having to change the traditional ownership structure. This feature makes them particularly well suited for family businesses that do not want to dilute their ownership. Neither the company nor the employee would have any tax consequences until the employee actually receives the cash. At that time, the employee reports taxable compensation income and the employer takes a tax deduction for the same amount. One downside to phantom stock plans and stock appreciation rights plans is that the accounting for them under GAAP is complicated. The company must treat them as compensation expense and prorate the amount over the vesting period adjusting for fluctuations in value.

> Phantom stock plans and stock appreciation rights are an ideal way to provide employees incentive compensation based on the increase in the company's value.

Employee Stock Ownership Plans (ESOPs)

An ESOP is a qualified retirement plan that primarily invests in company stock, thereby making the employees indirect owners of the company. The company sets up the ESOP by first establishing a trust to receive company stock and cash contributions. Employers can make tax-deductible contributions into the trust of up to 25% of the compensation of the eligible participants while the employees do not pay any tax on these contributions received on their behalf. Many small and medium-size companies have ESOPs to encourage employee ownership and commitment while at the same time maintaining liquidity. The company enhances its liquidity position by the tax benefit of the contribution of appreciated stock, which does not represent a related cash outflow. If you are a majority shareholder in a closely held business, you may want to consider establishing an ESOP as a business exit strategy or to diversify your portfolio. The ESOP can buy some or all of your shares with cash contributed to the plan.

ESOPs and Appraisals

The Employment Retirement Income Security Act (ERISA) stipulates that ESOPS should not pay more than "adequate consideration" for employer stock. Business valuators generally interpret this to mean the same thing as "fair market value" as it is defined in the Internal Revenue Service's Revenue Ruling 59-60, which is discussed in Chapter 4. In order to determine what is adequate consideration and to get the related tax benefits, you must hire an independent appraiser to professionally value the company every year. This means that you can't just use the CPA who audits your books or performs other regular services for you. You will need to find someone who regularly performs appraisals and who is not related in any way to your company. The appraiser actually will work on behalf of the trustee of the plan to give the trustee the information he or she needs to make good decisions on behalf of the participants. Since business valuators often use the discounted cash flow method to value a company for ESOP purposes, you will need to prepare income or cash flow projections for three to five years. An appraiser who fraudulently overstates the value of the company to the ESOP will be subject to civil penalties.

ESOP Valuation Issues

The specialized rules and circumstances related to ESOPs influence the value of the stock being sold to the ESOP. First, all shares are not treated equally. If an owner or owners are transferring stock over a period of time to the ESOP, the first shares transferred will be subject to lack of control discounts because the ESOP will be a minority shareholder of the stock. However, if a shareholder transfers even a minority interest to the ESOP, and those shares put the ESOP's holdings over 50 percent, the ESOP should pay a control price rather than a discounted minority price because the ESOP now has a controlling interest. Second, the marketability discount can be very different for the shareholder selling stock to the ESOP and the stock the ESOP purchases because of the required buyback provision. This buyback provision makes the stock in the ESOP very marketable and, therefore, not eligible for the same marketability discount applied to the original shareholder's shares. Thirdly, the value of the company stock can drop because of some of the fundamental financial changes that take place when the company starts an ESOP, particularly a leveraged ESOP. The main culprit in a reduced price relates to the fact that the ESOP liability will be reported on the balance sheet, but the ESOP will not appear as a corresponding asset item. You should consider all of these factors that generally act to depress the price of the sponsoring company stock when valuing the stock to be contributed to the ESOP so you do not overstate the price the ESOP has to pay for the stock.

Litigation

Although the United States does not have more than 70% of the world's attorneys, as Dan Quayle once claimed, this is a very litigious society with about 1 million lawyers, or one for every 230 people in the country. What do all of these lawyers do? Lawyers practice in many different areas including estate planning, employment law, real estate law, contracts, general business law, etc. In addition, many lawyers work in government, industry, and education. Even with all of these other jobs for lawyers, there are plenty of litigators to go around and plenty of opportunities for them to litigate. Leaving divorce suits out of the equation, damage cases are probably the most common litigation situations that can require a business valuation to establish the extent of the loss. Some examples include:

Breach of Contract—Wrongful nonperformance of a contractual duty—e.g., cancellation of an important sales contract between a buyer and seller.

Personal Injury—Wrongful conduct causing bodily injury or mental pain and suffering (including defamation of character, libel, slander, etc.) that prevents someone from continuing to work successfully in his or her business.

Antitrust—Infractions of the federal statutes preventing price-fixing, price discrimination, and other monopolistic practices.

Insurance Casualty Claims—Claims related to the physical loss of business assets or the interruption of business due to disasters like fire or hurricanes.

Lost Profits—Claims related to the inability of a company to operate and be open for business for a period of time.

Condemnation—Claims related to the government or a public utility taking a company's property for public use in exchange for some compensation.

These situations present some challenging valuation issues, because the valuator is often trying to value what is not there rather than what is. In addition, the business may not have adequate documentation to aid the valuator in determining the extent of damage. As you read Parts Four and Five of this book, you will learn more about all of the financial and nonfinancial considerations that go into a business valuation. If you think you may be subject to any of the above litigation, you may want to start keeping additional documentation that would be helpful in valuing your company. Especially keep in mind "before" and "after" information that could help the valuator come up with a value of the business or business unit before the damage and again after the damage has been done.

Bankruptcy

Business valuations and other appraisals of assets and real property play a major role in the bankruptcy and reorganization process. The court uses business valuations to indicate value for reorganization financing, restructuring, recapitalizations, turnarounds, and to determine whether the company even meets the legal definition of bankruptcy. Bankruptcy is when a business or individual is insolvent or unable to pay its debts. The two kinds of legal bankruptcy are defined by Chapters 7 and 11 of the 1978 Bankruptcy Act. Chapter 7 is an

The Three Rs of Bankruptcy— Reorganization, Restructuring, and Recapitalization

The Dictionary of Business Terms (Barron's Educational Services, 2000) defines reorganization as the "financial restructuring of a firm after it has filed for protection from creditors while it works out a plan to repay its overdue debt. Company reorganizations usually take place under Chapter 11 of the federal bankruptcy code under the supervision of a bankruptcy court. If the plan does restore the company's health, the company may be liquidated and its assets sold to pay off the claims of creditors and shareholders." Restructuring is the reorganization of a company to make it more profitable, usually by cutting costs, people, departments, etc. Restructuring is often a euphemism for downsizing, where the company lays off some employees. A recapitalization involves changing the capital structure of a firm, not the operations. Exchanging bonds for stock would be an example of a recapitalization.

involuntary process that gets started when one or more creditors go to court to have the bankruptcy judge rule that the debtor is insolvent. The judge determines, with information provided by a business valuator or other financial experts, whether or not the company does have more liabilities than assets. If that is the case, then the court appoints a bankruptcy trustee to run the business and secure interim financing so the company can liquidate in an orderly manner, with the goal of providing more funds for the creditors. Chapter 11 is theoretically voluntary, but what that really means is that the debtor initiates the process with the goal of a fair and orderly settlement of its liabilities. Chapter 11 protects the company so it can reorganize and become a viable business again, while paying off its debts in the process.

You may encounter other situations where you will want or need to know the value of your business such as loan applications, personal financial statements, or applying for financial aid for your children's college education. These are situations where you should be able to apply what you learn from this book to make your own calculations rather than paying an expert to value your company for you.

> **Chapter 7**

Types and Standards of Value

Part One

Part Two

Part Three

Part Four

Part Five

Part Six

Value Beyond the Numbers

The *American Heritage Dictionary* defines "value" as "an amount, as of goods, services, or money considered to be a fair and suitable equivalent for something else," and "worth in usefulness or importance to the possessor; utility or merit: the *value* of an education." This definition hints at the many types of value you encounter in your daily life, such as:

- Ethical value
- Religious value
- Environmental value
- Sentimental value
- Aesthetic value
- Potential value
- Economic value

All of these types of value can be factors in the value of a business. For example, you may be willing to pay more for a business that is run ethically than one that is more profitable but run by "a bunch of crooks." Or you may be willing to pay more for a business that incorporates good environmental practices than you would a similar business that saves money by disregarding environmental concerns. But the $64,000 question is "how much more might you be willing to pay?" In other words, how do you measure sentimental value, ethical value, environmental value, etc.? The short answer is that it is not easy to measure these types of values, and, consequently, you usually will not see any reference to these concepts in either the business valuation literature or in a formal business valuation. Just because you can't easily measure these values does not mean that you should not consider them as part of the intangible value of the company.

The Science of Value

Researchers in the fields of philosophy, mathematics, organizational behavior, and business management have developed some concepts that business owners and business valuators can use to augment the traditional methods of intangibles valuation in order to recognize value beyond the numbers.

Axiology, which comes from the Greek words "axios" (worth or value) and "logos" (logic or theory), is the science or theory of value. The cornerstone of axiology is the concept of a unit of measurement of value that is worth the same for everyone. Goran Roos, founder of Intellectual Capital Services in London, England, points out that even if you find such a unit of measurement—dollars, for example—one dollar will not be worth the same to a homeless person as it is to a multimillionaire. Roos is one of the leaders in the emerging field of intellectual capital, which he and others contend is the major value driver in modern knowledge-based businesses. Intellectual capital value is a major component in market value; in fact, it is a substitute for "intangible value" in the equation fair market value = net asset value + intellectual capital (intangible value).

Modern Axiology

Dr. Robert S. Hartman, the father of modern axiology or value science, created a mathematical system to order the value judgments of everyday life. He was nominated in 1973 for a Nobel Prize for his work involving the creation of the Hartman Value Profile, which incorporates three dimensions of value. Much of Dr. Hartman's work focused on individual human values, but you can apply his concepts and theories to the business valuation process to gain more insight into what is the "value" you are trying to capture. Intrinsic value is the individual value or the inherent value of the thing, person, or organization itself. For example, a company may be a "good" company because it "does well by doing good." Extrinsic value is the situational or comparative value of something. You can determine extrinsic value by classifying something by its similarity to other things. For example, SAS, Inc. often wins accolades for being one of the best companies to work for in the United States, compared to other companies. Systemic value is theoretical value and you can determine it by answering the questions "Does it meet the criteria to belong to this group?" and "Does it measure up?" For example, a company must be one of the largest 500 revenue-producing corporations in America to be a member of the *Fortune* 500 class or group. You can use traditional valuation methods to shed some light on the extrinsic and systemic value of closely held businesses, but you will need to embrace new concepts like intellectual capital or balanced scorecards to get

You can determine extrinsic value by classifying something by its similarity to other things.

a better picture of the intangible value of something like a work force of computer geniuses.

Measuring Intellectual Capital

What is intellectual capital? It is the intangible value of human resources, corporate culture, and relationships with organizations and people outside of the company. Verna Allee, in her article "The Art and Practice of Being a Revolutionary" (*The Knowledge Management Journal*, June 1997), poses the question "How long can we reconcile statements such as 'people are our greatest assets' with our balance sheets where they show up only as a liability and expense?" She goes on to describe how the three components of intellectual capital create business value using knowledge flows and a learning culture as catalysts. "With knowledge as the resource, this view captures the sense of a company in motion as it converts skills and knowledge into wealth and competitive advantage. The quality of the synergy among these three components of intellectual capital and the capacity for leveraging the flow of knowledge determines a company's capacity to generate sustainable value." The current economic era, known variously as the Intangibles Economy, the Knowledge Economy, the Experience Economy, and the Idea Economy, has created a new paradigm of thinking about value. This new perspective incorporates value concepts such as intellectual capital, knowledge value added, and balanced scorecards.

The "Balanced Scorecard"

Drs. Robert Kaplan and David Norton developed the "Balanced Scorecard" in the early 1990s as a strategic planning tool for businesses and other organizations. Since companies can't manage what they can't measure, Kaplan and Norton developed the balanced scorecard to measure the critical success factors of business in the new Knowledge Economy. The feedback components of the balanced scorecard enable businesses to use the information they collect as a management tool, not just a measurement tool.

Kaplan and Norton describe the balanced scorecard on the Balanced Scorecard Institute Web site, *www.balancedscorecard.org*: "The balanced scorecard retains traditional financial measures. But financial measures tell the story of past events, an adequate story for industrial age companies for which investments in long-term capabilities and customer relationships were not critical for success. These financial measures are inadequate, however, for guiding and evaluating the journey that information age companies must make to create future value through investment in customers, suppliers, employees, processes, technology, and innovation." The balanced scorecard measures a company from four perspectives: the learning and growth perspective, the business process perspective, the customer perspective, and the financial perspective. Like the intellectual capital model, the balanced scorecard model is an important tool to help understand and measure the value of intangibles in the Information Age.

Standards of Economic Value

Although noneconomic factors play a role in the overall value of a company, the focus of this book is on determining the economic value of closely held businesses. Economic value can be broken down into many different categories including:

- Fair market value
- Fair value
- Investment value
- Intrinsic value
- Going concern value
- Liquidation value
- Book value
- Transaction value

You can see from this list that you have a lot of choices about the definition or standard of value you will use to guide you in determining the worth of your company. Although you have a lot of flexibility to choose an appropriate definition, you do not have the flexibility to *not* choose a definition or standard of value. The standard of value alone can make a huge difference in the overall value of a company. Depending on the standard of value you choose you may or may not include discounts for marketability or minority interest, you may or may not choose certain valuation methodologies such as

You have choices about the definition or standard of value you will use in determining the worth of your company.

discounted cash flow, and you may or may not need to factor in the costs of selling assets, etc.

How do you decide which definition or standard of value to choose? You choose the standard of value based on the purpose of the valuation, and in some cases you need to research the case law to find out if the courts or other legal authorities have already made the decision for you. For example, if you are valuing your company for estate tax purposes, Internal Revenue Service Revenue Ruling 59-60 will direct you to use the fair market value standard of value.

Fair Market Value

Fair market value is the most important and widely used standard of value. The Internal Revenue Service defines "fair market value" in Revenue Ruling 59-60 as the "price at which the property would change hands between a willing buyer and a willing seller, when the former is not under any compulsion to buy and the latter is not under any compulsion to sell, both parties having reasonable knowledge of the relevant facts." This definition sounds very straightforward and reasonable, but you should note several important assumptions embedded in it. First, the willing buyer and willing seller are a hypothetical buyer and seller, not specific people or organizations with particular motives or characteristics. Secondly, you should assume that the economic climate at the time of the valuation is the one governing the transaction. Just because companies almost identical to yours sold at a certain multiple of earnings during the robust economy of the late 1990s does not mean that the value of your company will be the same during the economic downturn of the early 2000s. Finally, you must assume that the willing buyer and seller are able to buy or sell.

The price of publicly traded stock provides a good example of the definition of "fair market value." A securities market is comprised of many willing buyers and sellers, with the ability to buy and/or sell, who are buying and selling under current economic conditions. In addition, the efficient market theory posits that the market immediately takes into account all relevant information. The value of publicly traded stock is the average of the high and low prices on a given day with the market itself determining the value.

The market for closely held stock is not efficient, so you can benefit greatly from all the different kinds of analysis described in this book. In fact, the more analysis the better. In addition to choosing an appropriate valuation methodology, such as the discounted cash flow method or the excess earnings method, you also must consider whether discounts or premiums are applicable in arriving at fair market value. When should you consider discounts? The most common discount for closely held stock is the lack of marketability discount. By definition, "closely held" means that a market does not exist for the stock, so you will have to lower or discount the price in order to sell it. Similarly, if you are trying to sell a minority interest in the stock of a company you will often also take a minority interest discount to reflect the fact that one share of your stock is not as valuable as a share that is part of a controlling interest. Conversely, someone may be willing to pay a premium for shares of stock that would give him or her a controlling interest in a company.

Fair market value is the standard of value that the IRS requires for all tax matters, including gift, estate, and income taxes. Similarly, state governments follow suit in using the fair market value standard for gift, estate, inheritance, property, and income tax issues. In addition, the fair market value standard is the most widely mandated standard of value for all other valuation purposes. Real estate and fixed asset appraisers often use the term "market value" instead of "fair market value" to mean essentially the same

What Is the Efficient Market Theory?

Marketscreen.com describes the efficient market theory as the idea that publicly traded stock prices immediately incorporate all relevant information and expectations. "It says that you cannot consistently outperform the stock market due to the random nature in which most information arrives and the fact that prices react and adjust almost immediately to reflect the latest information. It assumes that every piece of information has been collected and processed by thousands of investors and this information is correctly reflected in the price . . . there is little to be gained by any type of analysis."

thing. The definition of "market value" or "fair market value" in a real estate context has the additional assumption embedded in it that the property is being put to its highest and best use. This assumption goes into the appraised value, whether or not the current owner has put the property to this highest and best use. This concept is important because several valuation methodologies incorporate the appraised fair market value of specific assets such as real estate and equipment into the calculation of the overall value of a closely held company.

Fair Value

The term "fair value" is often confused with "fair market value," which is understandable since they sound similar and they are often (incorrectly) used interchangeably. To be fair, "fair value" has a number of definitions. However, the definition you need to remember from a business valuation perspective is the one used in dissenting shareholder cases, which is the value of a proportional share of the total value of the company, not reduced by discounts. The courts have indicated that you should not apply the normal minority interest discount to a dissenting shareholder's stock because that might encourage controlling shareholders to "squeeze out" the minority shareholders at an unfairly reduced price. In other words, the minority shareholders would be subject to "double jeopardy"—they would not only have no power to stop major stock transactions, but they would also be penalized on the price they received for their stock if the controlling owners could discount the price to minority interests.

Dissenting or minority shareholder disputes arise when a corporation takes a major action, such as merging, selling, liquidating, declaring bankruptcy, establishing an ESOP, minority buy-outs, restructuring, etc., where minority shareholders do not feel they received a proper price for their stock. The dissenting shareholder statutes in most states provide that the minority shareholders have the right to receive cash for the "fair value" of their shares. You should consult the particular statutes in your state to make sure that you take into consideration any additional nuances or differences in the law.

Investment Value

Investment value is the value to a specific buyer or investor, not the hypothetical willing buyer and seller who determine fair market value. Generally, you would use the discounted cash flow method to calculate the investment value of a particular stock because you can use the rates of return that are appropriate for the specific investor. Investment value can approach or equal fair market value when the investment requirements of the particular investor are similar to the universe of hypothetical willing buyers and sellers in the marketplace. However, investment value usually is not the same as fair market value because specific individuals usually have different income projections, different rates of return reflecting a different risk/reward calculus, and different tax effects than the market as a whole. Often a company can be worth more to a particular buyer, such as a consolidator, when the purchase will provide strategic advantages or economies of scale. You would use the investment standard of value if you are considering buying or selling a company, especially if you have a target buyer or seller in mind.

Intrinsic Value

The Business Valuation Library at ✍ *www.bvlibrary.com* refers to the definition of intrinsic value from the *International Glossary of Business Valuation Terms*: "the value that an investor considers, on the basis of an evaluation of available facts, to be the 'true' or 'real' value that will become the market value when other investors reach the same conclusion." Discovering the intrinsic value of a stock, whether publicly traded or privately held, is the goal of all fundamental analysis. Fundamental analysis includes determining the value of the assets, projecting future earnings, assessing the appropriate growth rate, and so on, to determine the inherent value of the investment. In a publicly traded setting, analysts will

Protecting Against a Shareholder Lawsuit

Your best defense against a shareholder lawsuit is to make sure that you have treated all interested parties fairly. Barron's *Dictionary of Business Terms*, Third Edition, defines the Business Judgment Rule as the "deference given by the courts to the good-faith operations and transactions of a corporation by its executives. The rationale behind the rule is that stockholders accept the risk that an informed business decision, honestly made and rationally thought to be in the corporation's best interests, may not be second-guessed." To prevent "second-guessing," Ray Sheeler (in the article "Fairness Opinions and the Closely Held Business" at *www.cbizonesource.com*) suggests that closely held business owners and directors solicit fairness opinions. These are official reports by qualified experts stating that particular transactions do meet the criteria of the Business Judgment Rule. You can use a fairness opinion not only if you are sued, but also to avoid a lawsuit in the first place.

recommend that investors buy the stock if the fair market value is less than the intrinsic value, and they will usually recommend that they sell the stock if the intrinsic value is significantly less than the market price.

Premises of Value

In addition to choosing a standard of value, you also must choose a premise of value. The standard of value refers to the type of value you are calculating while the premise of value relates to the assumptions underlying the valuation itself. The most common premise of value is going-concern value, which assumes that the business will continue to use its assets to produce income and function as an ongoing business. For example, if you are valuing your company for gift tax purposes, you would use the fair market value standard of value and the going concern premise of value.

At the other end of the spectrum is the forced liquidation premise of value, which assumes that the assets will be sold piecemeal at deep discounts because they must be sold quickly. If you plan to use your business as collateral for a loan, the lender would value the company using the same fair market standard of value, but would probably use the liquidation premise of value to determine if you could pay back the loan in the worst-case scenario. Other premises of value include the assemblage of assets value and the orderly disposition value. In the assemblage of assets premise of value, the assumption is that although the assets are all together as they would be in a going concern business, they are not functioning or in use. The orderly disposition value assumes that the assets are going to be sold individually, allowing enough time to get reasonable prices. In other words, you will not have a "fire-sale" situation like you do with the forced liquidation premise of value.

Other Types of Economic Value

Book value is an accounting term rather than a valuation term, but you may see it used in a valuation context. The book value of a company is the net worth shown on the company's balance sheet, i.e., the historical net assets minus the net liabilities. Sometimes the definition is tweaked to subtract the reported intangible assets as well as the liabilities from the tangible assets, which produces "net asset value," also known as book value. Whichever definition of book value you use, you will be using historical cost numbers, which rarely have any relationship to fair market value. Consequently, you would not use book value to determine the worth of a company, but you can use book value as a tool for comparisons between years of the same company. For example, if the book value of the company is increasing from year to year that is a positive indicator.

The **transaction value** is the nominal value of the transaction and does not reflect the costs of actually completing a transaction, say the sale of a business. The different standards and premises of value all assume that the transaction will be consummated immediately for cash, a situation that rarely occurs when you are dealing with a closely held company. The terms of a sale of a closely held business usually include a down payment in cash and payments of the balance over a period of time at a below-market interest rate. The present value of these payments generally would not equal the stated sales price. In addition, if you paid a broker to help you sell your business, you would have commission expenses that reduce the amount of cash you actually receive in the transaction. You should think about the transaction value, particularly when you research comparable sales, to help you determine the value of a business. Although you may see reported transaction values, you do not know what the actual terms of the deals were that may have influenced the transaction prices either up or down.

The standard of value and the related premise of value you choose provide the framework for the valuation process. They answer the questions "Value to whom?" and "What are the underlying assumptions regarding the ongoing nature of the business?" If the purpose of your valuation is either tax related or in response to some type of litigation, you should consult legal counsel or a valuation professional to determine the appropriate standard of value in your state. In the next chapter you will learn more about how the purpose of a valuation influences the standard of value and the valuation methodologies you choose and, therefore, the value itself.

What If You Choose the Wrong Standard of Value?

The short answer to this question is that you come up with the wrong value for a company. In a worst-case scenario, the opposing counsel or the judge will embarrass you or your valuation expert in court and you lose your case, even if you or the valuation expert did everything else right.

Trial judges and attorneys are becoming more sophisticated about business valuation standards and methodologies. Attorneys will try to discredit your valuation expert by contending that they have not adhered to the standards of the profession. One of the basic standards of report writing for valuation professionals is to clearly state the appropriate standard of value being used. You or your expert could make a mistake regarding the standard in two different ways. Suppose you are doing a valuation for a dissenting shareholder suit and the legally required standard of value in your state is fair value. You could incorrectly state that the standard of value was fair market value and perform your valuation taking lack of marketability discounts, or you could refer to the fair value standard but inappropriately take lack of marketability discounts. Either way, you or your expert may have made a fatal error that could totally disqualify the valuation report and any further testimony.

> **Chapter 8**

How the Purpose of a Valuation Influences the Value

Part One

Part Two

Part Three

Part Four

Part Five

Part Six

PART THREE: BUSINESS VALUATION CONCEPTS

■ CHAPTER 7 Types and Standards of Value ■ CHAPTER 8 How the Purpose of a Valuation Influences the Value
■ CHAPTER 9 How the Size of the Company Influences Value

Primary Purposes

Y ou can categorize the multitude of reasons for valuing a business into five basic categories:

- Purchase and sale transactions
- Partner or shareholder agreements
- Financing purposes
- Tax-related purposes
- Litigation purposes

Each of these primary purposes represents several specific types of transactions or subsets of purposes. Many of the judgments and assumptions you make in the process of valuing a business are directly related to the purpose of the valuation. For example, if you are valuing a company for gift or estate tax purposes, you would use the fair market value standard of value and the valuation methodologies prescribed by the relevant IRS Revenue Rulings. On the other hand, if the same company was planning to sell out to a larger company, you may use the investment value standard of value and some aggressive projections of future earnings to arrive at an asking price. Sometimes you may be able to use a valuation that was performed for one purpose for another purpose, but be careful! For example, if you hired a professional valuation analyst to value your company for gift and estate tax purposes, you could probably use this same valuation for obtaining financing or setting up a buy-sell agreement with your business partners. A valuation analyst will often rely heavily on historical numbers when he or she performs a valuation for tax purposes. If the business is growing rapidly, this presumption may result in a conservatively low value. That is great for tax purposes. However, do you want that same conservatively low number if you need to borrow a lot of money from the bank? Would you be happy with that number if you die tomorrow and the company pays your estate that amount of money? Maybe, maybe not.

No matter what the purpose of the valuation and the methodologies you use, you must be able to support your conclusion of value. In addition, the value should fall within a reasonable range based on all of the valuation methodologies and assumptions you employ. If you start using valuation tools and techniques to prove a point or to arrive at a predetermined

Many of the judgments and assumptions you make in the process of valuing a business are directly related to the purpose of the valuation.

conclusion of value, you are turning into an advocate instead of a valuator. If you are valuing your own company, you will be presumed to be an advocate for your position, which is why in many cases you should hire an independent valuation analyst to avoid this problem. Even if you are going to be presumed to be an advocate, you should try to be as objective and thorough as possible in order to counter any arguments about subjectivity. You may be tempted to hire a valuation analyst whom you can turn into an advocate for your position in order to get more money, pay less money, pay less taxes, own more of the company, etc. However, this plan may backfire, especially if you end up going to court. The judge may disqualify your expert if the opposing counsel can prove that your expert has performed inconsistent valuations. For example, if your valuation expert testified six weeks ago that a 20% discount rate was appropriate and this week he or she is testifying that 7% is the appropriate discount rate for similar companies, someone has a lot of explaining to do.

Purchase and Sale Transactions

Business owners who are planning to sell their businesses need to look at both the investment value and the fair market value of their business. Investment value (see Chapter 7 for a discussion of investment value) is the value to a specific buyer or investor, while fair market value contemplates a market made up of numerous hypothetical buyers and sellers. If you are thinking about selling your business, the investment value you need to determine first is your own. In other words, you need to know "what is this business worth to you?" Secondly, you need to find out what the business is worth on the open market. When you make the calculation of what the business is worth to you, you will factor in your own positive perceptions of things like good customer relationships, established management, the prestige of owning your own company, and even sentimental value. Often the investment value of a closely held business is significantly higher than the fair market value of the same business in the hands of new owners. If you have a specific buyer or type of buyer in mind, then you should also determine the value of the business using the investment value standard tailored to the information you have regarding the potential investor(s).

Supply and Demand

No matter what value you place on your own business, the fair market value of the business will be subject to the economic laws of supply and demand. You will be trying to find the price at which the market demand will equal the supply. If your asking price is too high, you might not attract any potential buyers, or potential buyers may offer a lot less than your asking price. Conversely, if you price the company too low, you may get a number of competing bids, but even if a bidding war ensues, you may not get what you consider to be the value of the business. If you do a good job estimating the fair market value, then you can realistically expect someone to purchase the company at or near your asking price in a reasonably short period of time. If your price is too high, the laws of supply and demand would indicate that you would either need to lower your price or be prepared to wait for a longer time until someone comes along who values your business as much as you do. These same concepts apply to the buyer's side of the transaction as well.

Purchase and sale transactions have as much to do with economics as they do with underlying value. The ultimate goal of the process is to come up with a price and terms that two parties can agree upon. Some of the factors that go into the pricing decision include the tax effects of the transaction to both parties, the motivation of the seller to sell, the motivation of the buyer(s) to buy, the timing of the transaction, the overall economy, and individual considerations of the parties involved. When you value a company for sale purposes, you will incorporate some of these factors into the fundamental value of the company, some of them will be factors in choosing discounts or premiums, and others may just be considerations in the negotiation process.

> If your asking price is too high, you might not attract any potential buyers, or potential buyers may offer a lot less than your asking price.

"Desperate" Sellers and Good Deals

Why would you or another business owner decide to sell your company? Sometimes owners sell to maximize their investment dollars so they can look for another opportunity or retire comfortably in the south of France, or maybe the south of Florida. Many times, however, owners feel forced to sell due to circumstances such as failing health, the business is not profitable, the business needs an infusion of capital to grow, or they just don't enjoy some of the aspects of running a company. At the extreme, this can produce "desperate" sellers instead of "willing" sellers with a compulsion to sell and an inclination to not share all of the relevant facts. What does this do to "fair market value"?

If you are a willing buyer and you come across one of these desperate sellers, you should be able to get a good deal. But a good deal is not enough. Have you ever bought a jacket that was on sale because it was good quality and a great deal, only to have it sit in your closet unworn? As a potential buyer, you should determine what you are looking for in a business, what you can afford to pay, and only look for opportunities within these parameters. Shannon Pratt, et al., in their book, *Valuing Small Businesses and Professional Practices*, Third Edition (McGraw-Hill, 1998), provide a useful list of criteria for the budding entrepreneur to consider for a potential purchase:

1. The type of small business or professional practice.
2. Acceptable geographic locations.
3. The minimum and maximum size the buyer considers worthwhile and that he is realistically capable of managing.
4. The amount of cash available for purchase. (If outside sources are to be used, the buyer should at least explore the availability of funds from such sources before he goes shopping for a business.)
5. Whether, and for how long, the buyer will need assistance from existing management, and/or the duration and structure of a management transition period.
6. Whether the buyer wants a smooth-running and profitable operation or a "fixer-upper" (i.e., an operation currently not doing so well).

Valuation of Minority Shares

The valuation of a business in anticipation of the purchase or sale of less than full ownership is a variation on the fair market value calculation/investment value calculation that you make when you are contemplating a 100-percent deal. However, it is not as simple as multiplying the percentage you are buying by the total value of the business because a partial interest in a company is generally worth less than its percentage of the total. Why is that? When an owner has lack of control, they do not have the ability to make the decisions that set the course of the business. Consequently, you would need to use the investment value standard of value to determine what a partial share of the business is worth to you personally or to any other minority owner.

You can use several different methods of deriving the investment value of a minority share. Conceptually, the easiest method is to calculate the fair market value of the entire enterprise and then take an appropriate minority discount. For example, you want to buy 20% of the Great Scot Bagpipe Company, which you have valued at $1 million after lack of marketability discounts. You would initially take 20% of the total or $200,000 and then you would apply your minority discount to that number. Minority discounts can range from 20 to 40% depending on the specific circumstances of each situation. Assume that you determined that 30% was a reasonable discount; the value of your 20% interest in Great Scot would be $140,000 ($200,000 – (30% x $200,000)). See Chapter 23 for an in-depth discussion of minority interest discounts.

Valuation and Mergers

When two businesses merge, they exchange the stock of one company for the stock and assets of the other. The one that absorbs the assets of the other continues as the ongoing company and the absorbed business liquidates. Even though only one business ultimately continues, you will need to value both companies to determine the value of the stock and or assets you are exchanging. If one of the companies has publicly traded stock, then the market will determine the valuation of that company. In a merger you may use the investment value standard rather than fair market value because you have a specific "buyer and seller." In addition, you may only need to value the particular assets, divisions, etc., of the soon to be liquidated company if the ongoing company is not going to continue those operations in the same way. In fact, you may even need to use liquidation values for some of the assets if just acquiring tangible assets is the goal of the merger. On the other hand, if the liquidating company has significant goodwill or other intangible value that can be transferred, the acquirer may pay a premium.

> When two businesses merge, they exchange the stock of one company for the stock and assets of the other.

Partner or Shareholder Agreements

The presumptions that drive valuations for shareholder agreements such as buy-sell agreements, range from using a low number like book value, which has no relationship to fair market value, to using a high value that is backed up by life insurance for estate planning purposes. Partners or shareholders can agree on any value or method, as long as they mutually agree. Equally important as mutual agreement on the terms of the agreement is mutual understanding of what you have actually agreed upon. Although this sounds straightforward, business partners or shareholders can disagree, usually after the fact, with the definitions, intentions, or results of the terms of the agreement. For example, let's say you specify in a buy-sell agreement that you will value the company at fair market value to determine how much a retiring partner will receive. If you own 40% of Trinity News Corporation, which has a fair market value of $500,000 before any discounts, what will you receive? Is $200,000 ($500,00 x 40%) your fair market value interest? Since fair market value usually contains discounts for marketability and/or minority interests, your retirement nest egg probably looks more like $120,000 ($200,000 – 40% combined marketability and minority interest discounts.) See Chapter 7 for a discussion about the fair market value standard of value. Alternatively, you could specify that a partner would receive his or her pro rata portion of the value of the company as a whole upon retirement. In either case, you need to make sure that everyone understands these differences and has agreed upon the language that your attorney ultimately puts in the agreement.

One of the usual roadblocks to getting a buy-sell agreement implemented is that the owners cannot agree on the value or valuation methodology. Some of them want a high valuation number that is backed up by insurance so their spouse will receive a lot of money from the business when they die. Others want a relatively low valuation number so they can more easily buy out retiring owners or encourage younger associates to become partners or owners. Some are thinking ahead to estate taxes or even possible divorces. Just as you would use different valuation methodologies and standards of value for different purposes, you can specify different valuation methods for the different triggering events of a buy-sell agreement. However, most companies choose one of the following stipulations about how to value the company for purposes of all of the triggering events covered by the buy-sell agreement:

"Penny-wise, Pound-foolish"

Hiring someone to perform an independent appraisal of your company may cost tens of thousands of dollars, but having a supportable independent valuation can also save or make you potentially hundreds of thousands of dollars, depending on the size of your company. Sometimes, though, you can try to do too many things with one valuation. Courts often disregard the provisions of buy-sell agreements if the values produced are out of line with other valuations that other experts performed for the express purpose of the matter at hand. My advice is to separately consider each valuation purpose and not try to get an all-purpose valuation when you are drafting your buy-sell agreement. You also should not skimp on hiring professional valuators for other purposes such as tax-related issues, divorce proceedings, or other litigation.

- A specific dollar amount, with the caveat to update the price annually
- A formula approach—e.g., a multiple of gross revenue applied to the weighted average revenue of the last five years
- A valuation performed by an independent business appraiser

If you think that the provisions of the buy-sell agreement do reflect fair market value transactions, then you may be able to use the valuation for other purposes such as estate taxes or litigation. If you are planning for dual purposes, make sure the valuation is done in accordance with any legal or tax framework that would be controlling for the nonbuy-sell purpose. For example, make sure you clearly state that the valuation used the fair market standard of value if you want to use the valuation for tax purposes. More importantly, make sure that the fair market value standard of value is what you really want in your buy-sell provisions.

Financing Purposes

Lenders don't really care about the intrinsic value of your business or even the fair market value of it. They want to know if the business will support the debt service of any loan they make you, and, in the worst-case scenario, they want to know that they can liquidate your collateral to cover the debt. You may be able to convince someone to lend you more money based on a well-crafted valuation report using a fair market value standard of value and a going-concern premise of value. However, you will still want to show them what they need to see—evidence that they will get their money back. This will probably entail valuing the assets at liquidation value and conservatively projecting future cash flows and interest rates.

Tax-Related Purposes

The good news and the bad news about valuations for tax purposes is that you will find a lot of rules, regulations, statutes, and other guidance about how to perform your valuation. This is good news because it is always helpful to know the rules of the game so that you won't have any surprises in the future. The bad news is that you will need to research the statutes, case law, Revenue Rulings, and other relevant information to make sure you choose the appropriate standard of value, methodology, capitalization rate, discount rate, etc., or you will risk having the IRS or Tax Court repudiate your valuation report.

The general rule for valuations for tax purposes is that you will use the fair market value standard of value, which is laid out in Revenue Ruling 59-60. However, within this standard you will see some significant variations. Business owners usually would prefer a lower rather than a higher value for their company for tax purposes. The IRS and other taxing agencies usually prefer a nonspeculative value. Consequently, you should use valuation methods for tax purposes that are based more on historical numbers than projections of future cash flow. In addition, you should consider the market approach, which looks at comparable companies, because the IRS specifically mentions this approach in its Revenue Rulings. You can also factor in decreases in value for inheritance or estate tax purposes for loss of a key person or liquidation of assets at below market rates to satisfy tax liabilities. The combination of these two perspectives produces the unusual happy occurrence of both sides getting what they want—the business owner gets a conservative valuation and the IRS gets a valuation based on historical, proven numbers. However, you would not necessarily want to use this same conservative fair market value if you were trying to sell your business. This is a perfect example of how the same business can have different values for different purposes, all of them reasonable and legitimate.

If you are going to make a charitable contribution of your closely held stock, the same rules and presumptions apply. In addition, if the gift is over $5,000 you will need to attach a qualified appraisal report to your tax return along with Form 8283 detailing the gift and containing the signature of someone from the qualified charitable organization to which you gave the donation.

Litigation Purposes

"Litigation" means to engage in legal proceedings. If you are doing a valuation for purposes of a lawsuit, you need to arm yourself with legal knowledge. In addition to the usual factors you consider regarding the purpose of a valuation and its related methodologies, you need to research and understand state laws, legal precedents, and other guidance from the courts. Some states have statutes and case law that are in direct conflict with each other so it is very important to research the situation in your jurisdiction.

Types of Litigation

Some of the common types of litigation that involve business valuations include minority shareholder disputes, divorce, and damage cases. Minority shareholder disputes, also called dissenting shareholder disputes, arise when majority shareholders do not agree with a corporate decision such as a merger or a reorganization. State statutes provide a remedy, which directs the court to determine the value of their shares and force the corporation to buy the shares at that price. Although this is a business transaction, in a closely held company this can also be an emotionally painful experience. See the discussion in Chapter 7 about fair value and suggestions for preventing dissenting shareholder suits in the first place.

If you haven't been able to prevent a lawsuit, then you should review the statutes and case law in your jurisdiction to guide your valuation. Most state statutes specify that you must use the fair value standard; however, you have already seen that "fair value" can have many interpretations. You or your professional business appraiser should seek a legal opinion about the standard of value for your case in your jurisdiction.

Levels of Value

The primary differences between jurisdictions involve the level of control and marketability that you can and/or should factor into your valuation. Even within jurisdictions, the courts treat these factors inconsistently due to a lack of understanding of the relationship between different valuation methods and level of value they produce. The three levels of value are controlling interest, noncontrolling marketable interest, and noncontrolling nonmarketable interest. In general, what you are trying to get at is the value of the shares before the corporate action that the dissenting shareholders didn't think was fair. Although you would think that most dissenting shareholders would have noncontrolling, nonmarketable interests before the action, the fair value standard in most states indicates that you would not take a minority discount in these cases. You can see that a valuation for this type of litigation can produce a wide range of values, even if the methodology is the same, by virtue of applicable and nonapplicable discounts.

Valuation and Divorce

If you need to value your company or your spouse's company for a divorce, hire a professional business valuator. Unfortunately, the valuation process in a divorce can't be completely divorced from the divorce itself. If you are the nonowning spouse, you might find that it is difficult to get all of the information you need to value the business. In any case you will have legal issues, like the standard of value issue, that have ambiguous statutory guidance or conflicting case law precedents. You may have to value the business as of the date of separation, the date of the divorce, or the date of transfer, or some combination of these. In addition, you need to avoid or prepare to defend against "double-dipping" alimony as discussed in Chapter 5, depending on which side of the aisle you are (were) on. Because so many divorce cases actually go to trial rather than settling, attorneys and the courts dissect, scrutinize, and sometimes discredit the related business valuations. Consequently, you, or your independent business appraiser, need to be able to support all of your numbers, methodology, discount and capitalization rates, and discounts for control and marketability, especially as they relate to statutory requirements or other legal precedent. Even within all the legal parameters, you will often see two widely different values for the

A Timely Question

Just yesterday I received an e-mail question from an out-of-state valuation analyst who wanted to know if North Carolina allows minority interest discounts in divorce proceedings. I posed the question to Eddie Strange, CPA, one of the most respected business valuators and expert witnesses in divorce cases in North Carolina. He said that the way the question was asked, the answer is, yes; North Carolina *allows* minority discounts in divorce cases because the statutes do not *preclude* them. Neither do the statutes *require* minority discounts. In other words, the courts look at this issue on a case-by-case basis, so you might find some cases with minority discounts and some cases where minority discounts were not used. This question illustrates the many legal regulations and precedents you can encounter on a jurisdictional level when performing a valuation for any litigation purpose.

business, depending on who stands to gain and who stands to lose. Theoretically, the judge should decide the value based on the merits of the valuation reports and testimony. However, many times the court averages the two values to come up with a value that has no theoretical underpinning whatsoever. So you can see that the purpose really does influence the value.

Damage Cases

Valuations for damage cases can produce yet another value for a business. As discussed in Chapter 7, the purpose of a valuation in a damage case is to establish the value of the business or part of the business that was lost due to another party's wrongful action. How do you value something that isn't there? The before-and-after method is to value the company as if the damage did not occur and compare it to the current value. The difference would be the amount of the damage. Another way is to find a comparable company or division of the same company that was not damaged and compare the performance of the two companies or divisions to arrive at an estimate of the lost value. Finally you can use sales projections and rate of return projections to develop a sophisticated model of what the company would look like if the damage had never occurred. This method is similar to the before-and-after method, with the main difference being the reliance on projections. Even if you have good projections that were made before the damage incident, you should be aware that the court usually likes to see projected sales, growth rates, and rates of return that are based on historical numbers that they can digest relatively easily. Another factor that can influence the value of a company in a damage case is that if the case does go to trial, it will probably be a jury trial. You may have thought that you or your appraiser already had simplified the concepts and issues in your valuation report so a judge and opposing attorney could understand them. Be prepared to simplify them even more, so that a jury that doesn't hear these cases every day can understand what you are doing.

You have learned in this chapter about how different purposes for valuation influence the value of the company. In the next chapter, you will learn about how size itself can influence the value.

> **Chapter 9**

How the Size of the Company Influences Value

Part One

Part Two

Part Three

Part Four

Part Five

Part Six

PART THREE: BUSINESS VALUATION CONCEPTS

What Is a Small Business?

"Small business" is a term that has different meanings for different people. For the purpose of this book, the definition is a closely held company. The U.S. Department of Commerce defines it as a business that employs fewer than 100 people. The U.S. Small Business Administration's (SBA) Office of Advocacy defines it for research purposes as a business with fewer than 500 employees. For other purposes the SBA Office of Advocacy defines it differently based on number of employees and revenue. Although the number of employees in the definition is a moving target, the SBA definition of a small business specifies that it must be independently owned and operated and not have a large market share in its industry. The SBA definition of a large business is one that is not classified as a small business by the SBA. Shannon Pratt, Robert Reilly, and Robert Schweihs, in their book *Valuing Small Businesses and Professional Practices*, Third Edition (McGraw-Hill, 1998), define small businesses as employee- or family-owned businesses with less than $5 million in revenue. A large business to them would be one with revenues over $5 million where the owners are not employees.

Small Business Facts

The SBA Office of Advocacy publishes statistics about small businesses on their Web site, *www.sba.gov/advo/stats/sbfaq.html*. They gather the information from the U.S. Department of Commerce, Bureau of the Census, U.S. Department of Labor, Bureau of Labor Statistics, an Advocacy-funded study by Joel Popkin & Company, International Trade Administration, and the SBA Office of Government Contracting. They report that small businesses represent more than 99% of all employers; they employ 51% of private-sector workers and 38% of workers in high-tech jobs; they provide two-thirds to three-quarters of the net new jobs; and they produce 51% of private-sector output and represent 96% of all exporters of goods.

The statistics for 2001 show that about 10% of the estimated 5.75 million businesses with employees were new and about that same number closed. One-third of new companies with employees is that one-third shut down within the first two years. However, almost 40% of new companies survive over six years. Part of the failure rate might be related to the burden of regulation that small companies bear. The smallest firms spend about twice as much per employee than large companies, $6,975 versus $4,463, to comply with federal regulations alone. These high regulatory costs limit small companies' ability to invest in their own growth.

Small Businesses and Valuation

Valuation analysts consider small businesses to be riskier than big businesses for a variety of reasons including more limited debt and equity financing opportunities, reliance on a few key people, less market share, less formal organizational structure, and the public's perception of the risky nature of small businesses. The SBA Web site information indicating that one out of three new businesses fails within the first three years also contributes to this risky impression. This reality of greater risk translates into higher risk premiums in the calculation of discount and capitalization rates for small companies.

> Valuation analysts consider small businesses to be riskier than big businesses for a variety of reasons.

How Does Size Impact Rates of Return?

Ibbotson Associates conducts statistical studies of rates of return correlated to size, which the firm publishes annually in the *Stocks, Bonds, Bills & Inflation Yearbook*. These studies show that the small firms they tracked have returns about 5% higher on average than the large firms. Small companies for Ibbotson Associates are the smallest companies listed on the New York Stock Exchange, which means that they are big companies by closely held business standards—the average capitalization of these "small" companies is around $40 million. These studies and others like them are important because they confirm the inverse relationship between risk and return. Business valuators use the Ibbotson studies to determine how much they need to add to the discount rate of a small company to account for the additional risk due to small size. This additional amount is called the "size premium."

The discount rate is the interest rate you use to determine the present value of future cash flows. (See Chapter 13 for a discussion of the discounted cash flow method of valuation and Chapter 22 for a discussion of discount and capitalization rates.) The discount rate represents the company's cost of capital. The components of the discount rate or cost of capital for a closely held company are the risk-free rate, an equity risk premium, a size premium, and a premium for additional risk. A common method of determining the appropriate discount rate for a closely held company is the "build-up" method in which you "simply" add the components together. The first three components of the discount rate are pretty simple to identify, thanks to a lot of complicated work done by firms like Ibbotson Associates and Willamette Management Associates. These are the people who study rates of return and various correlations over time to come up with current numbers for the equity risk premium and the size premium. The foundation of the build-up method is the risk-free rate, which is represented by the rate of twenty-year Treasury bonds. You can find all of these numbers on the Web or in reference books such as Ibbotson's *Stocks, Bonds, Bills & Inflation*.

The last component of the build-up method is a premium for other risk factors including economic forces, industry trends, and company-specific characteristics. Unlike the first three components of the discount rate, you will have to make your own subjective judgment about how much of a premium to add for these risks. The company-specific risks are the most important to consider because they are the ones that you can control, and they have the most impact on the risk of your company compared to other companies. For example, if you own a CPA firm and you are still doing tax returns by hand, your risk is enormous, no matter what the trends are for the overall economy and the CPA profession in general. Any company that has not kept up with technology, discontinued unprofitable or outmoded services, and added new services to implement their vision for the future will require a significant risk premium even in good economic times. In contrast, if you own a CPA firm and you have augmented your tax practice with value-added services (such as business valuation, financial planning, and divorce planning), your risk premium will be substantially less, even if the economy is bad and the accounting industry is in a decline.

Even though the company-specific component of the risk premium is not a result of size, it may be related to size or be correlated with it. The CPA doing tax returns by hand in the above example could not support a large firm because she could not attain or maintain the quantity and quality of the output needed to cover the overhead of a large firm. (In addition, she probably could not find enough CPAs who know how to do returns by hand.) Because high risk factors are prevalent in small companies, the risk premium for small companies is higher than for large companies; therefore, the discount rate or required rate of return will be higher.

Bonds and Risk

A bond is a debt obligation, a promise to pay. If you buy a Treasury bond, you have lent money to the U.S. government. The bond is the government's promise to pay you back, with interest, at the date of maturity. The components of a bond are its face value, the interest payment or coupon, and the maturity date. Like any other loan, you will receive interest during the life of the loan and hope to get paid back the face of the loan at the due date or maturity date. Federal and state governments, municipalities, and corporations all issue bonds.

Why would you loan money to the government, a state, or a corporation in exchange for a bond? If you are going to tie up your money for ten, twenty, or even thirty years, you had better be looking at this as an investment. A bond is an investment with a specific return so you can count on getting regular payments, usually every six months. In addition, you generally will get your original investment back at the maturity date, so your risk of loss of principle is diminished. Treasury bonds may be risk-free because the U.S. government stands behind them, but the other bonds, especially corporate bonds, have some risk of not being paid back. Consequently, the rate of return you can get on a corporate bond will be higher to compensate you for the additional risk. If the interest rate on the corporate bond sounds too good to be true, it might be a "junk bond," which will have a greater risk of not being paid back. Other than the risk of not being paid back, the biggest risk of investing in bonds is the risk that inflation will erode the value. If you have a $100,000 twenty-year Treasury bond with a 5% coupon rate, what happens if inflation increases? If prices rise, the $2,500 interest payment you receive every six months will continue to come in, but it will buy fewer goods and services. In addition, the value of your bond on the open market will also be worth less.

> A bond is an investment with a specific return so you can count on getting regular payments, usually every six months.

Key Person and Organizational Risk Factors

One of the biggest differences between small businesses and big business is the organizational structure. Entrepreneurs start small businesses with a vision for the future and a lot of sweat equity. Often an entrepreneur is the key employee with responsibility for operations, research, human resources, marketing, and financing the business. Many times a small business is identified with its owner and vice versa. This can work to everyone's advantage for a while if the company is successful. However, even if the entrepreneur is doing a good job juggling all of these activities, the company has a huge risk exposure. If something were to happen to this one person, it would be the equivalent of losing all the top management of a larger company. Would the bank continue to loan money to the company? Would customers and suppliers continue to do business with the company on as favorable terms? Does someone else know the secret ingredient or have the knack for problem solving on the fly? Who is working on the next great idea?

> Often an entrepreneur is the key employee with responsibility for operations, research, human resources, marketing, and financing the business.

Sometimes the founder of the company lives up to the Peter Principle and is no longer working effectively. (The concept of Peter Principle, put forth by Laurence J. Peter in the late 1960s, is that employees get promoted up to their level of incompetence.) The entrepreneurial mindset of creativity, independence, urgency, and getting a business off the ground is sometimes incompatible with actually running a business. Running a business requires a managerial mindset of organization, people skills, interdependency, teamwork, financial accountability, etc. The founder may still be a key employee, but who is going to fire him or her from the chief operating officer job if he or she is incompetent in this role?

Creating Management Structure

Many times the organizational structure in a small business is very informal, and the relationships between the employees, owners, and managers become blurred. This may create a comfortable working environment that attracts good employees, but the company could have difficulty sustaining growth if it does not create some organizational and management structure. Often this informality carries over to the record-keeping system. Entrepreneurs frequently do not put a priority on the mundane aspects of running a business, such as having an effective accounting system that can produce the reports needed for tax and other compliance purposes. These same financial reports could be used as a management tool, but often they are not produced until several months after the fiscal year to comply with a tax-reporting deadline. Consequently, the budgeting and strategic planning that are an integral part of most large businesses are not possible with the small business.

As small businesses expand, they tend to rely on a small "inner circle" of loyal employees, friends, family members, or other investors to manage the company. The loyalty and good intentions of this group may not make up for lack of management experience or expertise. In contrast, large companies have the following characteristics that make them less risky than small businesses:

- The company is run by professional management.
- The company is financially and psychologically independent from the founder(s).
- Systems and people are in place to ensure that the company would survive the loss of a key person.
- The company operates as a business enterprise, not an extension of a charismatic individual.
- The company has sophisticated financial records and reporting systems.

Key Person Insurance

If you are the key person in your organization, you should start thinking about how you can reduce your company's risk that is directly related to you. Reducing risk by giving up control, delegating more, and perhaps hiring professional management is a long-term process. You might not be ready for this psychologically or financially. However, you can do one thing immediately that would increase your company's chance of survival if something happened to you. Buy key person insurance. How does it work? The company buys an insurance policy on your life, pays the premiums, and is the beneficiary of the policy. If you die, the company receives the proceeds so it can continue operating until you can be replaced. Key person insurance is not just for owner-employees. You may have other employees who are critical to the success of the business, so you should consider buying key person insurance on them as well. How much insurance do you need? Determine how much money the business would need to keep going until a key person could be replaced and buy that amount of insurance. Term insurance is relatively inexpensive if the insured employees are not particularly old or unhealthy. You can expect to pay between a couple hundred to a couple thousand dollars per key person per year, depending on the age and amount of insurance. You can reduce the overall risk of your small company by putting key person insurance in place, and you can also give your employees some assurance that their jobs will still be there even if you are not.

Succession Issues

The succession issues that small companies face are an outgrowth of the key person risk factors. If you put a professional management team in place to deal with the key person risks, then you have already gone a long way to dealing with the succession issues. However, if you are still running the business, then you need to start planning for your successor. Many small companies do not survive the death or retirement of the founder because they do not have a plan, or they don't have competent people to implement an existing plan. If you are valuing a small company, you would consider this situation to be very risky, which could significantly decrease the valuation.

If the business is a family business, the succession issue is even more problematic because of the emotional relationships you have with your potential successor(s) and other relatives. In addition, you may not be objective about your son or daughter's ability to lead the firm in the future. You may be overly pessimistic or overly optimistic about their skills, motivations, and ability to command the respect of the "troops." Whether you are considering a family member or a trusted employee to take over the management of the company, do them and the company the favor of giving them the tools to do a good job including:

- Having them work in a variety of jobs within the organization
- Being a mentor
- Paying for outside education and training
- Being honest with them about your expectations

- Delegating responsibility and holding them accountable
- Assessing their performance as objectively as possible

Debt and Equity Financing Opportunities

Small companies do not have the same access to either debt or equity financing opportunities that large businesses enjoy. Not having deep pockets or immediate access to the deep pockets of others is another risk factor for small companies. Public companies have access to capital through the public stock and bond markets, which allows them to tap into a large pool of individual and organizational investors around the world. Small, closely held companies are usually limited to the personal assets of their founders, family, friends, and bank debt. Lenders determine the relative risk of small companies and price their loans accordingly. Consequently, the smaller, riskier companies must pay higher interest rates to borrow money. This can hurt their cash flow and become a self-fulfilling prophecy—they do become less profitable and more risky.

Small businesses sometimes rely on asset-based financing, which is even more expensive than bank financing. Asset-based financing is a euphemism for factoring. Factoring is a financing strategy in which businesses sell their accounts receivables and use the money to pay for inventory growth. Factoring companies also make loans to their customers in anticipation of sales. At best, this is a "robbing Peter to pay Paul" strategy. At worst, it can become like a "loan shark" arrangement. Factoring companies are legitimate businesses offering a needed service to their business clients, but the use of factoring at a high cost to the company creates additional risk. The tendency for small companies to rely more on debt than equity financing in general is an additional risk factor.

This chapter explored the relationship of size to risk and value based on several characteristic differences between large and small companies. Even though size may not *cause* various risk factors, you can correlate these factors to the size of the company. Consequently, you can generalize that the smaller a company, the greater the risk and, therefore, the lower the value.

> Small companies do not have the same access to either debt or equity financing opportunities that large businesses enjoy.

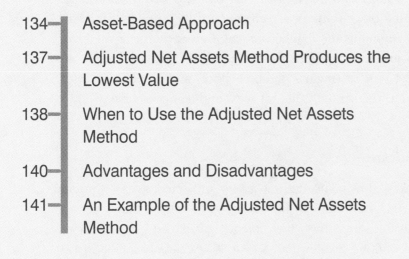

➤ **Chapter 10**

Adjusted Net Asset Method

Asset-Based Approach

The adjusted net asset method of business valuation focuses on determining the fair market value of the assets in a business and then subtracts the liabilities to arrive at the value of the company. The starting point for this calculation is the balance sheet of the company. The balance sheet is the financial statement that summarizes the capital structure of the business. It shows the assets, liabilities, and net worth of the business at a point in time. You can determine the book value of a company just by looking at the balance sheet—the assets minus the liabilities equal the net worth of the business. (Net worth is just another name for book value.) Assets are reported on the balance sheet at their original purchase price, and an allowance for depreciation is used to reduce the value for wear-and-tear over time.

Types of Assets

Assets are broken down into current assets and fixed assets. Current assets refer to cash or assets that can be converted to cash within a year—e.g., accounts receivable, inventory, investments, etc. Fixed assets refer to assets that have a useful life greater than a year. This category includes real estate, equipment, computer software, and intangible assets such as patents, copyrights, and purchased goodwill. Purchased goodwill arises when you buy another business or part of a business and pay more for it than the value of the underlying assets. This amount is recorded on the balance sheet and amortized, generally over fifteen years. The goodwill inherent in your own business does not appear on the balance sheet. In fact, determining the value of this missing number is the object of most sophisticated valuation methods. Fixed assets are depreciated or amortized over "useful lives" proscribed by Generally Accepted Accounting Principles (GAAP) or the IRS.

Why can't you just use book value as the value for your company? It certainly has the advantage of being simple, since all of the information is right there on the balance sheet. The problem is that balance sheets are historical in nature and subject to accounting and tax conventions that do not necessarily reflect the value of the reported assets. The assets are recorded at the price you originally paid for them, and they are depreciated on an arbitrary basis. In addition, if you take advantage of the IRS Code Section 179, then certain assets, namely tangible personal property, can be completely depreciated in the first year for tax purposes. If you use the same depreciation schedule for book and tax purposes, this can distort the value of your assets on the balance sheet. You can report the value of your inventory using certain conventions such as last-in, first-out (LIFO), first-in, first-out (FIFO), the average cost method, or specific identification. What about the value of assets that may have appreciated over time rather than depreciated? For example, if you purchased land for $100,000 and built a warehouse for $400,000 ten years ago, the total property value may be worth over $1 million now. Unfortunately, you can't increase the value of this property on your balance sheet and still be in compliance with Generally Accepted Accounting Principles (GAAP).

How Does an Accounting Principle Become "Generally Accepted"?

Generally Accepted Accounting Principles are the conventions, practices, rules, and procedures that accountants and other financial professionals use to report financial information consistently. GAAP is crucial to the business world and to society as a whole. You would not be able to compare the performance of two companies if they didn't follow the same rules for reporting their income and expenses and recording their assets and liabilities. In fact, you might not even be able to tell if either or both companies were making a profit.

Who makes these rules? Many of the rules have evolved over time in general practice, but the Financial Accounting Standards Board (FASB) has primarily set new accounting standards and interpreted the previously established rules and regulations. This is not an easy job because the number of standards is so large that complaints of "standards overload" are routinely heard in the accounting profession. FASB alone has issued more than 140 Statements of Financial Accounting Standards (SFAS), six concept statements (SFAC), and numerous interpretations and technical bulletins. In addition, GAAP includes several types of pronouncements by the American Institute of Certified Public Accountants (AICPA) including Accounting Research Bulletins (ARBs), Statements of Position, Industry Audit and Accounting

The Financial Accounting Standards Board (FASB) has primarily set new accounting standards and interpreted previously established rules.

Section 179 Expense Election

IRS Code Section 179 provides a tax incentive to purchase new business property; it allows an immediate deduction of up to $100,000 for taxpayers electing to treat certain newly acquired business property as an expense rather than as a depreciable capital asset. The eligible property, called Section 179 property, must be tangible Section 1245 property (like equipment, but not real estate), depreciable, and purchased for use in a trade or business. One limitation is that the Section 179 expense deduction can't exceed the total income from the business and you must reduce the deduction to the extent that you purchased over $400,000 of qualifying property during the year. The Jobs and Growth Tax Relief Reconciliation Act of 2003 raised the maximum Section 179 deduction to $100,000 but the sunset provisions of the law provide that the deduction will revert back to the pre-2003 amount of $25,000 after 2005.

Guides, Practice Bulletins, Accounting Interpretations, Technical Practice Aids, and issue papers. If this were not enough, Opinions of the Accounting Principles Board (APB), the predecessor of FASB, are still GAAP, as are standards set by other professional or regulatory bodies.

Even with all of these guidelines, or in some cases because of them, you have to use your judgment when reporting financial information. One thing that most generally accepted accounting principles have in common is that they involve historical numbers. When you manipulate the historical numbers on a financial statement to arrive at what you think is the correct fair market value of certain assets or the company as a whole, you are getting out of the realm of GAAP.

Reducing Asset Value by Value of Liabilities

Although GAAP doesn't really permit adjustments to fair market value, this is exactly what you do when you are using the adjusted net assets method of valuation. You adjust the book value of all of the tangible and intangible assets to their fair market value. If you have assets such as real estate and equipment, you may need to hire a separate appraiser to value these components of the business. After you have ascertained the fair market value of all of the assets, you subtract the value of any liabilities. Just as you adjusted assets, you may make adjustments to liabilities to recognize their fair market value and to record any liabilities that may not have made it onto the financial statements. Examples of unrecorded liabilities may include accounts payable in cash basis businesses, credit cards, and contingent liabilities.

Contingent Liabilities

Contingent liabilities are obligations of a business that have been created by a past event, but the magnitude and the terms of payment have not been determined. Examples of contingent liabilities include pending or threatened litigation or unasserted claims such as recall expenses for defective parts. You are required by GAAP to report contingencies on your balance sheet if you *probably* will have to make a payment to settle the obligation and if you can make a reliable estimate of the amount. "Probably" means "more likely than not" for these purposes. If you know that a contingent liability has been created, but you are uncertain whether you will actually have to pay to settle this obligation and you can't begin to quantify the potential effect, you should disclose this information in the footnotes to your financial statements. Have you heard about these rules before? Probably not, since most closely held business owners do not issue financial statements with disclosures such as footnotes and calculations of contingent liability costs. If you don't need to have your financial statements audited by an independent CPA firm to meet either bank or regulatory requirements, you don't need to comply with the fine points of GAAP disclosure rules. Although you may not need to report this information in your financial statements, you do need to consider it if you are valuing your company.

Adjusted Net Assets Method Produces the Lowest Value

Have you heard the old adage: "The whole is greater than the sum of the parts"? The adjusted net assets method is just the sum of the parts. This method doesn't place any value on the synergies inherent in the assets that comprise a business. Consequently, you can usually use this method to set the "floor" for the value of an enterprise since sellers would rarely sell their business for less than the fair market value of the assets. Why is setting the "floor value" so important to buyers and sellers?

Buyers want to know the best-case scenario—If you want to buy a business, you need to know the lowest price the seller would accept. However, you would rarely use this value in negotiations unless you knew that the business was performing poorly.

Buyers can compare this price to the cost of starting a new business— The adjusted net assets method is often a good approximation of what it would cost you to buy assets to start a company. If you decide to pay more for an existing business, you are paying for the synergies, goodwill, and other intangibles that make you feel that the company will be successful sooner than a startup.

Sellers want to know the worst-case scenario—If you want or need to sell your business quickly and you do not plan to remain for a transition period, this is the lowest amount you could expect to receive. Will it be enough to pay off all of your company-related liabilities?

Sellers can use the floor value to assess the reasonableness of any purchase offers—If a prospective buyer is offering you an amount at or below the adjusted net assets value, they may not be negotiating in good faith.

A variation of the net adjusted assets method produces an even lower valuation called the liquidation value. The liquidation value is the amount you could expect to receive if you sold your assets individually and did not plan to continue in business. When adjusting the assets to the liquidation value, you would also reduce the fair market value by any costs you might incur for selling the assets. For example, you might need to pay a commission to an equipment broker to sell your equipment.

When to Use the Adjusted Net Assets Method

You can use the adjusted net assets method to value capital-intensive businesses and nonoperating companies such as holding companies and investment companies. You would also use this method to value companies that aren't making a profit or companies that will be liquidated. The adjusted net assets method is most appropriate when you are valuing 100% ownership or at least a majority interest in the company because minority owners would have little control over the underlying assets being valued.

Capital-intensive businesses would include many manufacturers and companies involved in industries such as transportation and delivery if they own large fleets of cars, trucks, airplanes, or railcars. These types of companies are good candidates for the net adjusted assets method of valuation because their income is directly related to their productive assets. Consequently, these capital-intensive companies usually have good information regarding the value of their tangible assets, which will facilitate the process.

Holding companies are businesses that own stock of other companies and direct the management of those companies. The holding company does not own business operating assets nor does it directly employ the workers who are working in the core business. In some cases, holding companies, like Warren Buffett's Berkshire Hathaway, own stock in many different companies. In other cases, the holding company may own a majority of shares in one company, such as a bank holding company. Large, publicly traded holding companies, like Berkshire Hathaway, are valued by the marketplace, but smaller, closely held holding companies, such as a local bank holding company, can be valued using the net adjusted assets method. The value of the holding company is directly related to the value of the underlying assets, namely the stock it owns in the bank.

Investment companies are defined as businesses with more than 80% of their assets invested in marketable securities, real estate investment trusts (REIT), or regulated investment companies (RIC). Investment companies can avoid paying income tax on much of their investment income if they distribute at least 90% of this income annually to their investors who pay the tax on the income received. The value of an investment company is directly related to its underlying assets; however, discounts may be appropriate since regulations reduce the control of the owners.

You can also value other nonoperating companies effectively with the adjusted net asset method. An example of a typical nonoperating company would be an LLC that holds the land and building that you use in your operating business. Your business rents the property from the LLC, just as it would from any other landlord. Again, the underlying assets are the basis for the value of the LLC, and you may need to consider discounts. In this case, the owners' control is reduced because the LLC members own an interest in an LLC that owns the property, not a percentage of the property itself.

The adjusted net assets method is a good way to value companies that consistently lose money. You don't want to use past earnings as an indicator of future earnings when these "earnings" are negative. Although you can use projections of future earnings, the reliability of these numbers

> Holding companies are businesses that own stock of other companies and direct the management of those companies.

What Are REITs and RICs?

These acronyms stand for "Real Estate Investment Trust" and "Regulated Investment Company." Both of these investment vehicles are highly regulated entities that provide an opportunity for individual investors to participate in large real estate or investment deals in a tax-favored environment. How do they work? REITs are mutual funds that invest in real estate and mortgages. In addition to strict requirements on ownership composition and asset value, REITs must distribute at least 95% of their income to their shareholders on an annual basis to avoid corporate income tax on these earnings. RICs are more traditional stock and security mutual funds that distribute dividends, interest, and capital gains directly to their shareholders, thereby avoiding corporate income tax. The individual investors in REITs and RICs pay the income tax on the distributed profits.

is often questioned, especially if there is a history of losses. Remember to include the value of any intangible assets that are not on the balance sheet—just because a company is losing money does not mean that it doesn't have some valuable intangibles.

Companies that are going to be liquidated are good candidates for valuation using the adjusted net asset method. You adjust the asset values to liquidation value, which assumes the assets are being sold and you don't add unrecorded intangible assets to the balance sheet. However, you may need to add unrecorded or contingent liabilities to the balance sheet.

Advantages and Disadvantages

The adjusted net assets method has many advantages:

1. Conceptually, it is easy to understand the idea that the value of the component parts add up to the value of the entire company.
2. The starting point and ending point of the analysis is the company's balance sheet, which should be familiar territory to most business owners.
3. This method is helpful when structuring an actual sale of the company because different components can be taken out without compromising the rest of the analysis. For example, sellers often want to retain the cash from the business so this number would be eliminated from the reconstructed balance sheet.
4. This method facilitates the allocation of the sales price to different assets after a sale. This allocation is important for tax and financial statement purposes.
5. This method makes it easier to secure appropriate financing since the asset values are delineated rather than included in a lump-sum value for the business.

One of the disadvantages of the adjusted net asset method is that all of the assets and liabilities of a company must be valued separately. This can be very costly and time consuming if you hire several specialists such as real estate appraisers and specialized equipment appraisers. If you don't hire these specialists, then the accuracy and integrity of the valuation will suffer, especially if these assets comprise a major part of the total value of the company.

Another disadvantage of the adjusted net assets method is that it is difficult to properly value intangible assets, especially goodwill, using an asset-based approach. You can deal with this problem by using a hybrid method such as the excess earnings method, which will be discussed in Chapter 12. Otherwise, you should use this method for companies that do not have any goodwill or that will be sold in a manner that negates the goodwill that is there, e.g., liquidations.

An Example of the Adjusted Net Assets Method

Potteryshed, Inc. is an S corporation owned by John Clay and his wife Sally. They are both potters and the only employees of the company. They have been in business making decorative and utilitarian pottery for five years. They sell their wares on a wholesale basis to a few craft galleries in their home state of Pennsylvania, and they have a small retail outlet in their building. They have been able to make a living but have never been really profitable. A representative of a large tableware manufacturer, Plate and Bowl, Inc., saw their work and wanted to hire them as designers and consultants. As part of the contract, Plate and Bowl has agreed to buy Potteryshed, Inc. John and Sally need to know the value of their business to determine a fair asking price in this arm's length transaction. Potteryshed, Inc. has the following GAAP balance sheet (**Chart 10-1**) as of December 31, 2003 (see next page).

CHART 10-1

POTTERYSHED, INC.

Balance Sheet
As of December 31, 2003

ASSETS

Current assets:

Cash	$25,000
Accounts receivables	30,000
Prepaid expenses	2,000
Inventory	15,000
Total current assets	72,000

Noncurrent assets:

Land	20,000
Buildings	100,000
Equipment	25,000
Fixtures	15,000
Total property, plant, and equipment	160,000
Less: accumulated depreciation	42,000
Net property, plant, and equipment	118,000

Other noncurrent assets:

Trademarks	5,000
Total other noncurrent assets	5,000

TOTAL ASSETS	**$195,000**

LIABILITIES AND OWNERS' EQUITY

Current liabilities:

Accounts payable	$15,000
Taxes payable	5,000
Total current liabilities	20,000

POTTERYSHED, INC.

Balance Sheet
As of December 31, 2003

CHART 10-1
(continued)

Noncurrent liabilities:

Notes payable	10,000
Mortgages payable	95,000

Total noncurrent liabilities — 105,000
Total liabilities — 125,000

Owners' Equity:

Capital stock	1,000
Additional paid-in capital	5,000
Retained earnings	64,000

TOTAL LIABILITIES AND OWNERS' EQUITY $195,000

This December 31, 2003, balance sheet for Potteryshed, Inc. is the starting point for a valuation using the adjusted net assets method. The balance sheet is prepared according to Generally Accepted Accounting Principles (GAAP); therefore, it is on a historical cost basis. The first step in using the adjusted net assets method is to analyze each of the balance sheet accounts to determine if any adjustments need to be made to reflect fair market value.

Cash—Cash is reflected at the correct current balance; however, John and Sally don't plan to transfer the cash to the new owners so this account is adjusted to zero.

Accounts receivable—This account needs to be adjusted to reflect $7,500 of receivables that were booked in the first year of business that probably won't be collected

Prepaid expenses—This account properly reflects prepaid expenses.

Inventory—Inventory needs to be valued upward by $5,000 to reflect purchases that have been improperly expensed but are on hand in inventory.

Property, plant, and equipment—This account has been valued upward by $50,000 to reflect the current real estate value according to a recent appraisal that John and Sally used for refinancing purposes. The account has also been increased by $2,500 to reflect the fair market value of equipment and fixtures that are worth more than their depreciated cost basis indicates.

Trademarks—This account reflects the cost of acquiring the Potteryshed trademark, but John and Sally never had the time or resources to promote this name beyond their local area. Since John and Sally haven't leveraged the trademark, the historical cost basis for this asset seems reasonable.

Current liabilities—These accounts fairly represent the outstanding short-term liabilities of the company.

Noncurrent liabilities—The notes payable and mortgages payable accounts accurately reflect these liabilities.

Contingent liability—A jealous competitor sued Potteryshed, Inc. claiming that John and Sally stole their secret recipe for an unusual glaze. Although the Clays think the claim is unwarranted, they plan to offer their adversaries $10,000 to go away.

The next step in using the net adjusted assets method is to make these adjustments to the balance sheet as follows in **Chart 10-2.** Retained earnings is adjusted by the net amount of the above changes, thereby balancing the balance sheet.

CHART 10-2

POTTERYSHED, INC.

Adjusted Balance Sheet
As of December 31, 2003

ASSETS	HISTORICAL COST	FAIR MARKET VALUE
Current assets:		
Cash	$25,000	$—
Accounts receivables	30,000	22,500
Prepaid expenses	2,000	2,000
Inventory	15,000	20,000
Total current assets	72,000	44,500
Noncurrent assets:		
Land	20,000	40,000
Buildings	100,000	130,000
Equipment	25,000	27,500
Fixtures	15,000	15,000
Total property, plant, and equipment	160,000	212,500
Less: accumulated depreciation	42,000	42,000
Net property, plant, and equipment	118,000	170,500
Other noncurrent assets:		
Trademarks	5,000	5,000
Total other noncurrent assets	5,000	5,000
TOTAL ASSETS	$195,000	$220,000
LIABILITIES AND OWNERS' EQUITY		
Current liabilities:		
Accounts payable	$15,000	$15,000
Taxes payable	5,000	5,000
Total current liabilities	20,000	20,000

Chart 10-2 continues ▶

CHART 10-2

(continued)

POTTERYSHED, INC.

Adjusted Balance Sheet
As of December 31, 2003

	HISTORICAL COST	FAIR MARKET VALUE
Noncurrent liabilities:		
Notes payable	10,000	10,000
Mortgages payable	95,000	95,000
Contingent liability	—	10,000
Total noncurrent liabilities	105,000	115,000
Total liabilities	125,000	135,000
Owners' equity:		
Capital stock	1,000	1,000
Additional paid-in capital	5,000	5,000
Retained earnings	64,000	79,000
TOTAL LIABILITIES AND OWNERS' EQUITY	$195,000	$220,000

The final step in the adjusted net assets method of valuation is to sum all of the fair market values for the assets and subtract all of the liabilities. For the Potteryshed, Inc. the value is $220,000 in total assets, less $135,000 in total liabilities, producing a valuation of $85,000. This amount represents the total value of the Owners' Equity Section of the Adjusted Balance Sheet.

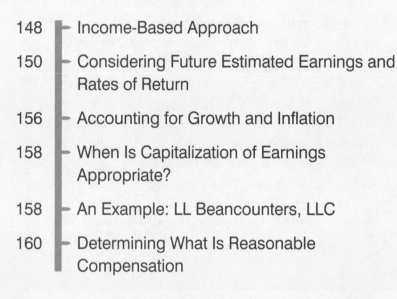

➤ **Chapter 11**

Capitalization of Earnings Method

Part One

Part Two

Part Three

Part Four

Part Five

Part Six

PART FOUR: BASIC VALUATION METHODS

■ CHAPTER 10 Adjusted Net Asset Method ■ CHAPTER 11 **Capitalization of Earnings Method** ■ CHAPTER 12 Excess Earnings Method ■ CHAPTER 13 Discounted Cash Flow Method ■ CHAPTER 14 Rule of Thumb Methods

Income-Based Approach

The underlying philosophy of the capitalization of earnings method, like all income-based methods, is that the whole is greater than the sum of the parts. Or to rephrase an old television commercial—"parts is not parts." Income-based approaches don't distinguish between the tangible and intangible assets of a company. They look to the earnings of the company to provide an indication of the total value of the company. The theory is that the ability to generate anticipated future earnings is really what someone is buying when they purchase a business, regardless of the underlying assets. Consequently, it is important to identify any nonoperating assets or liabilities that contribute income or expense to the bottom line. You should remove these assets or liabilities and adjust your income statement accordingly. For example, if you own a restaurant and you used some excess cash in the company to invest in a growth stock portfolio, the earnings or losses associated with this investment are unrelated to the operations of the restaurant and should be adjusted out of your earnings. On the other hand, if you temporarily invest excess cash in CDs or money markets to earn interest until you need the funds for the business, this income could be included in your income from operations.

The Basic Formula

The capitalization of earnings method is "simple, yet elegant." The entire valuation method can be reduced to one basic formula. Shannon Pratt, the guru of business valuation, delineates it in the book *Valuing Small Businesses and Professional Practices,* Third Edition (McGraw-Hill,1998), as follows:

$$PV = \frac{E}{c}$$

Where:
PV = present value
E = expected economic income
c = direct capitalization rate

The capitalization rate is a rate of interest used to convert future income streams to a single present value. This rate is based on expectations in the marketplace about what rates of return can be expected on alternative investments. The beauty of this simple formula is its versatility. If you know any two of the variables, you can calculate the third. For example, let's say you are interested in buying a restaurant that has earned $50,000 each year for the last five years. You use a capitalization rate of 10 percent, which reflects the risky nature of the business and the rate of return you would need to achieve in order to make this type of investment. Apply the formula:

$$\frac{E}{c} = PV \qquad \frac{\$50,000}{10\%} = \$500,000$$

This scenario indicates that you would be willing to pay $500,000 for the restaurant.

> The capitalization rate is a rate of interest used to convert future income streams to a single present value.

Assessing Different Scenarios

What if the seller counters your offer with a price of $625,000? You can use the capitalization of earnings method formula to assess the viability of this offer by rearranging the formula according to the basic rules of algebra. Algebraic formulas allow you to solve for any unknown variable as long as you have values for the other variables. In the basic capitalization of earnings formula, you know the earnings and the interest rate and you are determining the present value. In this case, you know the value, $625,000, and the earnings, $50,000, so you are determining what interest rate would produce that value with those earnings. You rearrange algebraic formulas by multiplying or dividing each side of the equation by the same variable. In this case, you would divide each side by "E" in order to isolate the "c" variable. When the same variable appears on one side of the equation as both a numerator and denominator, they cancel each other out and become "1" because any number divided by itself is "1."

$$\frac{PV}{E} = \frac{1}{c} \qquad \frac{\$625,000}{\$50,000} = \frac{1}{c} \qquad 12.5 = \frac{1}{c} \qquad c = 8\%$$

Since you know that the earnings have historically been $50,000 per year, a value of $625,000 would mean that the capitalization rate would have to be 8%, as opposed to the 10% rate of return you originally expected or required. You may need to do further research regarding the appropriateness of this interest rate in the marketplace. Can you borrow money at this rate to purchase the business? Can you invest in a safer business or investment vehicle and still make this level of return? The answers to these questions are not necessarily easy to determine, but you will have to answer them to decide whether you are willing to reconsider the price you are willing to pay for the business.

Other Configurations

Another configuration of the capitalization of earnings method formula will tell you what the earnings would need to be to produce a given value at a given capitalization rate. Using your original capitalization rate of 10% and the seller's asking price of $625,000, what earnings would need to be produced to make this a viable deal? By multiplying each side of the formula by "c", you can isolate "E" and solve for the required earnings:

$$c \times PV = \frac{E}{c} \times c \qquad c \times PV = E \qquad 10\% \times \$625,000 = \$62,500$$

You can see from this calculation that the company would need to earn $62,500 annually rather than $50,000 to produce a value of $625,000 with a 10% capitalization rate. Perhaps an analysis of the income and expenses would indicate some areas of opportunity for increased earnings or decreased expenses. In any case, using the capitalization of earnings method can give you a good sense of whether you and the seller are in the same ballpark.

Considering Future Estimated Earnings and Rates of Return

Although the concept of the capitalization of earnings method is simple, it is not always so easy to estimate the future earnings and choose the appropriate rate of return for the calculation. Earnings can be measured several different ways, all of which may be appropriate for the capitalization of earnings method of valuing a company.

Which definition of earnings should you use?

- **EBIT**—Earnings before interest and taxes
- **EBITDA**—Earnings before interest, taxes, depreciation, and amortization
- **Net Cash Flow**—Income adjusted for noncash items
- **Free Cash Flow**—Cash flow adjusted for management compensation

> Earnings can be measured several different ways, all of which may be appropriate for the capitalization of earnings method of valuing a company.

You calculate earnings before interest and taxes (**EBIT**) by starting with the company's net profit and adding back any interest expense that was used to finance the company. For example, the interest expense on shareholder loans, mortgages, or equipment loans would be added back. However, you should consider whether some of the interest expense on the income statement relates to ongoing operations rather than financing the company. If you historically finance inventory purchases or use a line of credit to manage cash flow needs in a seasonal business, these interest expense items would not be added back. The assumption would be that a buyer would have these same operating interest costs.

Next, you add back any *income* taxes that were deducted in arriving at net income. Adding taxes back to net income can be like a "trick question" because income tax expense usually shows up on the income statement only after net profit has been calculated. Caveat: Don't add back something that hasn't been subtracted. Also you can't just go to the "taxes" line on the income statement and add that number back to net profit. Most, if not all, of the taxes in this category are ordinary operating expenses such as property taxes and payroll taxes that do need to be included in the net income calculation. Why, you might ask, would analysts adjust net income for interest and income taxes when valuing a company? The theory is that these costs relate to the financing of the company and the tax structure of the organization. You can "level the playing field" by adjusting for these items so that you can compare different businesses or investment opportunities.

The Importance of a "Level Playing Field"

Dahlia Bloom wants to buy a flower shop so she can own a business in which her unusual name will be an asset. She has two opportunities: Bud's Florist, which is a C corporation, or Rose's Petals, which is an S corporation. Dahlia used the capitalization of earnings method with a capitalization rate of 20% to value both companies and determined that they were each worth $350,000.

Then, she remembered that Bud told her that he originally bought the business from someone else so she added the related $7,500 of interest expense back to the earnings. She also realized that the C corporation's earnings had income taxes subtracted from them, whereas the S corporation's net income did not include taxes since it is a flow-through entity in which taxes are paid by the individual shareholders. She added another $5,000 to Bud's income to adjust for the tax differential. When she recalculated the value with the additional $12,500 income, the value of Bud's Florist became $412,500. Even though Dahlia originally thought that these two businesses were very similar, you can see that the financing and tax structures of the two businesses are responsible for a $62,500 swing in the value of the two companies. This difference represents more than 15% of the total value. The "level playing field" allowed Dahlia to more accurately compare the relative values of the operating businesses once the tax and financing costs were removed.

Incorporating Depreciation and Amortization

Earnings before interest, taxes, depreciation, and amortization (**EBITDA**) goes a step further than EBIT by adding back the expenses of depreciation and amortization. Why add back depreciation and amortization? Both Generally Accepted Accounting Principles (GAAP) and the Internal Revenue Code proscribe arbitrary methods of accounting for the wearing out or obsolescence of assets over time. Depreciation is the name of the method used for tangible assets, and amortization is the name of the method used for intangible assets. (See Chapter 4 for a detailed discussion of depreciation and how to calculate it.) Because depreciation and amortization are accounting constructs, no cash is expended to correspond to the annual depreciation or amortization expense. Consequently, these amounts are added back to EBIT to more closely approximate the earnings that would be available to shareholders or other owners.

Net Cash Flow

Net cash flow means what it says—it is the income adjusted for all noncash items. In many cases you need to make a lot of adjustments, underscoring the fact that net profit does not equal net cash flow. What the business owner or prospective business owner really wants to know is how much *cash* is available to pay dividends and increased salaries or to grow the business. In addition to adding back depreciation and amortization, you make adjustments such as subtracting the purchases of long-term assets and the payment of loans and dividends, while adding back the proceeds from the acquisition of loans, the sale of fixed assets, or a stock issuance. Businesses whose financial statements are issued in accordance with Generally Accepted Accounting Principles (GAAP) already have a cash flow statement in addition to a balance sheet and income statement. Most valuators use net cash flow in the capitalization of earnings method because they feel it best represents the earnings that would be available to owners.

The Cash Flow Statement of Moneyflow, Inc. for the year ended December 31, 2003 (**Chart 11-1**) shows how profit before taxes is adjusted to arrive at net cash flow.

> Net cash flow means what it says—it is the income adjusted for all noncash items.

CHART 11-1	MONEYFLOW, INC.	

Calculation of Cash Flow
For the Year Ended December 31, 2003

CASH FLOWS FROM OPERATING ACTIVITIES	
Profit before tax	$2,000,000
Adjustments for items not requiring cash:	
Depreciation	50,000
Operating profit before changes in working capital	2,050,000
Adjustments for:	
(Increase)/Decrease in trade receivables	(200,000)
(Increase)/Decrease in loans and advances	(500,000)
Increase/(Decrease) in current liabilities	(250,000)
Net increase in working capital	1,100,000
Adjustments for:	
Income tax	**(250,000)**
NET CASH FLOWS FROM OPERATING ACTIVITIES	**850,000**
CASH FLOWS FROM INVESTING ACTIVITIES	
Purchase of fixed assets	(75,000)
Interest received	25,000
NET CASH USED FOR INVESTING ACTIVITIES	**(50,000)**
CASH FLOWS FROM FINANCING ACTIVITIES	
Net proceeds from stock issuance	500,000
Dividend paid	(60,000)
NET CASH FLOWS FROM FINANCING ACTIVITIES	**440,000**
NET INCREASE IN CASH	**$1,240,000**

Free cash flow takes this concept one step further to refine the calculation of actual cash flowing into a business and thus available to owners. Free cash flow is often defined as operating cash flow reduced by necessary expenses to run the business such as interest, taxes, and a maintenance level of capital spending. If you are calculating the value of a closely held company, you would also add back any salary the owner is taking and subtract what you would need to pay a manager. This normalizing adjustment differentiates between the income that is available to owners by virtue of investing their capital, the essence of ownership, and the income that would be available to an owner who was investing sweat equity. Even if you are an owner investing sweat equity in the business, it is a good idea to quantify what is a reasonable salary for the actual work you perform. Only the excess cash inflow over that amount represents the earnings available to an ownership interest.

Capitalization Rates

Once you have decided what definition of earnings or cash flow you are going to capitalize, you must choose an appropriate capitalization rate. See Chapter 22 for a discussion of the sophisticated calculation of appropriate capitalization and discount rates. In the meantime, you can select a more accessible rate that still captures some of the nuances of the relationship between risk and return. Chad Simmons sets forth the following interest rate choices in the *Business Valuation Bluebook*, (Facts on Demand Press, 2002):

Once you have decided what definition of earnings or cash flow you are going to capitalize, you must choose an appropriate capitalization rate.

- Federal lending rate
- Prime lending rate = P
- Small business lending rate = P + <2.00%
- SBA lending rate = P + 2.25–2.75%
- Safe rate = >5 year CDs

Simmons recommends using the small business lending rate because it takes local market conditions into account as well as the risk inherent in financing a closely held company—just the type of business you are valuing. If you choose a different rate, such as the safe rate, you may need to make adjustments to the rate to reflect an appropriate level of risk. If you don't make these kinds of adjustments, you will inflate the value of the company. Take the example of Moneyflow, Inc. You divide the net cash flow of $1,240,000 by the appropriate capitalization rate. If you use a small business lending rate of 7%, the value of Moneyflow, Inc. becomes $17,714,286. On the other hand, if long-term CDs were earning 5%, the safe rate calculation would be $24,800,000. Another way to look at this is—why would anyone invest $24,800,000 in a small business when they could get the same projected rate of return by investing in risk-free long-term CDs?

Accounting for Growth and Inflation

The simplicity of the capitalization of earnings method is partially compromised when you start examining the underlying assumptions. Is current cash flow, for example, really representative of expected future cash flow? If not, how do you account for projected growth or decline in the earnings? What if you use another measure of income such as EBITDA? Does it make a difference if you calculated EBITDA based on a five-year weighted average versus the most recent fiscal year? What if you make a projection for the coming year? The combinations and permutations of types of earnings and the time period for which they are measured or projected seem limitless. Because all of these nuances do make a difference, selecting the appropriate capitalization rate becomes the key to an accurate valuation. The capitalization rate is derived from the discount rate; the rate of return you use to convert future income streams into present value. You should take into account the following factors when selecting a discount rate:

1. The risk-free rate—e.g., the rate of twenty-year Treasury bonds
2. A risk premium for investing in stock
3. An additional risk premium for investing in a small company
4. An additional risk premium for investing in a nonmarketable investment
5. Additional risk premiums for other factors such as the particular industry

The difference between the discount rate and the capitalization rate is that you use the discount rate to convert a *series* of expected income streams to present value, while you use the capitalization rate to convert *one* measure of income to present value. Consequently, the capitalization rate incorporates a factor to account for projected growth. Thus, the relationship between capitalization rates and discount rates is born—the capitalization rate is equal to the discount rate less the growth rate projected for the duration of the investment.

How do you account for the effects of inflation? You need to incorporate an inflation factor into the growth rate when determining the appropriate capitalization rate. For example, if you expect the inflation rate to be 5% over time and you are projecting real growth in income to be 10% a year, you would subtract 15% from the discount rate to get the appropriate capitalization rate. In a world with no inflation, you would value a company with projected net cash flow of $100,000, a discount rate of 25%, and a growth rate of 10% as follows:

$$\frac{100,000}{25\% - 10\%} = 666,667$$

If you incorporate the effect of inflation in the same example, you get a higher value because the effective growth rate is 15% instead of 10%. This assumes that the growth of the company is not only keeping up with inflation but also growing an additional 10%

$$\frac{100,000}{25\% - 10\% - 5\%} = 1,000,000$$

When Does the Capitalization Rate Equal the Discount Rate?

A simple formula describes the relationship of the capitalization rate to the discount rate: capitalization rate = (discount rate – growth rate). When you look at the equation, you can see that eliminating the growth rate would result in capitalization rate = discount rate. This means that you have an investment that will continue to earn the same amount year after year. When you analyze this formula, you also see that you should develop the capitalization rate in exactly the same way you would develop a discount rate. The only difference is the subtraction of the growth rate after the capitalization/discount rate is determined. If you foresee declining earnings rather than growth, you should add the rate of decline to the capitalization rate.

When Is Capitalization of Earnings Appropriate?

The theoretical underpinning of the capitalization of earnings method is that the growth rate used in the calculation is a rate that can be sustained over the long-term. Consequently, you should use the capitalization of earnings method to value companies with predictable and steady earnings. If you think a company's growth rate will vary significantly, especially in the near term, you should probably use the discounted cash flow method. (See Chapter 13 for a full discussion of this method.) The capitalization of earnings method is usually a good way to value professional service firms or other companies with the following characteristics:

> You should use the capitalization of earnings method to value companies with predictable and steady earnings.

1. Income is generated by people, not assets.
2. Specialized education is usually required.
3. Loyalty and trust reside with the professional.
4. The industry is regulated, such as by certification, licensure, and ownership structure.
5. New business comes via referrals.

Companies with the above characteristics generally have predictable earnings and don't have rapid growth due to the very factors listed above.

In contrast, the capitalization of earnings method would not be a good way to value a capital-intensive business such as an automobile manufacturer. Since a large part of the value of any manufacturing company is the actual assets used to produce the product, a method with an asset-based component may be more appropriate.

An Example: LL Beancounters, LLC

LL Beancounters, LLC is a financial consulting firm that has been in business for thirteen years. Beancounters has four employee-owners, one is a CPA (certified public accountant), one is a CFP (certified financial planner), one is a CVA (certified valuation analyst), and one of them has an MBA from a prestigious southern business school. A large national consulting firm has approached them about selling. Although the partners never thought about selling out to a larger firm, they decided that this was a good opportunity to see what their company was worth and maybe do a deal. They decided to approach the valuation using the capitalization of earnings method because they do not have a capital-intensive business, they have predictable earnings with a steady growth rate, and they have heard that these large firms are only interested in a target's ability to generate future earnings. The first step is to calculate the cash flow of LL Beancounters, LLC.

LL BEANCOUNTERS, LLC

Cash Flow Calculation

CHART 11-2

REVENUE	$1,000,000
OPERATING EXPENSES	(950,000)
NET PROFIT	**50,000**
Adjustments for:	
Interest	$20,000
Taxes	-
EBIT	**70,000**
Adjustments for:	
Depreciation	$25,000
Amortization	1,000
EBITDA	**96,000**
Adjustments for:	
Owners' "excess salary"	$100,000
CASH FLOW	**$196,000**

The owners of LL Beancounters, LLC added back $100,000 of "excess salary" because they determined that they had each received $25,000 more in salary than they would have earned based on the amount of services they each provided to the firm. If they were to continue working for the new company, they would only be paid a fair salary based on services provided and revenue generated. (See Chapter 17 for a full discussion of normalizing adjustments.) Therefore, the $100,000 of "excess salary" is added back to the cash flow of the company to reflect the additional earnings—making this additional value available to the purchaser.

They chose a capitalization rate of 25%, which reflects a risk-free rate of 5% and additional risk premiums for size, illiquidity, and equity. Their growth has been able to keep up with inflation, but not exceed it, so they chose a growth rate of 5%, which is what they think the long-term inflation rate will be. Using these assumptions, they calculate the value of LL Beancounters, LLC as follows:

$$\frac{196,000}{25\% - 5\%} = 980,000$$

The owners of LL Beancounters, LLC feel comfortable putting forward an asking price of $980,000 for their company. Although they are willing to negotiate, and they understand that the ultimate terms, taxes, etc., will probably reduce the amount of cash they ultimately will receive, they know what price range they need to be in to do a deal. For example, if the larger firm offered them $500,000 paid in installments of $100,000 over five years, they would probably turn it down because they have valued their business at almost twice that amount, assuming a cash deal. The underlying basis for their valuation is that they are generating almost $200,000 per year of cash flow, so under normal circumstances they should not accept an offer of less than that amount. On the other hand, if the firm offered them $1 million paid in $100,000 installments over ten years they may agree to that. Or they might not. At this level, they would have to calculate the present value of the future cash flows, the tax effects, etc., in addition to considering nonfinancial issues such as when the partners want to retire to make a decision. Valuing the company is only the first step, not the final answer.

Determining What Is Reasonable Compensation

In the case of LL Beancounters, LLC, the question of whether the employee-owners were receiving reasonable compensation was a significant factor in its valuation.

Reasonable compensation means different things to different people, but everyone needs to be aware of what the IRS considers reasonable compensation. The IRS looks at the reasonableness of compensation on both ends of the spectrum—in other words they will try to get you "both coming and going." On the low end, the IRS wants to make sure employee-owners of S corporations are taking enough compensation to reflect the value of the services they provide to the company. This is a payroll tax issue. If an S corporation shareholder has a $40,000 salary and takes $100,000 in distributions, the IRS would probably determine that she was trying to avoid social security tax and that her compensation should have been higher. How much higher? First, look at the services the owner is providing to the company—how much would an employee doing similar tasks earn? Does the owner have some special skills that would warrant an even higher salary? If you start here with a baseline reasonable salary, then you need to look at the relationship of salary to dividends. The IRS does not have a strict rule, but in operating businesses where the owner performs significant services, the owners' salary should definitely be more than the dividends. We usually suggest to our S corporation clients that dividends should be less than half the amount of compensation, preferably closer to one third.

On the other end of the spectrum, the IRS does not want companies to have a tax deduction for compensation that they consider unreasonably high. At this level, they want distributions to be dividends that are not deductible at the corporate level but are taxable at the individual shareholder level. Yes, the IRS can "have their cake and eat it too." The most important aspects of reasonable compensation are the employee's qualifications and performance. Many times an employee-owner of a closely held company actually performs several jobs, has specialized knowledge, or difficult to develop business contacts. These factors would warrant a higher than "normal" salary. When you are planning your executive compensation package, you should consider what you would pay someone else who could perform all of your job duties, even though all entrepreneurs know that nobody else could possibly do it. The IRS and the Tax Court look at the facts and circumstances of each case. In the H&A International Jewelry Ltd. Case, TC Memo 1997-467, the Tax Court found that the president's salary of $600,000 was unreasonable even though he was the person primarily responsible for the company's success. In the Automotive Investment Development Inc. case, TC Memo 1993-298, the Tax Court determined that

> The most important aspects of reasonable compensation are the employee's qualifications and performance.

the president's salary of over $2 million in 1985 was reasonable and deductible. One of the important factors in this case was that the company computed the owner's large bonus using a bonus formula common in the industry. You can't rely on a rule of thumb or a safe harbor amount to avoid charges of unreasonable compensation, but I would suggest using the "smell test." Does it seem reasonable? How does it compare to other executive salaries in the industry? What would you pay someone to do your job? What is it you do anyway?

> **Chapter 12**

Excess Earnings Method

Part One

Part Two

Part Three

Part Four

Part Five

Part Six

PART FOUR: BASIC VALUATION METHODS

■ CHAPTER 10 Adjusted Net Asset Method ■ CHAPTER 11 Capitalization of Earnings Method ■ CHAPTER 12 Excess Earnings Method ■ CHAPTER 13 Discounted Cash Flow Method ■ CHAPTER 14 Rule of Thumb Methods

A Hybrid Method Based on Assets and Earnings

The **excess earnings method** is a combination of the adjusted net asset method and the capitalization of earnings method. This method is conceptually similar to the adjusted net asset method in that the value of a business is determined by ascertaining the fair market value of all of the assets individually and then adding these values together. However, the excess earnings method separates the tangible and intangible assets—the tangible assets are valued using the adjusted net assets method and the intangible assets, notably goodwill, are valued by capitalizing the excess earnings. Excess earnings are those earnings over and above a "reasonable" rate of return on the adjusted net assets of the company. The theory is that if a company earns more than other similar companies, it must have goodwill, and you can quantify the amount of that goodwill by capitalizing the excess earnings.

The excess earnings method is also known as the Treasury method because it first appeared in Appeals and Review Memorandum 34 (ARM 34), which was issued by the U.S. Treasury in 1920. This ARM was promulgated to help taxpayers in the alcoholic beverage industry and related industries determine how much intangible value they lost when they had to liquidate their businesses due to Prohibition.

The relationship of the excess earnings method and the Treasury Department is still very important. The Internal Revenue Service branch of the Treasury Department has issued a number of Revenue Rulings that clarify and expand on the relationship between excess earnings and goodwill. Probably the most important of these is Revenue Ruling 59-60, which defined the concept of "fair market value" and set out a number of factors that need to be considered in every business valuation. Revenue Ruling 59-60 was issued specifically to help taxpayers value closely held businesses for gift and estate purposes. Just as ARM 34 developed a broader usage, so did Revenue Ruling 59-60. Because of this IRS pronouncement, the excess earnings method is widely accepted for most tax valuation purposes and many nontax purposes. Revenue Ruling 68-609 took ARM 34 and Revenue Ruling 59-60 one step further by setting out a formula approach for valuing goodwill using the excess earnings method, if no better basis for the valuation is available. Revenue Ruling 68-609 also specified that the formulaic excess earnings method was only appropriate to value the intangibles of a business, not the entire enterprise.

Goodwill Hunting

"Goodwill Hunting" may bring to mind the Robin Williams/ Matt Damon film about the uneducated mathematical genius and his psychiatrist. "Goodwill hunting" in the business valuation context is less about raw genius than it is about disciplined analysis and judgment. The goodwill you consider when valuing a business is an intangible asset that makes a company worth more than the sum of the tangible assets. Companies create goodwill by fostering customer and supplier loyalty, being good corporate citizens, building a better mousetrap, controlling a large share of the market, etc. Even though the concept of goodwill is intangible, the additional value of a business due to these factors can be quantified.

The goal of the excess earnings method is to value the goodwill derived from such factors. Another way to think of goodwill is as the difference between a company that has been profitable for many years and a similar company that is either new and/or not profitable. A buyer will only pay an amount over the fair market value of the assets if the goodwill is leading to earnings greater than a fair return on the assets.

Goodwill Accounting

When large corporations pay a premium to acquire another company, they are paying for goodwill in the same way the purchaser of a closely held company does. How is this premium treated on the company's financial statements? The total amount appears as an intangible asset, "Goodwill." Until 2002, this amount was amortized over forty years for financial statement purposes. The concept of amortization is to reflect the diminishing value of an asset over time. Consequently, large companies involved with mergers and acquisitions have written off huge sums in goodwill amortization. According to M•Cam, a Virginia company specializing in intellectual property and intangible asset information

What Are Revenue Rulings?

Revenue Rulings are published opinions of the Internal Revenue Service that indicate how the Service is interpreting the tax code, related statutes, tax treaties, and regulations. The purpose of Revenue Rulings is to inform and guide taxpayers, IRS personnel, and professional advisors about tax issues to improve voluntary compliance and consistent application of the tax laws. Revenue Rulings have the force of law until they are specifically superseded or unless the Tax Court rules otherwise. The National Office of the IRS issues these rulings throughout the year, and each ruling is identified by the year issued and a consecutive number based on the number of rulings in that year. Generally, Revenue Rulings are very technical in nature and very specific in their application. However, since they do constitute substantial authority for taking a position on a tax issue, they are interpreted and reinterpreted themselves, which leads to much broader application and importance than perhaps the IRS originally intended.

(✒ *www.m-cam.com/goodwill.html*), U.S. companies have written off billions of dollars in goodwill amortization. For example, Verizon Communications has reduced earnings by over $3 billion, Nortel Networks wrote off $12 billion, and Vodafone tops the list at $141 billion in goodwill amortization. These numbers can make a material difference in earnings per share and other financial benchmarks that the market uses to compare companies.

What is wrong with this picture? Why are companies writing off an asset that is supposed to be an indication of additional value and not a depreciating asset? GAAP (Generally Accepted Accounting Principles) dictated this treatment until FASB (the Financial Accounting Standards Board) changed the rules as of January 1, 2002, to eliminate amortization of goodwill for financial statements. (Purchased goodwill continues to be amortized over fifteen years for tax purposes.) Now companies only write off goodwill if they determine that its value is impaired.

The Adjusted Net Asset Method Revisited

As Yogi Berra would say: "It's déjà vu all over again." You can refer to Chapter 10 for an in-depth discussion of the adjusted net asset method. The underlying theory of the adjusted net asset method is that the total value of an enterprise is determined by adding up the fair market values of all of the component assets. If you have technical equipment or real estate, you may need to engage a specialized appraiser to determine the fair market value of these assets. You should especially consider hiring a separate appraiser if these assets make up a large portion of the total assets and/or capital assets are the major income-producing factor in the company. When the tangible assets do not constitute a major portion of the value of the company, you can estimate the fair market value of these assets. If you don't have anything better to use, you can start with the book value of the tangible assets. Book value is the number recorded on the balance sheet that reflects what the asset originally cost, less accumulated depreciation and amortization. You can see by that definition that the book value of an asset does not necessarily have any relationship with fair market value of the asset. However, if the assets are relatively new or represent a small portion of the value of the company, you can usually safely proceed with this gross simplification.

How do you treat intangible assets such as purchased goodwill, patents, trademarks, or computer software that are already on the balance sheet? You can deal with these assets in one of two ways. First, you can exclude them completely from the other balance sheet assets to which you will apply the adjusted net asset method. The theory is that the value of goodwill you determine by valuing all of the intangible assets, recorded and unrecorded, using the capitalization of excess earnings method will represent the total intangible value of the company. This goodwill value is then added to the value of the rest of the assets you found by applying the adjusted net asset method. The second way to approach recorded intangibles is to value them individually and include them in the assets you will consider in your analysis using the adjusted net asset method. If you choose this strategy, the goodwill value you calculate using the capitalization of excess earnings method will represent only the residual goodwill of the company, i.e., the goodwill that can't be attributed to a specific intangible asset.

If you decide that you want to value recorded intangibles separately before applying the capitalization of excess earnings method to determine the residual goodwill, how do you value these intangibles? You can value intangible assets using a cost, income, or market approach. An example of a cost approach would be determining in today's dollars how much a company would have to spend to recreate the current level of brand awareness for its products. You capitalize this amount to represent the intangible value of a brand or trademark. You can use the income approach to determine the value of intangibles such as favorable contracts, patents, and below-market leasing arrangements. With each of these situations, you quantify the competitive advantage in terms of additional income or relative savings provided. For example, if your company owns a patent that allows you to sell either more of your product than the competition or sell your product at a higher price or higher profit margin, this competitive advantage can be quantified. First, you determine the additional income due to the patent, and then you capitalize it to determine the fair market value of the patent. You would use the market approach in situations where you could buy a similar asset on the open market. For example, you purchased a computer program to monitor and control your inventory three years ago for $10,000. The asset value has decreased on your balance sheet because of amortization, but in reality it is more valuable to you because your resident

> You can value intangible assets using a cost, income, or market approach.

What Are Patents, Trademarks, and Copyrights?

A *patent* is a property right that the U.S. Patent and Trademark Office grants to inventors, which "excludes" others from making, using, or selling their invention in the United States for a period of twenty years. There are three types of patents: utility patents are for any new and useful process, equipment, improvement, etc.; design patents relate to ornamental designs; and plant patents are for discovering new plants and asexually reproducing them. In order to get a patent, the inventor must come up with something new, useful, and sufficiently different from other inventions. *Trademarks* prevent others from using a similar mark, rather than preventing them from manufacturing or selling the same products or services. *Copyrights* are for the protection of authors, artists, musicians, and other producers of original works. Copyright owners have the right to reproduce and distribute their work and to preclude others from doing so.

computer geek has customized it to allow you to implement an effective "just in time" inventory system. You have seen these customized systems at trade shows and know that they sell for $50,000, so you value your system at $50,000.

How do you decide whether to value intangibles discretely or collectively? The theory of valuing intangible assets discretely seems very straightforward; however, it is very difficult in practice. For example, how do you determine how much income is due to a patent versus a trademark versus a computer software system? Because it is difficult to separate the income related to specific intangibles, you can easily double-count income, thereby inflating the value of the assets when using an income approach. Consequently, most analysts use the capitalization of excess earnings method to calculate the total value of the intangibles collectively as goodwill.

What other adjustments should you consider making to the assets on the balance sheet? If your goal is to value the business as an operating entity at fair market value, you should remove nonoperating assets, obsolete assets, and certain real estate. Removing obsolete assets is self-explanatory, but why remove nonoperating assets such as investments and owner-occupied real estate? Business owners generally don't sell investments such as stocks, bonds, or mutual funds when they sell their companies, so it makes sense to remove these assets from the calculation. Also, if you are valuing a company such as a professional practice or other service business, real estate is generally not part of the operating business and often would be retained and rented to the buyer or sold separately. Consequently, you should remove this type of real estate from the balance sheet and make an adjustment on the income statement to reflect a fair market rent expense. You need to use your judgment about whether assets such as real estate constitute operating or nonoperating assets and then make adjustments accordingly. A good rule of thumb is to consider those assets you would sell with the business to be integral operating assets and the assets you would retain to be nonoperating assets.

After you determine the fair market value of the assets, you estimate the net asset value by subtracting the liabilities. Generally, you subtract only the current liabilities from the value of the financial and tangible assets (and any intangible assets valued separately). The value of the long-term liabilities is subtracted at the end of the process to arrive at the value of the equity. You could subtract all of the liabilities to arrive at the net tangible asset value; you would just need to use a different capitalization rate for the excess earnings.

Calculate Excess Earnings and Choose Appropriate Interest Rates

In order to determine excess earnings, you must first determine "normal" earnings. Revenue Ruling 68-609 is suspiciously silent on the definition of "earnings" to be used in the capitalization of excess earnings method. See Chapter 11 for a discussion of different types of earnings that may be capitalized to produce an entity value. Most valuation professionals use net cash flow to represent earnings in the capitalized excess earnings method because it represents the cash available to the owner of the business. Generally, analysts also use an average of the last three to five years' earnings, either on a weighted or unweighted basis, to estimate future earnings. Once you settle on a definition of earnings, you still need to make some adjustments for the following items:

Nonoperating income—You will remove any income from investments or other nonoperating assets that were removed from the balance sheet in the process of determining the adjusted net asset value.

Nonrecurring items—You will remove any extraordinary income or expense items such as gain from the sale of assets not in the ordinary course of business or unusual writeoffs related to a discontinued line of business.

Excess compensation—You should determine what the company would have to pay a manager to perform the duties of the owner. Any compensation that the owner is receiving above this amount of "reasonable compensation" is added back to income.

Tax effects—You should make adjustments for tax effects in certain situations such as when a corporate buyer would have to pay taxes on "flow-through" income of an S corporation or sole proprietor that is not taxed at the entity level.

You have a lot of choices regarding which definition of earnings to use and whether the earnings are before or after tax. Even though there aren't any right or wrong choices, you will be making a mistake if you apply an inappropriate rate of return or capitalization rate to the earnings you select. In other words, if you are using the Net cash flow definition, which has taxes subtracted, you need to use an after-tax rate of return and capitalization rate. If you are using EBITDA (earnings before interest, taxes, depreciation, and amortization), you need to use before-tax rates of return and capitalization rates. Selecting the appropriate rates of return and capitalization rate is the most difficult aspect of the capitalized excess earnings method.

Once you determine the earnings measure you are using for the valuation, you must determine a reasonable rate of return for the net tangible assets that you have previously identified and adjusted to fair market value. This reasonable rate of return will be multiplied by the tangible asset value to determine the "normal earnings." You will then subtract the "normal earnings" from the total earnings to arrive at the "excess earnings."

How do you determine the appropriate rate of return to apply to the net tangible assets? First, consider the universal relationship between risk and return—the riskier an investment or an asset, the higher the required rate of return. Investing in a company's assets is no different in this respect than investing in the stock market. You will calculate the "weighted cost of capital" by first analyzing the underlying assets to determine how much outside financing you could get based on these assets and assuming that the rest will be supported by owners' equity. Then based on the relative proportion of debt to equity financing and the relative interest rates for each, you calculate the weighted average cost of capital. For example, if you have tangible assets (e.g., receivables, inventory, and equipment) with a value of $1,000,000, you might determine that you could go to the bank and borrow $600,000 at 7% using these assets as collateral. By default that means you would have to make an equity investment of $400,000 ($1,000,000 − $600,000) to purchase the assets. The cost of equity is always more than the cost of debt because the owner is taking more risk than the bank, so the required rate of return is higher. See Chapter 22 for a discussion

> The riskier an investment or an asset, the higher the required rate of return.

of how rates of return are calculated and some of the risk factors that influence the calculation. Assume for this example that you have determined that the cost of equity is 14%. Before making the final calculation, you should adjust the cost of debt to reflect that business interest on bank debt is tax-deductible. You make this adjustment by multiplying the interest rate by one minus the tax rate. Assuming the business has a combined federal and state tax rate of 35%, the calculations would be as follows for the above example:

$600,000 Debt	@ 4.55% (7% x (1 − 35%))	x 60% ($600,000 / $1,000,000) = 2.73%
$400,000 Equity	@14%	x 40% ($400,000 / $1,000,000) = 5.60%
		Weighted average cost of capital = 8.33%

Now that you have calculated an appropriate rate of return on net assets using the weighted average cost of capital method, how do you calculate the appropriate rate to capitalize the excess earnings? When you recall the relationship of risk and return, you will intuitively know that the capitalization rate for excess earnings is going to be much higher than either the debt or equity rate that you can apply to tangible assets because intangible assets are inherently riskier than tangible assets. Another component of the risk/return equation specific to the capitalization of excess earnings method is that the greater the uncertainty about the level and duration of the excess earnings, the greater the risk and, therefore, the greater the interest rate. Shannon Pratt, in the book *Valuing Small Businesses and Professional Practices*, Third Edition (New York: McGraw-Hill, 1998), indicates that the most common capitalization rate is $33\frac{1}{3}$ percent, which represents paying for three years of excess earnings. A capitalization rate of 25% would indicate a relatively high degree of certainty that the present level of excess earnings will continue at least for four years into the future. If you have earnings that are not consistent or without any apparent trends, you should choose a higher rate of return to reflect the inherent riskiness of an uncertain future. Chapter 22 includes a detailed discussion of how to determine the capitalization rate.

Putting It All Together

The basic steps you take to value a company using the excess earnings method are:

1. Estimate the future earnings of the business. Generally you can use an average of the past five years' historical numbers on either a weighted or unweighted basis.

2. Determine the value of the net tangible assets. You adjust the different assets on the balance sheet to their current fair market value and subtract current liabilities.

3. Calculate a reasonable rate of return on net tangible assets using a weighted cost of capital.

4. Multiply the net tangible assets by the reasonable rate of return to determine the portion of total earnings allocable to the net tangible assets.

5. Calculate the "excess earnings" by subtracting the earnings allocable to net tangible assets from the total earnings. These excess earnings are then allocated to the intangible assets or goodwill of the company.

6. Choose an appropriate capitalization rate for the excess earnings.

7. Divide the excess earnings by the capitalization rate to arrive at a total value for goodwill.

8. Add the goodwill value calculated by capitalizing the excess earnings to the fair market value of the net tangible assets to arrive at a total value for the business.

An Example: Holy Terroir Winery

The owner's of Holy Terroir Winery, Frank B. and Ed J. Gallows, want to value their C corporation so they can start gifting shares of stock to their heirs to reduce estate taxes. They are using the excess earnings method described in Revenue Ruling 68-609 because they want to use a method that will be accepted by the IRS if their gift tax returns are audited. The relevant financial information is as follows:

- The five-year weighted average net cash flow is $24 million
- The fair market value of adjusted net tangible assets is $32.1 million
- The company's average cost of debt is 9%
- The company's cost of equity is 15%
- Frank B. and Ed J. can finance 50% of the assets with bank loans

- Holy Terroir Winery pays tax at a combined federal and state rate of 43%
- The appropriate after-tax capitalization rate for Holy Terroir is 25%

The Gallows calculate the value of their company as follows:

Estimate future earnings	$24,000,000	**CHART 12-1**
Fair market value of net tangible assets	$32,100,000	
Reasonable rate of return on net tangible assets	10.07%	

Weighted cost of capital calculation:
  Debt—5.13% (9% x (1 – 43%))   x 50% = 2.57%
  Equity—15%   x 50% = 7.50%
                                                      10.07%

Earnings allocable to net tangible assets	$3,232,470
$32,100,000 x 10.07%	
Excess earnings	$20,767,530
$24,000,000 – $3,232,470	
After-tax capitalization rate	25%
Value of goodwill	$83,070,120
$20,767,530	
25%	
Value of Holy Terroir Winery	$115,170,120
$83,070,120 + $32,100,000	

When Is the Excess Earnings Method Appropriate?

The excess earnings method is probably the most widely used method for valuing closely held businesses, and it is probably the most maligned method in the professional press. It is the most widely used method because, conceptually, it is easy to understand and work through the formula, and because the IRS sanctions its use by including it in Revenue Ruling 68-609. It is the most maligned method because many inexperienced valuators use it due to its simplicity and, in the process, make some simple mistakes. Some of the most common mistakes to avoid include:

"The Excess Earnings Method—Let the User Beware"

This is the title of an article written by Gary Trugman, one of the leading authorities on business valuation today. His article, which appeared in his firm's Web-based publication, "Valuation Trends—Winter 1999," found at *www.trugman valuation.com/Archive/Winter1999.html*, emphasizes that you should use the excess earnings method only when you can't find a better method. Even the IRS cautions in Revenue Ruling 68-609 that you should only use the formula method when no better method is available. He also points out that the excess earnings method is a method for valuing intangibles, not the stock of a company.

- Using historical earnings that don't reflect expected future earnings
- Failure to adjust for owner's compensation in sole proprietorships and partnerships
- Failure to adjust for excess owner's compensation in corporations
- Using the rates of return included in Revenue Ruling 68-609 for return on net assets and capitalization of excess earnings (These rates were published in 1968 and reflect the economic realities of that time)
- Using after-tax rates of return with before-tax earnings and vice versa

If you are careful to avoid these common mistakes, you can use the excess earnings method very successfully to value a wide variety of businesses. This method is most appropriate for valuing companies that have a goodwill component and a readily ascertainable value of net tangible assets such as professional practices, retailers, small manufacturers, and restaurants. The excess earnings method is appropriate for most IRS applications such as estate and gift taxes and calculating built-in gains for C corporations electing S status as well as legal matters such as divorces and damage cases.

> **Chapter 13**

Discounted Cash Flow Method

PART FOUR: BASIC VALUATION METHODS

■ CHAPTER 10 Adjusted Net Asset Method ■ CHAPTER 11 Capitalization of Earnings Method ■ CHAPTER 12 Excess Earnings Method ■ CHAPTER 13 Discounted Cash Flow Method ■ CHAPTER 14 Rule of Thumb Methods

Using the Basis of Future Projected Income

The discounted cash flow method is an income approach that is truly future oriented. The basic concept underlying this method is that the total value of a company can be determined by calculating the present value of the future earnings and adding this number to the present value of the terminal value. The terminal value is the value at the end of the last period of your projections. Most valuation methods use historical figures, albeit adjusted, to represent expected future earnings. Although you may be tempted to extrapolate past numbers into the future, you would not be playing by the rules of the discounted cash flow method. The discounted cash flow method requires someone to make actual projections of earnings into future years.

Who is that "someone" who will be making the projections? Ideally, a member of the management team of the company should prepare the projections because company insiders should have the best sense of where the company is heading. Sometimes even a prospective buyer will prepare the projections. Credible projections are the essence of the discounted cash flow method. So a professional valuation analyst would review the projections made by either of these interested parties to verify their reasonableness and perhaps suggest adjustments. In cases where the company has not made projections, the valuation analyst will prepare the projections in conjunction with management. Large businesses with accounting staffs, controllers, and financial officers generally prepare projections as part of the normal budgeting and strategic planning process. Because small businesses do not have the luxury of having CPA's and financial analysts on staff, they do not generally prepare formal earnings projections. This is the main reason why the discounted cash flow method is used more frequently to value larger companies than it is used to value small companies.

The discounted cash flow method is the common name for what might be more properly described as the discounted earnings method or the discounted economic income method. Some of the measures of earnings, in addition to net cash flow, that you can use in the discounted earnings method include:

- **Net Income**—Income based on GAAP (Generally Accepted Accounting Principles)
- **Operating Cash Flow**—Net income plus interest and noncash charges
- **After-Tax Cash Flow**— Operating cash flow after taxes

> Most valuation methods use historical figures, albeit adjusted, to represent expected future earnings.

- **Discretionary Cash Flow**— Cash that would actually be available to a purchaser
- **EBIT (Earnings Before Interest and Taxes)**
- **EBITDA (Earnings Before Interest, Taxes, Depreciation, and Amortization)**

You can use net financial statement income in the discounted earnings method calculation if you think it is similar to cash flow. Net income and cash flow are similar in some service businesses or professional firms that don't have a lot of noncash items such as depreciation, capital expenditures, or debt.

All of the other earnings measures are really variations of cash flow. If you do choose an earnings measure other than net cash flow, make sure that you are using the appropriate discount rate, e.g., a before-tax rate for EBITDA (earnings before interest, taxes, depreciation, and amortization.)

Even though you can use other earnings measures, the reason this method is commonly known as the discounted cash flow method is because professional valuation analysts prefer to use net cash flow in the calculation. They prefer it for several reasons. First, cash flow represents what buyers want: the money they can take out of the business. Secondly, valuators rely on a myriad of studies and databases that are based on net cash flow information to help them choose the appropriate discount rate.

Once you decide which measure of earnings you will project into the future, how do you decide how far into the future to make the projections? The easy answer is to make projections as far into the future as possible. The qualifier is that you need to have a reasonable basis for making the projections. So, as a practical matter, you should try to project cash flows, or other earnings measures, for at least five years and determine a terminal value at the end of the period. Beyond this period, your numbers will lose their credibility unless you are valuing a company with very stable earnings or growth.

Defining "Present Value"

Present value is one of the most important concepts of economics and finance. It refers to the value today of an amount or amounts you will receive in the future. Another term for present value is "time value of money." Either way, the concept is the technically correct way of saying " a

What Is the Terminal Value?

The *terminal value* in a discounted cash flow analysis is the number that represents the present value of all of the future cash flows that you are not going to individually forecast. For example, say you did project five years of unique cash flows and discounted them back to present value. You would probably have a difficult time projecting discrete cash flows beyond that point, so what do you do? You develop a number that represents the present value of all of these subsequent cash flows. This number is called the terminal value. You can calculate the terminal value either using a capitalized economic income method or using earnings multiples from comparable companies.

bird in the hand is worth two in the bush." Intuitively, we know that a dollar today is worth more than a dollar next year or at any time in the future because of factors like inflation. You calculate the present value of an amount to be received in the future by multiplying it by an appropriate compound interest rate. Published present value tables and financial calculators make this computation relatively easy. However, if you want a challenge, you can work through the mathematical formula. Remember that numbers in scientific notation are multiplied by themselves for the number of times indicated by the superscript.

$$\text{Present Value of } \$1 = \frac{1}{(1 + i)^n}$$

Where i represents the interest rate and n is the number of years

For example, assume the interest rate is 5% and you want to know the present value of a dollar you plan to receive five years from now.

$$\text{Present Value of } \$1 = 1 \div (1 + 5\%)^5 = \$.78$$

The same dollar would be worth only \$.61 if you received it ten years from now with a 5% interest rate, $[1 \div (1 + 5\%)^{10}]$ or \$.57 $[1 \div (1 + 12\%)^5]$ if you received it five years from now with a 12% rate.

You can use the present value theory to calculate how much you would need to invest in today's dollars to reach a specific monetary goal in the future. You can also calculate the present value of future streams of income, referred to as an annuity, using these same techniques.

Discount Rate

The term "discount rate" sounds like the mechanism retail store managers would use to calculate the price of merchandise they wanted to "mark down" to sell quickly. In the business valuation realm, "discount rate" is the interest rate you use to determine the present value of future cash flows. It is the interest rate component of the question: "How much do I need to invest today, at a certain compounded interest rate, to receive a dollar in the future?" Another way to look at it is the rate of return you could get in the marketplace on a similar investment, i.e., one that has the same risk and marketability. You may remember the following components of the discount rate from Chapter 12:

1. The risk-free rate—e.g., the rate of twenty-year Treasury bonds
2. An equity risk premium that reflects that stocks are riskier than cash or bonds
3. A small company risk premium that reflects that small businesses are riskier than large companies
4. A liquidity premium that reflects that nonmarketable closely held companies are riskier than publicly traded companies
5. Additional risk premium for other factors such as specific industries, locations, and the complexity of the investment

The way you calculate the appropriate discount rate is to start with the risk-free rate and add to it in increments to reflect the different types of risk inherent in the investment you are valuing. The risk-free rate is an interest rate that covers inflation plus the relatively small amount of "real rate of return" you could expect to earn from investing in something where you are sure to get your money back—for example, twenty-year Treasury bonds. As the risk factors increase, the rate of return you would need to receive for investing in a riskier investment also increases. Statisticians describe this relationship between risk and return as being "highly correlated." You also need to correlate the discount rate with the earnings measure you have chosen, e.g., you use pretax discount rates with pretax earnings measures such as EBITDA and you use after-tax discount rates with after-tax earnings measures such as net cash flow.

Correlation Analysis

Correlation analysis is a type of statistical analysis that measures the relationship between two things or concepts. When interest rates rise, the price of bonds goes down—this is an example of a negative correlation. The components of correlation analysis are the dependent variable, the independent variable, and the correlation coefficient. The correlation coefficient measures the extent to which a change in the independent variable causes or predicts a change in the dependent variable. A correlation coefficient of +1.0 means that the two items are perfectly positively correlated while a correlation coefficient of –1.0 means that the two items are perfectly negatively correlated. A correlation coefficient of zero means that the items have no relationship whatsoever. Very few things are perfectly correlated, but many things are positively or negatively correlated. Statisticians consider correlation coefficients of ± 0.70 to represent highly correlated relationships. If you determine that two things are highly correlated, you can use that information to make predictions and informed decisions. For example, Chapter 9 discussed how the size of a company influences its value. Size is the independent variable and value is the dependent variable. Size and value are highly negatively correlated, which means that the smaller the company, the lower the value. Therefore, if you were comparing two companies in the same industry, you would predict that the smaller one would be less valuable, even if the net earnings were the same.

Calculating Discount Rates

You can use several different "build-up" methods to calculate the appropriate discount rate for your company. Professional valuation analysts often use the "Ibbotson Build-Up Method," which was developed by Roger Ibbotson and Rex Sinquefield. This method uses historical data published and updated annually by Ibbotson Associates in their *Stocks, Bonds, Bills and Inflation Yearbook* (Ibbotson Associates, 2003). However, using the Ibbotson Build-Up Method is not as simple as looking in a book and picking out the right number. You need to understand some very sophisticated economic concepts such as the Capital Asset Pricing Model (CAPM) and beta as well as be able to make appropriate additional adjustments for companies that are much smaller than the smallest companies ($200 million in capitalization) considered by Ibbotson. A hypothetical example of the Ibbotson Build-Up Method for a privately held company is as follows:

Risk-free long-term government bond rate	6.7%
Long-term equity risk premium	7.5%
Small company risk premium	3.5%
Specific company risk premium	5%*
Discount rate	22.7%

*An additional risk premium based on the appraiser's judgment of specific company risks

What do you do if the preferred Ibbotson Method sounds good in theory but is impossible to really use in practice? If you are valuing a company for tax purposes, equitable distribution, or other litigation, you should pay someone to do a formal valuation and make these sophisticated calculations and judgments. If, on the other hand, you just want to get some idea of what your company may be worth for planning purposes, you could use a more subjective method such as the Schilt's Risk Premium Method. James H. Schilt developed a guide to risk premiums based on the general characteristics of the business rather than the analysis of the almost overwhelming amount of historical information inherent in the Ibbotson Method. Schilt updated and published his theories in the June 1991 edition of the American Society of

What Is Beta?

Beta in a business or valuation context refers to the volatility of a stock, relative to other stocks of the same class. Beta is a sophisticated mathematical concept that portfolio analysts use to predict the behavior of stocks. Another way to look at beta is as the correlation coefficient between two things, say an individual stock and the rest of the market. A stock with a beta of one is perfectly correlated with the market; therefore, you would expect its price to move in concert with a broad market index like the S&P 500. If you were evaluating a stock with a beta greater than one, you would expect it to be more volatile than the market, measured by the S&P 500 index. This stock would be inherently more risky; therefore, you would need to receive a higher rate of return.

Appraisers publication, *Business Valuation Review,* in an article entitled "Selection of Capitalization Rates-Revisited." He categorizes companies into one of the following five categories and assigns a risk premium accordingly.

1. Established businesses with a strong trade position that are well financed, have depth and management, whose past earnings have been stable, and whose future is highly predictable. (6–10 percent)
2. Established businesses in a more competitive industry that are well financed, have depth and management, have stable past earnings, and whose future is fairly predictable. (11–15 percent)
3. Businesses in a highly competitive industry that require little capital to enter, no management depth, and have a high element of risk, although the past record may be good. (16–20 percent)
4. Small businesses that depend upon the special skills of one or two people, or larger established businesses that are highly cyclical in nature. In both cases, future earnings may be expected to deviate widely from projections. (21–25 percent)
5. Small "one-man" businesses of a personal service nature, where transferability of the income stream is in question. (26–30 percent)

You add the risk premium, calculated above, to the risk-free rate, just as with the Ibbotson Method. The calculation of the discount rate for a privately held company in the 35% tax bracket using the Schilt's Build-Up Method is as follows:

Risk-free long-term government bond rate	6.7%
Risk premium for category 4 company	25%
Pretax discount rate	31.7%
Convert pretax rate to after-tax rate	
(31.7% x (1-35%))	20.61%
(31.7% x (1 – 35%))	

You can see that the two methods did not produce the same discount rate, but the Schilt's Method does approximate the Ibbotson Method. By using the Schilt's Build-Up Method you have a reasonable theoretical framework with which to proceed with a discounted cash flow calculation of your company's value. The benefit is that this method is conceptually understandable and relatively simple to apply; the downside is that you would have a difficult time defending your ultimate discount rate in a court proceeding because it is so subjective.

A Theoretically Sound Method

The theory behind the discounted cash flow method is that someone will only purchase an investment today at a price that represents the earnings they anticipate in the future. The investor discounts the future earnings using the rate of return they could receive on other investments of comparable risk. Investors use this same analysis implicitly when they buy a publicly traded stock—if you pay $100 per share for a stock, you should expect to receive at least that much in dividends and appreciation over your time horizon after discounting at an appropriate rate. If you did not have this anticipation of future earnings, you would just invest in safe vehicles such as certificates of deposits and Treasury bills.

> Someone will only purchase an investment today at a price that represents the earnings they anticipate in the future.

When you look at the valuation of a company as an investment decision, all of the other valuation methods become proxies for the discounted cash flow method. Whether you employ an asset, income, or market approach to valuation, the process of determining fair market value is the process of estimating what you are ultimately going to get out of the investment. Consequently, you should always make an attempt to perform a discounted cash flow analysis to corroborate the reasonableness of any other valuation methods you use. The difficulty is estimating the projected future cash flows—so you frequently must use the other methods that start with more accessible input information.

The basic steps for using the discounted cash flow method are:

1. Determine the appropriate discount rate by finding the risk-free rate, usually twenty-year Treasury bills, and adding risk premiums to reflect the level of risk inherent in the business.

2. Project the amount and timing of future cash flows for at least five years.
3. Determine the terminal value at the end of the projection period by capitalizing the final year's earnings.
4. Discount the future earnings and the terminal value to the present using the discount rate calculated above.
5. Add the discounted future earnings and discounted terminal value to determine the total value of the business.

The "total value of the business" can mean different things to different people. You must be clear about whether you are valuing equity or total invested capital. Equity refers to ownership interests such as stock in a corporation and capital accounts in a partnership. Invested capital includes not only these ownership interests but also includes debt used to finance the business. Depending on which value you want, you will make adjustments to your cash flow calculation to make sure you are using the appropriate type of cash flow. For example, if you are valuing only equity, you would add back any principal payments on long-term debt to net cash flow, and if you are valuing total invested capital, you would add back the tax-affected interest expense and any preferred dividends. The following comparison summarizes Shannon Pratt's discussion of "Valuing Equity versus Invested Capital" in the book *Valuing Small Businesses and Professional Practices,* Third Edition (McGraw-Hill, 1998).

> Equity refers to ownership interests such as stock in a corporation and capital accounts in a partnership.

Net cash flow for equity valuation	Net cash flow for invested capital valuation
After-tax net income	After-tax net income
+Noncash expenses	+Noncash expenses
–Net capital expenditures	–Net capital expenditures
–Changes in working capital	–Changes in working capital
+Changes in long-term debt	+Interest expense net of tax benefit
+Preferred dividends	
= Net cash flow for equity	= Net cash flow for invested capital

The Difficulty of Real World Application

The discounted cash flow method is like the theory of relativity; conceptually, both theories make a lot of sense, but the average person doesn't have all the necessary information (or brainpower) to work through all the calculations. The first difficulty is making a projection of future cash flows. Most small businesses don't have predictable earnings, and past earnings are not necessarily good predictors of future earnings, especially in start-up or high-growth scenarios. You will need to make "best estimate" projections regarding the amount and timing of anticipated future earnings. Generally, the larger and more stable the company, the easier this is to do.

The second difficulty is choosing the appropriate discount rate. The appropriate rate is the risk-free rate plus additional percentage points reflecting the risk inherent in the particular company you are valuing. You can pick a risk-free rate pretty easily by looking up the yield of long-term government bonds or other safe investments. Professional valuators usually use the rate of twenty-year Treasury bills, but you could choose from a number of other risk-free rates. So you can't even choose a risk-free rate without the risk of choosing an inappropriate one.

However, the most difficult challenge you face in choosing the discount rate is applying the appropriate premiums to reflect the risk inherent in the business you are valuing. See Chapter 22 for a detailed discussion of risk premiums. You can use a variety of methods to quantify the risk premiums you will add to the risk-free rate. Some of these methods are relatively subjective and easy to apply, but the results they produce are not grounded in documented statistical studies. You can use other more mathematically and statistically rigorous methods that are based on research and information from large companies. However, these methods are very complicated and, in addition, you need to make further adjustments to these methods to reflect the risks inherent in small companies. Consequently, selecting the appropriate discount rate becomes more like an art than a science.

In real estate, the phrase "location, location, location" reflects the fact that value is mainly determined by location. In the discounted cash flow method of business valuation, you determine value by using "assumptions, assumptions, assumptions." Just as good location is essential for a good real estate value, good assumptions are essential for a good business valuation.

When Is the Discounted Cash Flow Method Appropriate?

Investment banks, large consulting firms, merger and acquisition advisors, and other firms employing MBAs use the discounted cash flow method extensively. These firms have the resources and the talent to apply this theoretically sound method to real world cases. Consequently, the discounted cash flow method is used mostly to value large companies that are being bought or sold. However, the discounted cash flow method is becoming more widely accepted in many venues as MBAs and professional valuation analysts proliferate.

Situations in which you should consider using the discounted cash flow method include:

- Purchase or sale of the business
- Regular and irregular cash flows can be projected
- Start-up companies with no earnings history
- Rapidly growing businesses
- Damage cases that involve a loss of income
- Other litigation such as dissenting stockholders' cases

The discounted cash flow method is ideal for determining the purchase price of a business if you have good projections of future income because it answers the investor's question: "What can I expect to get out of this investment?" Investors are not interested in what the business has earned historically, unless they can expect to receive the same or greater returns. The discounted cash flow method is also very useful when you want to value companies without a history of earnings or whose earnings are very irregular. Many of the other valuation methods require assumptions of stable earnings or growth; therefore, they aren't appropriate for start-up companies or businesses with irregular earnings.

Historically, you might not have used the discounted cash flow method to value a business for any type of litigation, but as judges become more sophisticated, they are allowing the discounted cash flow method in divorce, malpractice, and even some gift and estate cases. Generally though, valuators do not use the discounted cash flow method for valuations for

> The discounted cash flow method is used mostly to value large companies that are being bought or sold.

divorce because the method is based on future earnings, which come after the date of separation, the major demarcation line for determining what is marital and separate property. In addition, some state statutes preclude the inclusion of goodwill in the value calculation for a divorce, which would make using the discounted cash flow method to determine a total value for the business problematic. However, the main reason you would not use the discounted cash flow method for divorce and many other litigated matters is that you need to make a lot of assumptions and projections into the future that are difficult for everyone to grasp. Generally, you would not use the discounted cash flow method for gift and estate tax cases because practitioners and the courts are still heavily relying on Revenue Rulings 59-60 and 68-609, which emphasize the excess earnings method.

An Example: Dreamweavers, Inc.

Dreamweavers, Inc. is a small company that makes woven silk throws and decorative pillows. Dreamweavers has been in business for five years but has had somewhat erratic earnings. The owners, Wendy and Peter Darling, have just wanted to make a good living from the company and pay for their children's education while providing beautifully crafted products of high quality that would enhance the lives of their customers. However, they have just employed their son, David, who recently completed his MBA. David learned a lot of things in business school including the mantra that the only reason to own a business is to grow it and sell it. Armed with this knowledge and the ability to do discounted cash flow analyses in his sleep, David set out to value the business. David projected that the company's earnings would grow significantly now that he was going to help run the business. David's process for calculating the value of Dreamweavers, Inc. is as follows:

DREAMWEAVERS, INC. PROJECTED ANNUAL CASH FLOWS: CHART 13-1

2003	$20,000		2006	120,000
2004	50,000		2007	130,000
2005	100,000			

CHART 13-1
(continued)

The after-tax discount rate is 25%

The after-tax capitalization rate is 35%

Calculate the present value of the projected cash flows. (Algebraic formulas are used here instead of scientific notation.)

2003 $16,000   ($20,000 / 1 + .25)
2004   32,000   ($50,000 / ((1 + .25)(1 + .25)))
2005   51,200   ($100,000 / ((1 + .25)(1 + .25)(1 + .25)))
2006   49,152   ($120,000 / ((1 + .25)(1 + .25)(1 + .25)(1 + .25)))
2007   42,598   ($130,000 / ((1 + .25)(1 + .25)(1 + .25)(1 + .25)(1 + .25)))
      $190,950

Calculate the terminal value by capitalizing the last year's earnings

$130,000 / .35 = $371,429

Calculate the present value of the terminal value

$371,429 / ((1 + .25)(1 + .25)(1 + .25)(1 + .25)(1 + .25)) = $121,710

Add the present values of the cash flows and the terminal value

$190,950 + $121,710 = $312,660

Wendy and Peter were surprised that their mom-and-pop business could be valued at close to $300,000 and decided that it was a good idea to think about selling in a few years so they could retire. Since their mortgage was paid off and they had been contributing to a SIMPLE IRA plan, they felt that they would have plenty of money to fund their modest lifestyle during retirement. David, on the other hand, was dismayed that the company was only worth about $300,000, so he was determined to look at every facet of the business to find inefficiencies and opportunities for major improvements.

➤ **Chapter 14**

Rule of Thumb Methods

Part One

Part Two

Part Three

Part Four

Part Five

Part Six

PART FOUR: BASIC VALUATION METHODS

■ CHAPTER 10 Adjusted Net Asset Method ■ CHAPTER 11 Capitalization of Earnings Method ■ CHAPTER 12 Excess Earnings Method ■ CHAPTER 13 Discounted Cash Flow Method ■ **CHAPTER 14 Rule of Thumb Methods**

Basing Valuation on Income, Assets, or Actual Transactions

The *American Heritage Dictionary* defines a "rule of thumb" as "a useful principle having wide application but not intended to be strictly accurate or reliable in every situation." The *Oxford English Dictionary*, Second Edition, refers to how rules of thumb came into existence in its definition: "A method or procedure derived entirely from practice or experience, without any basis in scientific knowledge; a roughly practical method." Rules of thumb abound for all kinds of situations. For example, a rule of thumb for writing is that every page of double-spaced typing yields about 250 words. Of course the actual number depends on the size of the type, margins, and whether you have any illustrations or charts. Rules of thumb for business valuation are very similar—they state a general rule, and then state a lot of disclaimers about what could make the general rule inapplicable. In other words, "rules are made to be broken."

Rules of thumb are usually industry specific and primarily used to value companies for purchase or sale. Rules of thumb allow you to make a "quick and dirty" valuation of a business, in order to get a rough idea of how much a business is worth. Rules of thumb are widely used because you can apply them to easily available information from the company's financial statements. Consequently, business brokers use them all the time to help their clients set a price for their business. The primary types of rules of thumb are as follows:

- Multiple of gross income
- Multiple of net income (or cash flow, EBITDA, etc.)
- Multiple of book value
- Multiple of a unit of production or revenue (e.g., people, rooms, subscribers, etc.)

Rules Based on Multiples of Earnings

The discounted cash flow method of valuing a small business makes the most theoretical sense because it quantifies the return an investor can expect to receive from projected future cash flow. Similarly, rules of thumb that use multiples of earnings are conceptually more reasonable than others because they too are trying to estimate the ultimate return to the investor.

The first step in using an earnings multiplier is similar to the first step in making the discounted cash flow calculation, and that is selecting the earnings measure you are going to use. Projected cash flow is probably the best earnings measure; however, you may not have enough information to accurately calculate it. In addition, because cash flow is not readily visible on most small company financial statements, the rules of thumb for the industry probably use some other measure. Generally, you should substitute current or historical net income, EBIT (earnings before interest and taxes) or EBITDA (earnings before interest, taxes, depreciation, and amortization) to approximate cash flow. If you are valuing a business in which the owner has an inflated salary or a lot of perks, you should consider making adjustments to normalize the earnings.

How do you pick the multiple that you are going to apply to the earnings measure? You will base the multiple on the perceived risk of the business, just as you would choose a discount or capitalization rate based on relative risk. Generally, you will see multiples in the three to five times earnings range. These multiples coincide with an expected return of 33% for three times earnings and 20% for five times earnings, which approximate the discount or capitalization rates you might derive from the more sophisticated build-up methods discussed in Chapter 22. Another way to look at these multiples is to relate them to the number of years it will take an investor to recoup their investment; i.e., an investor would expect to get back their initial investment in five years if they paid five times earnings for the company.

Making Adjustments

Theoretically, multiples of gross revenue are meaningless unless you can translate them into earnings. However, small business owners often try to reduce net income to reduce taxes, so net earnings are not reflective of the true profitability of the company. Consequently, you can use

What Is Discounted Cash Flow?

Discounted cash flow is a sophisticated technique you can use to estimate the present value of future cash streams. The "discount rate" is an interest rate that has a double meaning. The most common definition is the rate that the Federal Reserve charges banks for loans that are backed by government securities. However, the second meaning of this expression is the one of interest to business valuators, financial analysts, and anyone else who wants to know how much a series of payments in the future is worth in today's dollars. The discount rate in this context is an interest rate that is based on the cost of capital to the company. The discounted cash flow method, which you can explore in depth in Chapter 13, projects anticipated cash flows into the future and "discounts" them back to the present value using the "discount" rate.

multiples of gross revenue as a proxy for multiples of earnings in industries with relatively low capital requirements and similar cost structures. For example, business brokers generally apply a multiple of gross income approach to value accounting and CPA firms. The theory is that all accounting firms are structured similarly, so revenue will be a good determinant of value. They would have difficulty using a multiple of earnings method because the net income or net cash flow is purposely kept to a minimum, so it is not reflective of future returns to an investor. If you want to use a multiple of earnings method to value a professional practice, you should make adjustments to the income statement to arrive at a true cash flow number, just as if you were performing a more rigorous valuation such as the discounted cash flow method. Of course, making a lot of adjustments reduces the attraction of a rule of thumb—the ability to apply a simple formula to easily accessible data.

Even when industries adopt a particular type of rule of thumb to value companies within the industry, the specific rules of thumb are not always the same. Looking at the accounting profession again, you will see that the industry uses multiples of gross income to value individual firms. Although the industry is in general agreement about the type of multiplier to use, several different rules of thumb exist. They range from 100 to 150% of annual revenue on the high side to 90 to 110% of gross revenue on the low side. Depending on the rule of thumb you choose, you could value a CPA firm with $800,000 in revenue anywhere between $720,000 and $1,200,000. You still need to make judgments about the relative risk of the company related to others in the industry and take into consideration factors such as the national and local economy, the geographical location of the business, and critical success factors within the industry.

When you use either a gross income or net earnings multiplier to value a business, you are generally calculating the total value of the company including capital assets and goodwill. This makes sense unless the company has some significant assets that don't contribute to the production of income, e.g., real estate. In this case you should value these assets separately and add them to the value you derived from using the rule of thumb method. If you are using an earnings approach, you would adjust the income statement by adding rent expense at a fair market rate, which will reduce the earnings before you apply the multiplier.

Other Rule of Thumb Methods

Book value is the historical representation of the owner's equity of a company, which is determined by subtracting all of the balance sheet liabilities from the balance sheet assets. The book value includes all of the previous years' earnings, unless the company has paid dividends. Consequently, you can use book value, with or without a multiplier, as a rule of thumb valuation method. The problem with book value is that historical costs, what you paid for assets less the depreciation you have taken, do not necessarily represent current fair market value. In addition, book value doesn't usually reflect any goodwill that the business has developed.

> The book value includes all of the previous years' earnings, unless the company has paid dividends.

Multiples of a unit of production or revenue are a variation on the multiple of gross revenue approach. These multiples focus on the critical success factors for a particular industry. For example, a rule of thumb in the motel industry is $20,000–$30,000 per room, while a rule of thumb in the trucking industry is $2,000–$5,000 per driver.

Sources for Rules of Thumb

Where do all of these rules of thumb come from? Industry trade groups and professional organizations collect data on actual sales of companies within their industry, and with this information they have developed some of the rules of thumb as algorithms to aid their members in setting reasonable prices for the purchase and sale of their businesses.

Because business owners and brokers can use rules of thumb to quantify and compare the value of different companies with only a little readily accessible information, rules of thumb have become very widespread. In fact, rules of thumb have gone beyond being a shorthand summary for actual sales and have taken on a life of their own to become the valuation standard in some industries.

The Role of Business Brokers

Business brokers are people who work with both buyers and sellers to help them realize their business ownership goals. The broker helps the seller determine the value of the business and develops a marketing plan to

When an interested buyer makes an offer, the broker negotiates the price and terms of the deal and helps the buyer obtain financing.

locate and screen potential buyers. When an interested buyer makes an offer, the broker negotiates the price and terms of the deal and helps the buyer obtain financing.

Business brokers can add value in several ways. First, they take on the most time-consuming responsibility of marketing your business and screening potential buyers so that you only have to evaluate and talk to the best candidates. In addition, their experience and contacts give them greater access to and knowledge of the marketplace, which can lead to identifying more than one competitive bidder for your business. Business brokers can help you value your business using any of the techniques in this book; however, they also see a lot of actual sales and can tell you if businesses of your type are being sold at certain rule of thumb values.

How much does all of this cost? Of course it varies with each broker and each transaction, but the "rule of thumb" is that brokers charge from 6 to 10% of the sales price. In addition, they charge initially for valuing your business and analyzing the market. This usually costs from $5,000 to $10,000, but brokers often apply these fees against the sales price if an actual transaction occurs. You may incur other fees for consulting and drafting documents. Is it worth it? Only you can decide after taking into account your particular circumstances.

Bad in Theory

Rules of thumb are the opposite of all of the great ideas that are good in theory but not practical for use in the real world—they are bad in theory but "good" in practice. Rules of thumb aren't even really that "good" in practice, but business owners, brokers, and appraisers use them extensively.

Rules of thumb are bad in theory because they are arbitrary formulas based on unsubstantiated data applied to undifferentiated company financial information. Rules of thumb assume that you are valuing an "average" company in the industry, which is similar to analyzing the "average" American family with 2.3 children. Just as you won't find any average American families with 2.3 children, you won't find an average American company that you can accurately value with a shorthand formula. For example, if you use a midrange accounting industry rule of thumb of 100% gross revenue, you might determine that a CPA practice generating $800,000 in annual revenue would be worth $800,000. This process does not even take into account whether the practice is profitable. What if the firm has lost money for the last five years without taking excessive partner compensation? What if the firm has taken on a lot of debt to buy out a retiring owner? What if the firm has lost a key employee? What if the firm has just lost its major client? What if the firm is located within a geographical area that has been preferentially hard-hit by an economic downturn? What if the business is operating out of a company-owned building that is now worth $1,000,000? You can't address any of these important questions if you are just going to apply a multiplier to the gross revenue on the balance sheet. In fact, you won't even know to ask these questions unless you venture off the income statement. If you do discover some information, financial or otherwise, that will substantially change the value, you could make some adjustments to the earnings measure or to the multiplier. For example, you could add back "excess compensation" and perks, or you could use your judgment and choose a factor in the low-range for the earnings multiplier. However, you would be fine-tuning a process that did not have a theoretical basis in the first place.

Rules of Thumb as Self-Fulfilling Prophecies

George Berkeley, an eighteenth-century philosopher, is famous for the Latin phrase "esse est percipi," which translates as "to be is to be perceived." He meant that something must be perceived in order for it to exist. Advertising executives and pop psychologists of the late twentieth and early twenty-first centuries have taken this concept one step further to produce the mantra "perception is reality," which implies that even if something does not exist but people think it does, they will act as if it exists, and, therefore, in essence, it exists.

Despite the flawed logic, this principle applies to valuation rules of thumb. Even though rules of thumb do not have a theoretical underpinning, many business owners, brokers, and industry groups think they are valid, these people act as if they are, and, therefore, they are. In other words, they produce a self-fulfilling prophecy. Consequently, you should not completely disregard valuation rules of thumb, particularly in industries where business owners do in fact use rules of thumb to value their businesses for sales and purchases. You can use rules of thumb as a starting point for a valuation to get an idea of how the industry estimates the worth of companies in that industry. Alternatively, you can use rules of thumb to test the reasonableness of a company valuation that you have calculated based on one or more of the other more professionally recognized methods. If the rule of thumb corroborates your other value, you can feel vindicated. Conversely, if the rule of thumb method produces a value that is not even close to your other calculated values, you can dismiss it, citing the fact that there is little theoretical basis for using it.

> You can use rules of thumb to test the reasonableness of a company valuation that you have calculated based on one of the other more professionally recognized methods.

Where Do You Find Rules of Thumb?

Rules of thumb are everywhere and they seem to come from everywhere. Some are handed down orally like folklore or urban legends with no theoretical basis whatsoever and some are downloaded from cyberspace. Many industry and trade groups compile information on completed transactions and establish rules of thumb based on the data collected. Business brokers also often publish information about rules of thumb based on their experience and/or research in particular industries.

Thomas West and Glenn Desmond are the authors of the two most highly respected books regarding small business valuation formulas. Desmond's book, written with John A. Marcell, Richard Kelley, and Sandra Storm (Editor), *Handbook of Small Business Valuation and Rules of Thumb*, Third Edition (Valuation Press, 1993) contains formulas and rules of thumb for thirty-one industries and just rules of thumb for an additional forty-seven industries. West's book, *The Business Reference Guide* (Business Book Press, 2003) includes more than 1,000 business valuation rules of thumb for more than 350 different businesses.

The following chart includes a sample of some rules of thumb from the 2003 *Business Reference Guide* (BRG) published by Business Brokerage Press, reprinted here with permission of Tom West:

BRG = Business Reference Guide
FFE = Furniture, fixtures, and equipment
SDC = Seller's discretionary cash flow (amount owner can take out for themselves)
EBT = Earnings before taxes

TYPE OF BUSINESS	RULE OF THUMB 1	RULE OF THUMB 2	CHART 14-1
Accounting firms	100%–150% annual revenues	100%–115% annual fees + FFE	
Auto dealers	2–4 times net income	Goodwill = 1–3 x EBT Parts = current cost FFE = book value + ½ depreciation New vehicles = dealer cost Used vehicles = as agreed	
Book stores	15% annual sales + inventory	1.6 x SDC + inventory	
Day care centers	2–4 x annual cash flow	$1,500–$3,000 per child	
Dental practices	50%–70% annual collections +FFE	1–1.5 x SDC+FFE+inventory	
Dry cleaners	70%–100% annual sales	2.3–2.5 x SDC	
Gas stations	3 x monthly sales + FFE+ inventory	2.5 x SDC	
Gift shops	2.5–3 x SDC + inventory	32% annual sales + inventory	
Janitorial services	45% annual sales	1.5 x SDC	
Law practices	40%–100% annual fees	100% annual fees-estate practices	
Liquor stores	2 x SDC + Liquor license + Inventory	28% – 40% annual sales + Inventory	
Restaurants	2–3 x SDC	30%–45% annual sales	

As you can see, all rules of thumb are not created equally, so you should proceed cautiously and utilize other more reliable valuation methods in addition to rules of thumb.

An Example: LL Beancounters, LLC

You may remember LL Beancounters, LLC from Chapter 11—it is a financial consulting firm that has been in business for thirteen years. The firm started out as an "average" CPA firm but the partners embraced the CPA Vision Project and focused more on value-added consulting projects for their clients and less on compliance engagements, which were starting to become commodities in the marketplace. Even though the company still performs a lot of tax and accounting work for businesses and individuals, the partners decided to market the firm as a financial consulting firm rather than a CPA firm to emphasize their new focus. The partner who was a CVA (certified valuation analyst) recommended valuing the company using the capitalization of earnings method. However, the CPA partner had heard for years that the rule of thumb for valuing accounting firms was 100% of annual revenue, and she felt that it was reasonable to value LL Beancounters, LLC using this method because the firm was still really a CPA firm, just a progressive one.

The CPA researched the rules of thumb in the industry a little further and determined that they could use a range of multipliers rather than one number. The range was from 90 to 125% of annual revenues, so the CPA did the natural thing and averaged those numbers to come up with a multiplier of 107.5%. She then multiplied the firm's annual revenue of $1,000,000 by 107.5% to come up with a value of $1,075,000, which she liked a lot better than the $980,000 value that they calculated using the capitalization of earnings method. (She did find it interesting to learn that if she had used the legendary rule of thumb of 100% of annual revenue, her value of $1,000,0000 would have been very similar to the $980,000 capitalization of earnings value.)

What did the partners do with this conflicting information about the value of LL Beancounters, LLC? They decided to use $1,075,000 as the asking price for the firm, knowing that they could reduce the price through negotiations to $980,000 and still have a fair deal.

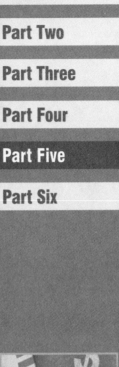

> ➤ **Chapter 15**

Analyzing the Balance Sheet

Basic Accounting Concepts

What is accounting? The American Institute of Certified Public Accountants describes accounting as "the art of recording, classifying, and summarizing in a significant manner and in terms of money, transactions and events which are of a financial character and interpreting the results thereof." Although this inscrutable definition sounds like a committee developed it, it does allude to several important accounting concepts, which are the basic assumptions that accountants rely upon to provide useful financial information to all interested parties. The most important accounting concepts are:

The Business Entity Concept—Accountants treat the business separately from its owners.

The Going Concern Concept—Accountants treat the business as if it will exist for a long time, and, therefore, they record expenses or investments that will have a long-term benefit differently than they record short-term expenditures.

The Money Measurement Concept—Accountants only record transactions that can be expressed in terms of money.

The Cost Concept—Accountants record all transactions for the amounts actually paid or received and they prepare the financial statements on a historical cost basis.

The Accounting Period Concept—Even though the going concern concept indicates that a business will have a continuing existence, accountants break this time down to smaller, more manageable increments such as years. Businesses can report on either a calendar year basis or a fiscal year basis that may better reflect their business cycle.

The Fundamental Accounting Equation—Assets = Liabilities + Net Worth. This equation embodies the concepts that each transaction has two sides, debits = credits, and sources of funds = uses of funds.

The Realization Concept—Accountants record transactions that have already happened so they report revenue when it is earned, e.g., when cash or an obligation to pay is received.

The Matching Concept—Accountants match revenues with the costs to produce those revenues during a specific period in order to determine the profit or loss of that accounting period.

The Accrual Concept—The accrual basis of accounting records revenues when a transaction occurs and the company receives the right to cash in the future (accounts receivable) or incurs the obligation to pay cash in the future (accounts payable). The accrual basis is distinguished from the cash basis where accountants record revenues only when cash is received and report expenses only when cash is paid, even if the obligations to do so were previously incurred.

The Consistency Concept—Accountants apply the same concepts and accounting conventions year after year so that a company's financial statements will be comparable. For example, if a company starts using the accrual basis of accounting for reporting they cannot alternate with the cash basis method.

Nobody would be able to meaningfully prepare or interpret a company's financial statement without understanding these accounting concepts. They all appear self-evident, but if you think about a financial statement that did not incorporate even one of these concepts, you will realize how important they are taken together as the theoretical and practical underpinning of all financial statements. For example, if a company does not match revenues with the related expenses, the profit or loss for the period and succeeding periods will be skewed. Similarly, if a company disregards the realization concept and reports expected sales rather than actual sales, their financial statements will be misleading and not comparable to other companies in their industry.

Accountants must also incorporate accounting principles, specifically Generally Accepted Accounting Principles (GAAP), into the preparation of financial statements. GAAP represents the recognized body of accounting methods and conventions used in practice, which are based on the theoretical concepts listed above. In order to promote financial statement consistency and reliability, various accounting and financial organizations have codified these generally accepted accounting principles and practices into standards that are collectively referred to as GAAP. Some of these accounting-related

> If a company starts using the accrual basis of accounting for reporting they cannot alternate with the cash basis method.

and regulatory organizations are FASB (Financial Accounting Standards Board), APB (Accounting Principles Board), and AICPA (American Institute of CPAs). In addition to basic principles, GAAP includes so many esoteric standards that even CPAs have difficulty keeping up with them and knowing which ones apply to a given situation. Accountants try to manage this generally recognized "standards overload" by referring to the GAAP Hierarchy outlined in SAS 69 (Statement of Auditing Standards 69) and summarized below in order of highest authority to least authority:

1. FASB Statements and Interpretations, APB Opinions, and AICPA Accounting Research Bulletins
2. FASB Technical Bulletins, AICPA Industry Auditing and Accounting Guides
3. AICPA Practice Bulletins and Consensus Opinions of the FASB Emerging Issues Task Force
4. AICPA Accounting Interpretations, FASB Implementation Guides (Q and A's), and widely recognized industry practices
5. Accounting literature, textbooks, AICPA publications, and pronouncements of other regulatory bodies and professional associations

As you analyze and adjust financial statements to value a company, you may find it helpful to understand how and why financial statements are prepared in a very proscribed way. Also, if you are using industry comparisons or databases, you need to know the accounting principles that the other companies in the industry use to report their financial information. GAAP requires accountants to report financial information in three different financial statements: the balance sheet, the income statement, and the statement of cash flows. The balance sheet reports the assets of the company at a point in time and how they are financed—i.e., debt and equity. The income statement shows the revenue and related expenses for the accounting period, usually a year, and the statement of cash flows shows the various sources and uses of cash in three categories: operations, investing, and financing. These three statements taken together give the user of the statements good information about the current financial position of the company and how it got there.

Are Fiscal Years Fiscally Responsible?

Before you start using accounting principles over a fiscal year, you need to know what the term means and how it is used. A fiscal year is any consecutive twelve-month period that an organization uses to account for its financial transactions. Some industries use a 52/53-week tax year that ends on a particular day of the week. For example, Whole Foods Market, Inc. reports in their Form 10-K filed with the Securities and Exchange Commission for the fiscal year ended September 30, 2001, that they use a 52/53-week year ending on the last Sunday in September. Fiscal year 2001 had fifty-three weeks and the previous fiscal years ending on September 24, 2000; September 26, 1999; and September 27, 1998 all had fifty-two weeks.

> A fiscal year is any consecutive twelve-month period that an organization uses to account for its financial transactions.

Almost all individuals have a fiscal year that coincides with the calendar year and since the Tax Reform Act of 1986, so do most closely held businesses that are pass-through entities or professional service corporations. Congress mandated this change (with some limited exceptions) so that business owners would not be able to defer paying tax on their income by taking advantage of different individual and business year ends.

The main reasons businesses and other organizations, including the federal government, use fiscal years is to account for their finances consistently with their business cycle or to avoid having to spend time on accounting and tax compliance when they are the busiest. This is why retailers often have a January 31 year-end, unless they are a pass-through entity with a required December 31 year-end. They don't want to be counting inventory and preparing for the year-end close at the busy Christmas selling season. In addition, having until the end of January gives them a chance to reduce their inventory with after-Christmas sales, which represent the end of their business cycle.

Understanding the Balance Sheet

You may have heard the adage that the balance sheet is a "snapshot" of the financial condition of a company at a given point in time. Usually the point in time is the end of the year, which is December 31 for most companies or the end of the fiscal year (a twelve-month period ending at the end of a month other than December). What is included in this snapshot? The fundamental accounting equation (Assets = Liabilities + Net Worth), which encompasses everything on the balance sheet, in addition to showing the relationship of the different components. When you increase or decrease assets, you must make a corresponding opposite change to liabilities and/or net worth to keep the equation equal, or in balance. Applying the rules of algebra, you can rearrange the equation to show that Net Worth = Assets – Liabilities or Liabilities = Assets – Net Worth.

The double entry system of bookkeeping is what makes this equation work. The double entry system is based on another fundamental equation— Debits (DR) = Credits (CR). Contrary to popular belief, debits do not always represent negative or reducing transactions and credits do not always represent positive or increasing transactions. However, debits are *always* on the left and credits are *always* on the right. Accountants show credit balances with parentheses or a minus symbol, just to symbolize that they are credit balances, not to indicate negative numbers.

> Debits do not always represent negative or reducing transactions and credits do not always represent positive or increasing transactions.

Asset accounts have debit balances and you increase them with debits, whereas liability and net worth accounts have credit balances and you increase them with credits. Consequently, you often see assets on the left side of a balance sheet and liabilities and net worth on the right side. Look at a very simple balance sheet of a startup company where the owner put in $1,000 of her own money and the company borrowed $1,500. All this money went into the asset account "Cash." You can see that the assets equal the liabilities and the net worth, and the debits equal the credits.

Assets (DR)	=	Liabilities (CR)	+	Net worth (CR)
$2,500 cash		$1,500 loan		$1,000 Owner's equity

Assets

The asset section of the balance sheet shows all of the recorded resources of the company that can be used to produce income. (GAAP does not permit businesses to record intangible assets such as goodwill on the balance sheet unless the company purchased the intangibles in a prior transaction.) Assets are listed on the balance sheet in order of liquidity, i.e., how quickly they can be converted to cash. Current assets are those assets that a company can convert to cash within a year:

Cash—This account includes currency, checking and savings accounts, and drafts.

Cash equivalents—This account includes highly liquid investments such as money market funds and U.S. government securities.

Investments—This account includes marketable securities including stocks and bonds.

Accounts receivable—This account represents the obligations of customers who purchased goods or services on credit.

Notes receivable–short-term—This account includes notes receivable that are payable on demand, the amount of long-term debt that is payable within a year, and any other note receivable that is collectible within a year.

Inventory—This account represents the stock or materials on hand that the business will sell in the future. Manufacturing companies have raw materials inventories, work-in-process inventories, and finished goods inventories.

Other current assets—This account includes prepaid expenses such as insurance, taxes, and rent.

Items reported under noncurrent or long-term assets fall into four main categories:

Fixed assets—This category includes property, plant and equipment used in the operations of the business.

Accumulated depreciation—This account reflects the reduction in value of the fixed assets, due to an accounting convention whereby the company deducts a ratable portion of the purchase price over time.

Intangible assets—This category includes purchased goodwill, trademarks, patents, computer software, etc. The assets are reported at the original purchase price or cost to develop them.

Other noncurrent assets—This category includes investments in related companies, fixed assets not used in the business, and other assets not included elsewhere.

Liabilities and Net Worth

Liabilities represent what a company owes to other businesses and individuals. The liability section of the balance sheet is broken down into current and long-term liabilities. As with current assets, current liabilities are those obligations that are expected or required to be paid within one year, and long-term liabilities represent all debts with a longer time horizon. By comparing the current liabilities to the current assets, you can determine whether the company can meet its upcoming obligations with available cash or short-term assets that will soon be cash. Current liabilities include:

> Current liabilities are those obligations that are expected or required to be paid within one year.

Accounts payable—This account represents goods or materials purchased on credit. Suppliers generally offer terms for thirty to ninety days and sometimes offer a discount if the invoice is paid within ten days. Consequently, accounts payable should be converted to cash much more quickly than a year.

Bank loans—This account includes unsecured loans, secured loans, and lines of credit; all of which will be satisfied within one year. These loans are often acquired to help with poor cash flow during slow seasons or to finance growth.

Notes payable–current portion—This category includes notes payable on demand, short-term borrowings, and the current portion of long-term debt from individuals or other companies. Notes payable—shareholders is a subcategory of notes payable that is usually broken out separately.

Other current liabilities—This category includes all of the remaining obligations of the company that are payable within a year or otherwise considered short-term, e.g., accrued payroll and income taxes, accrued wages and vacation pay, and deposits received for work or goods not completed.

Long-term liabilities are obligations that are due after one year, including long-term bank debt, equipment debt, and mortgages. Payments on these amounts are often made in installments. (An amount representing the upcoming twelve months of principal payments is deducted from the long-term debt balance and included under current liabilities.)

The final section of the balance sheet is the net worth section. You may know this section by one of its many aliases: shareholders' equity, owner's equity, partners' capital accounts, or book value. Whatever you call it, this section represents what would be left over for the owners after they liquidated the assets to pay the liabilities. In sole proprietorships, partnerships, and LLCs, the owners' capital accounts include the owner's or partners' initial investment, plus additional capital contributed, plus retained profits, minus any losses, minus any partner withdrawals. In corporations, the net worth section includes stock, additional paid-in capital, and retained earnings less any dividends paid.

Valuation Issues

How do accountants decide what numbers to report for all of these accounts? How do these numbers compare to fair market value? Are there any important assets that the company may not have reported on the balance sheet? Accountants use GAAP and the basic accounting concepts to help them determine what numbers to report. Even so, there is not always one "right" number—accountants must use their judgment to prepare financial statements. Because of these proscribed accounting conventions, the asset section of the balance sheet would rarely reflect the fair market value of the assets.

Basic Concepts Affecting Value

What value is reflected? Several basic accounting concepts influence the value at which accountants record assets on the balance sheet. The most important of these concepts is historical cost, also known as book value. Accountants report most assets at the original price paid to acquire the asset and then use a depreciation convention to arbitrarily reduce the value on an annual basis to reflect wear and tear.

The second important concept is conservatism, which has perhaps had an influence on many accountants' political views as well as their balance sheets. Conservatism in the accounting sense means that accountants must choose the lowest value for an asset when they have two viable options, e.g., they report at the "lower of cost or market value." So, even if accountants have access to a reliable fair market value for an asset, they can't always adjust the financial statements upward to reflect it.

Cash is perhaps the only asset where historical cost and fair market value are the same. The historical cost of cash equivalents may not be the same as fair market value if the account includes any long-term vehicles subject to interest rate risk that could influence their value. The investment account is one of the few where accountants can consider the fair market value of the assets, but the rules are different depending on the type of investment and its intended purpose. For example, marketable securities held as long-term investments are reported at book value and any related investment income is reported on the income statement. But the same marketable securities held for sale would be reported at market value with unrealized gains and losses being reported in the net worth section of the balance sheet instead of on the income statement. If the same marketable securities were purchased so they could be actively traded, they would be valued at fair market value with the unrealized gains and losses being reported on the income statement. The rules change again if a company makes a significant investment, but less than a controlling interest, in another company. These investments are reported at book value, which is adjusted to reflect the pro rata share of the target company's earnings and reduced to account for any dividends received. When a company has a controlling interest investment in another company, the rules totally change, in fact, the acquisition is not even shown as an investment. The controlling company must report the assets and liabilities of the other business in a consolidated format on its own balance sheet, and if there are any minority shareholders, their portion is shown as a liability.

Accounts Receivable and Notes Receivable

Accounts receivable are recorded at the invoice amount at the time of the sale. The primary valuation issue related to accounts receivable is the determination of the amount that won't be collected. Companies can reduce accounts receivable prospectively by creating an allowance for doubtful accounts based on the percentage of receivables that they have historically not collected. Alternatively, they can reduce accounts receivable when they determine that a particular account won't be collected. You should look at the accounts receivable aging report that shows the detail of the accounts receivable shown on the balance sheet. If a large proportion of the company's receivables are more than 90 or 120 days old, you need to do some more investigating. Does the company have a poor collection system? Was the quality of the product or service substandard? Do you need to adjust the accounts receivable balance downward to reflect more bad debts? The answers to these questions may influence your valuation of the company as a whole.

The value of notes receivable–short-term should be pretty straightforward since the time horizon for receiving the funds is within one year. However, you should compare the amounts in this account to the amounts in the same account for the previous year to see if appropriate payments have been made. If short-term or demand notes have not been paid off within the last year, perhaps they need to be restructured and "termed out." Also, check to see that proper interest is being charged and collected, especially when shareholder loans are involved. Nonpayment of loans or interest can indicate poor cash flow, potential bad credit risk, and/or a disregard for the rules; all of which may reduce the value of the company as a whole.

Demand Notes

Demand notes are loans that are payable immediately when the lender presents them to the borrower and demands payment. Consequently, they are recorded on the balance sheet as a short-term liability—not only might they be due and payable within a year, they may become payable tomorrow. This sounds like a pretty risky type of debt for a company to hold, but, in fact, the company often has more flexibility with its demand notes than any other type of debt. Demand notes usually have two sources: the bank and the owners. When a bank issues a demand note, it does usually have a maturity date, so you don't have to worry about your banker appearing on your doorstep totally unannounced ready to collect. In addition, you often have to just pay monthly interest on the loan instead of regular payments of principal and interest each month. At some point the loan will be due, but you may be able to get the loan renewed until you can pay it down in lump sums or have the balance termed out over time. If it is termed out, it becomes a term or installment loan instead of a demand note. When owners make demand notes, they are often more like capital contributions than bona fide loans. Unlike the banker, who will be a stickler on interest and

> Demand notes usually have two sources: the bank and the owners.

payment by a certain date, the owner is often the last person to be paid in a small company. Sometimes owners do not even receive the stated interest payments in the loan documents, much less recover the principal. Look at the payment history for shareholder demand loans and consider whether you should make a normalizing adjustment, just for purposes of the valuation, from short-term liabilities to equity to better reflect their character.

Inventory

A company has several options to choose from when valuing inventory: specific identification, FIFO, LIFO, and weighted average. Specific identification means that the company records the individual cost of each item in inventory and tracks it along with the movement of that particular piece. This method is most often used where there are relatively few, but relatively expensive items such as antiques or custom jewelry. The FIFO (first-in, first-out) method is an accounting convention that assumes that the oldest goods or materials in inventory will be the first ones sold. From a valuation standpoint, FIFO usually results in inventory being valued close to fair market value because the most recent purchases are deemed to be in inventory. LIFO (last-in, first-out) produces the opposite effect—inventory is valued closer to the historical cost of the oldest items purchased; therefore, it is not reported at or near fair market value. Why, then, would a company choose to use the LIFO system to record its inventory? The managers of most companies are more interested in what happens on the income statement than they are in what is recorded on the balance sheet because that is where the profit and loss is determined. An important by-product of the net profit calculation is the amount of income taxes the company will have to pay on those profits. This is where LIFO comes in—in periods of inflation, using the LIFO method will reduce income and thereby reduce income taxes. The weighted average method lumps all the purchases together to come up with an average cost that is used for both inventory and cost of goods sold. If inventory turns over frequently, the value of goods remaining in inventory will be similar to fair market value. How do you compare companies that use different inventory valuation methods? You can make adjustments to LIFO inventories and the related cost of goods sold section of the income statement using information that must be included in footnotes to

> The FIFO (first-in, first-out) method is an accounting convention that assumes that the oldest goods or materials in inventory will be the first ones sold.

the financial statements of companies using LIFO. Companies using LIFO must report the difference between a LIFO and FIFO inventory value as the LIFO reserve.

Fixed Assets and Intangible Assets

Accountants report fixed assets at historical cost and reduce their value annually for wear and tear through depreciation. See Chapter 4 for a more detailed discussion of depreciation. Generally, companies use straight-line depreciation for financial reporting and accelerated methods for tax reporting. However, some companies use accelerated depreciation for both purposes rather than keeping two sets of books. In any case, depreciation is just an accounting convention, not an accurate method of adjusting value, so you may need to look beyond book value when trying to ascertain the value of fixed assets. Some assets may be appreciating assets, so reducing their value on an annual basis through depreciation is increasing the disparity between reported value and fair market value.

Companies must treat intangible assets differently depending on how they are acquired. If a company purchases an intangible asset, such as a patent or trademark, they report it at book value and amortize it over its useful life. If, instead, the company develops the intangible asset internally, they do not report it as an asset, even though it may be one of the most valuable income-producing resources of the firm. Goodwill is treated similarly—if it is acquired in the purchase of another company, it is put on the books and amortized. Otherwise, determining the value of unrecorded goodwill becomes the objective of many business valuation methodologies.

The values of other noncurrent assets on the balance sheet are influenced by the concepts already discussed. For example, you should look for assets recorded at book value that are perhaps appreciating, such as nonproductive real estate.

Liabilities

Accountants record liabilities at historical cost, just as they do assets. The historical cost of current liabilities should be pretty similar to fair market value because the obligations are due within one year. Long-term bank loans valued at historical cost are also being reflected at or near fair market value. If the company issued bonds or other debt instruments whose value was affected by interest rate fluctuations, the changes in value would not be made to the balance sheet. However, if the bonds were sold originally at a discount or premium (less or more than face value), these amounts would be amortized over the life of the debt.

Amortization of Bond Premiums and Discounts

Bond premiums and discounts could be amortized using the straight-line method over the life of the bonds, but that would be too easy. The preferred GAAP method is the "effective interest method." This method computes the interest cost for each period by multiplying the book value of the bonds at the beginning of the period by the effective interest rate at which they were issued. This is a present value calculation, which combines the present value of the principal amount of the bond and the present value of the anticipated cash flows represented by semiannual interest payments. In order to make this calculation, prepare a bond interest amortization schedule to record the semiannual interest payment and amortization of bond premium or discount which will be added or subtracted from the bonds payable account on the balance sheet.

Other Obligations

Just as with intangible assets, companies may have some liabilities that are true obligations but have not been reported on the balance sheet. For example, long-term lease obligations, employee benefits, retirement benefits, and deferred taxes. Often in closely held companies, these items are expensed on the income statement, as they are paid rather than recognized on the balance sheet as liabilities. So the best place to start to uncover unrecorded liabilities is the income statement, but you can't end there. You must go to the source documents backing up these accounts, e.g., lease agreements, summary plan descriptions, and employee census information for retirement plans, tax returns, and employee benefit plan documents.

The net worth section of a corporate balance sheet includes common and preferred stock recorded at book value and retained earnings.

> Companies may have some liabilities that are true obligations but have not been reported on the balance sheet.

Accumulated dividends that have not been paid to preferred shareholders are added to the value of the preferred stock on the balance sheet. Most closely held companies do not reflect the value of any outstanding stock options in the equity section of the balance sheet due to the difficulty in coming up with a value for a transaction that has not occurred. The accounting concepts of realization, conservatism, and historical cost are at work to keep this potentially significant item off the balance sheet. However, companies should be reporting the existence of options in their footnotes, if they are not on the financial statements, so you should be able to make some adjusting calculations of your own.

What Can You Learn from the Balance Sheet?

Analyzing the balance sheet, for the current and previous year, and related source documents can give you answers to the following important questions:

- Can the business pay its debts, both short- and long-term?
- Does the company have too much debt?
- Is the company adequately capitalized?
- How much of the financial burden are the owners bearing?
- Do the asset values approximate fair market value?
- Are any significant assets or liabilities not recorded?
- Is the company growing?
- Does the balance sheet conform to GAAP?

The answers to these questions are important when you are valuing a company. They may lead you to make adjustments to the reported numbers, or they may indicate that the company in question is riskier than other companies in the industry, which would require adjustments to the discount or capitalization rates used in any valuation calculations. Now that you have looked beyond the superficial level of a company's financial position at a point in time, you can move on to an analysis of the other financial statements that reflect performance over a period or periods of time.

> **Chapter 16**

Analyzing the Other Financial Statements

Part One

Part Two

Part Three

Part Four

Part Five

Part Six

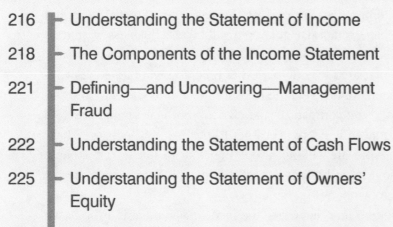

PART FIVE: BASIC BUSINESS VALUATION CALCULATIONS AND ANALYSIS

Understanding the Statement of Income

I f the balance sheet can be compared to a snapshot, a picture at a point in time, then the **income statement** is more like a video, a record of what happened over a period of time. The income statement, also known as the *profit and loss statement, statement of earnings,* or *statement of revenues and expenses*, shows a company's revenues and related expenses, including income taxes, for a specific period. Companies always prepare annual statements at the end of the calendar or fiscal year, but sometimes also prepare additional quarterly statements. Businesses prepare statements at regular intervals to promote comparability, but an income statement could be prepared for any period of time you want to examine.

The income statement answers the question everyone wants to know—how much money did the company make? When you hear sayings like "All that matters is the bottom line," or "Let's get to the bottom line," or "That's it, bottom line!," people are talking about the bottom line of an income statement. The all-important bottom line of the income statement is the net profit (or loss) of the company.

As the term "bottom line" indicates, the income statement is a top-down construction: you start at the top with the income and move down by subtracting the expenses until you get to the bottom line. This contrasts with the balance sheet, which is a right-left construction to coincide with the fundamental accounting equations: Assets = Liabilities + Net Worth and Debits = Credits. Although the income statement and balance sheet are constructed differently and report different important financial information, they are inextricably related. Because of the double-entry bookkeeping system and debits equaling credits, some income statement transactions also affect the balance sheet. For example, the other side of the transaction that reduces income by depreciation expense (a debit) increases the accumulated depreciation account on the balance sheet (a credit). More importantly, the net profit from the income statement, the bottom line, is transferred to the equity section of the balance sheet where it becomes part of retained earnings.

What are the basic elements of the income statement? Although you may report more or less detail on an income statement, the following is an example of an income statement for the candy maker, Sweet Treats and Good Eats, Inc.:

> The income statement answers the question everyone wants to know—how much money did the company make?

SWEET TREATS AND GOOD EATS, INC

CHART 16-1

Income Statement and Statement of Retained Earnings
For the Years Ending December 31, 2003 and 2002

	2003	2002
Net sales (in thousands)	$423,496	$427,054
Cost of goods sold	(216,657)	(207,100)
Gross margin	206,839	219,954
Selling, marketing, and administrative expenses	(109,117)	(105,805)
Amortization of intangible assets	(3,778)	(3,420)
Earnings from operations	93,944	110,729
Other income, net	6,843	7,079
Earnings before income taxes	100,787	117,808
Provision for income taxes	(35,100)	(42,071)
Net earnings	$65,687	$75,737
Retained earnings at beginning of year	$180,123	$158,619
Net earnings	65,687	75,737
Cash dividends ($.28, $.26 per share)	(14,021)	(13,350)
Stock dividends	(70,444)	(40,883)
Retained earnings at end of year	$161,345	$180,123
Earnings per share	$1.30	$1.49
Average common and class B shares outstanding	50,451	50,898

IRS Code Section 263A-Uniform Capitalization (Unicap) Rules

Whenever you see an IRS code section, it usually means that something is so complex that you have to use the code section to even talk about it. The IRS requires businesses with gross receipts over $10 million to use the uniform capitalization rules under section 263A to calculate the value of their inventory. The purpose behind the unicap rules is to prevent businesses from taking large current tax deductions for operating expenses that are related to either manufactured goods or property acquired for resale that are still in inventory. The direct costs of material and labor to produce goods are always included in inventory, but under the unicap rules you must allocate a percentage of indirect costs to inventory, such as repairs and maintenance, utilities, rent, depreciation, indirect supervisory wages, administrative costs, insurance, and retirement plans. (You do not need to allocate a percentage of marketing, advertising, or distribution expenses.)

The Components of the Income Statement

The **net sales number** represents the total income from all sales of goods and services to customers during the period less any discounts, rebates, returns, allowances, etc. The net sales number is the starting point for the income statement because it represents the amount of cash that the company can hope to collect, and it facilitates comparisons with other companies. The **gross profit** or **gross margin** represents the difference between the sales and what it cost to produce them and it is calculated by subtracting the cost of goods sold from net sales. The cost of goods sold is a specific accounting term and it is calculated as follows:

Beginning inventory
+ purchases
+ manufacturing labor
+ factory expense
– ending inventory
= cost of goods sold

The gross profit is one of the most critical numbers on the income statement because it shows how much profit the company is making on its basic business before paying administrative, overhead, and other operating expenses. If a company has a healthy gross margin, it will have the resources to invest in marketing, advertising, research, technology, etc., which will enable it to continue to grow and/or return more profits to the investors. If a company does not have an adequate gross margin, it may not be able to fund its basic operating expenses much less invest in the future. Look for changes in the gross profit to indicate potential changes in the overall profitability of the company, which may ultimately impact the value of the company.

The Sweet Treats and Good Eats, Inc. Income Statement (**Chart 16-1**) shows a gross margin of $206,839, or 48.8%

($206,839 / $423,496). This means that it costs the company a little over half of its net sales to manufacture its product. This appears to be more than adequate to pay for the operating expenses with enough profit left over to pay both cash and stock dividends to shareholders. In fact, the company distributed more dividends than in the previous year. However, if you compare the gross margin to the previous year, you will see that it has decreased. Since sales have decreased, you would expect the actual dollar amount of the gross margin to decrease, but you would not necessarily expect the gross margin percentage to decrease. But that is what occurred; not only did sales decline, but the cost of manufacturing the goods that were sold increased. The gross margin percentage for Sweet Treats and Good Eats, Inc. declined between 2002 and 2003 from 51.5% ($219,954 / $427,054) to 48.8%

When you see changes in critical financial benchmarks like the gross margin, you should investigate further to understand whether these changes appear to be trends or isolated incidents. In a closely held company, you may need to ask management to explain these changes if they are not included in any notes to the financial statements. If you *are* management, you need to understand and be able to explain any changes in the critical gross profit/cost of goods sold section of the income statement.

Earnings from operations represent the overall profit generated by the company's core business. You calculate it by starting with the gross margin and then you deduct general operating expenses, depreciation, and amortization. General operating expenses include such normal expenses as salaries, rent, marketing expenses, office expense, and employee benefit plans. General operating expenses do not include interest expenses, investment income, extraordinary income or expenses, or anything else that is not part of day-to-day operations.

Take another look at the income statement for Sweet Treats and Good Eats, Inc. You can see that earnings from operations are a healthy $93,944; however, this number is down from the previous year, and earnings from operations as a percentage of net sales has decreased from 25.9% in 2002 ($110,729 / $427,054) to 22.2% in 2003 ($93,944 / $423,496). Based on the analysis of the changes in gross margin, it appears that most of the decrease in earnings from operations can be attributed to the decrease in gross margin.

Earnings before interest and taxes (EBIT) is just what it sounds like: all of the income and expenses of the business, with the exception of interest expense and income tax expense. In addition to operating income, EBIT includes any income (or expense) not related to the operations of the business, e.g., investment income in a manufacturing company. It also includes any extraordinary items, which are transactions that are both rare and unusual, e.g., acquisition of another company, sale of appreciated real estate, or the uncovering of management fraud. The notes to the financial statements for Sweet Treats and Good Eats, Inc. indicate that other income includes interest income, dividend income, and net miscellaneous income. An immaterial amount of interest expense was included with other income rather than broken out separately.

Net earnings (or net loss) is the bottom line. Net earnings represent *all* of the income less *all* of the expenses from every source. This is the most important number for investors because it determines what return, if any, they will receive on their investment. Most closely held companies do not report huge net earnings. Smaller companies usually have smaller net sales to begin with, but the common financial goal of providing a good return to the shareholders is often achieved differently in closely held businesses. Some closely held companies like Sweet Treats and Good Eats, Inc. pay dividends to their shareholders, whereas many closely held companies often pay above-market-rate salaries to their owner-employees along with giving them numerous perquisites. This strategy allows small companies to reward their investors (who are also employees) and deduct the cost of it as operating expenses, thereby reducing the company's tax burden. Dividends are not tax deductible, so they are used to a lesser extent in small companies unless they have a few passive investors.

Retained earnings are the net earnings less the dividends paid to shareholders. Although companies are not required to pay dividends, many companies, especially large ones, have a policy or history of doing so. When an investor buys stock in a company that pays dividends, he expects to receive a regular return on his investment as well as to benefit from some long-term growth in value of the company. When an investor buys stock in a company that does not pay dividends, she expects to receive a larger return in the future when she sells her stock or the company itself is sold. The expected return is greater because the risk of the investment is greater. If the company has net earnings and does not pay dividends, it means that it is reinvesting all of the retained earnings back in the company. If the company does not have net earnings, or reports a loss, it may mean that the business is not profitable, or it may mean that the management has made tax-deductible payments to owners instead of paying dividends. In any case, you need to understand what is causing the company to report a net loss, and if you *are* management, you need to be able to explain it.

The ending retained earnings number is transferred over to the equity section of the balance sheet to complete the accounting cycle.

Defining—and Uncovering— Management Fraud

Management fraud is the intentional misrepresentation or concealment of material amounts or disclosures on a company's financial statements. Employee fraud, such as embezzlement, usually involves directly stealing money or otherwise diverting funds for personal use. Businesses can implement sophisticated systems of internal control to prevent this type of fraud and to identify it if it does occur. In contrast, the goal of management fraud is to mislead the users of the financial statements in order to retain investors, debt financing, public confidence, etc. This kind of fraud is not so easy to prevent or detect because when management inflates the value of the company, all the employees benefit in the short term due to continued growth and job stability. However, artificially propping up the stock price will preferentially benefit managers who receive incentives in the form of cash or stock options for reaching performance goals.

Barbara Apostolou, John M. Hassell, and Sally A. Webber published an article entitled "Forensic Expert Classification of Management Fraud Risk Factors" in the *Journal of Forensic Accounting*, Vol.1 (2000), pp.181–192, which details twenty-five management fraud risk factors. The most important factor they identified was "significant compensation tied to aggressive accounting practices." Other factors relate to the characteristics of management, condition of the industry, and operating and financing characteristics.

Does Paying Dividends Pay Dividends?

Dividends are non-deductible payments that the company (as decided by its board of directors) makes to its shareholders out of retained earnings. Dividends are personally taxable to the shareholder receiving them. Large companies pay dividends as a way to acquire or retain investors, and small companies pay dividends to reward the owners, who are often also the management and the board of directors. Companies who need all of their cash for reinvestment and growth generally don't pay dividends. Small closely held companies may intermittently pay dividends to reward shareholders for profitable years or other occasions. Companies usually pay dividends in cash, but sometimes they award stock dividends, which don't use any of the company's money but do dilute the ownership of the firm. Thus the managers of companies that pay dividends do so to reap future "dividends" in the form of investment capital and owner loyalty.

Understanding the Statement of Cash Flows

Generally Accepted Accounting Principles (GAAP) require companies to prepare a **statement of cash flows** in addition to the balance sheet and income statement. However, because most closely held companies do not have their financial statements audited, they do not prepare it. If the company you are analyzing does not have a statement of cash flows, you can create one by converting income statement accrual items to the cash basis, adding back non-cash items, and making adjustments for changes in the balance sheet accounts. The purpose of the statement of cash flows is to report the sources and uses of cash for the same period covered by the income statement. The sources and uses are classified into three categories:

- Cash provided by or used for operations
- Cash provided by or used for investing activities
- Cash provided by or used for financing activities

The totals of each classification are summed to determine the net increase or decrease in cash for the period. The statement of cash flows uses both the income statement and the balance sheet to determine where cash has come from and where it has gone. **Chart 16-2** illustrates how to prepare and understand the statement of cash flows.

CHART 16-2

SWEET TREATS AND GOOD EATS, INC.

Statement of Cash Flows
For the Years Ended December 31, 2003 and 2002

	2003	2002
CASH FLOWS FROM OPERATING ACTIVITIES:		
Net earnings	$65,687	$75,737
Adjustments to reconcile net earnings to net cash provided by operating activities:		
Depreciation and amortization	16,700	13,314
Gain on retirement of fixed assets	—	(46)

CHART 16-2
(continued)

Changes in operating assets and liabilities, excluding acquisitions:		
Accounts receivable	3,096	(4,460)
Other receivables	(2,100)	4,486
Inventories	910	(768)
Prepaid expenses and other assets	(8,857)	(7,903)
Accounts payable and accrued liabilities	(224)	(1,717)
Income taxes payable and deferred	4,402	5,691
Post-retirement health and life insurance	494	399
Deferred comp and other liabilities	1,206	337
Other	191	(189)
Net cash provided by operating activities	81,505	84,881
CASH FLOWS FROM INVESTING ACTIVITIES:		
Acquisitions of businesses, net of cash acquired	—	(74,293)
Capital expenditures	(14,148)	(16,189)
Purchase of held to maturity securities	(243,530)	(156,322)
Maturity of held to maturity securities	228,397	176,576
Purchase of available for sale securities	(64,640)	(78,993)
Sale and maturity of available for sale securities	74,166	82,754
Net cash used in investing activities	(19,755)	(66,467)
CASH FLOWS FROM FINANCING ACTIVITIES:		
Issuance of notes payable	—	43,625
Repayments of notes payable	—	(43,625)
Treasury stock purchased	—	—
Shares repurchased and retired	(1,932)	(32,945)
Dividends paid in cash	(14,168)	(13,091)
Net cash used in financing activities	(16,100)	(46,036)
Increase (decrease) in cash and cash equivalents	45,650	(27,622)
Cash and cash equivalents at beginning of year	60,882	88,504
Cash and cash equivalents at end of year	$106,532	$60,882
Supplemental cash flow information:		
Income taxes paid	$30,490	$35,750
Interest paid	$356	$1,067

First, start with the net income from the Sweet Treats and Good Eats, Inc. income statement: $65,687. Then, add back noncash items such as depreciation and amortization. Next, move on to the balance sheet, where you will record all the changes in the accounts as either increases or decreases to cash as if you were converting an accrual basis balance sheet to the cash basis. If a current asset account has increased over the period, you will show it as a use of cash because you do not have your money yet. For example, Sweet Treats and Good Eats, Inc.'s other receivables and prepaid expenses increased between 2002 and 2003, so they are shown as cash outflows. Conversely, accounts receivable and inventories decreased over the same period, so they are shown as sources of cash or cash inflows. When accounts receivable are reduced or if inventory is sold, that means that you have more cash.

Current liability accounts work in the opposite way; if accounts payable go up, it means you haven't spent your cash, and, therefore, this increase becomes a source of cash. If the short-term liabilities go down, it means you have paid them, so the difference becomes a use of cash. Looking at the Sweet Treats and Good Eats, Inc. statement of cash flows again, you can see that accounts payable decreased and this change was treated as a use of cash. The other short-term liabilities increased, so they were treated as sources of cash. Totaling this section of the cash flow statement shows the net cash provided by operations, $81,505. This is the most important number on the statement of cash flows from a valuation perspective, because it is the starting point for calculating the earnings measures used in income or discounted cash flow valuation methods. You should also compare the net cash provided by operations in 2003 with the net cash flow from operations in the previous year, $84,881. Although the net earnings were down by $10,050 between 2002 and 2003, the net cash provided by operations only decreased by $3,376.

The next section is cash flows from investing activities. The primary activities in this section are the purchase of fixed assets and the purchase and sale of long-term investments. You can see that Sweet Treats and Good Eats, Inc. purchased about $14,000 of new property, plant, and equipment and that their major use of invested cash was to purchase long-term securities, $243,530. They also sold $228,397 in long-term securities that are treated as a source of cash from investing activities. The purchase and sale of securities mostly offset each other for the period ended December 31, 2003, so the major component of net cash used in investing activities, ($19,755) is the purchase of fixed assets.

The final classification is cash flows from financing activities. The major transactions reflected in this section are the acquisition and retirement of debt, and equity transactions such as retiring stock and paying dividends. Increases in debt are shown as sources of cash, and payments of principal are shown as uses of cash. Dividends paid are a use of cash, as is the retirement of any stock or purchase of treasury stock. In 2002 Sweet Treats and Good Eats, Inc. borrowed some money and paid it back in the same year. Other than that, they have not had to finance their activities, which would make them a less risky investment than a similar company with more debt. This type of information is important when valuing businesses, especially in the process of determining capitalization and discount rates.

Understanding the Statement of Owners' Equity

The **statement of owners' equity** reflects the components of net worth and ties the income statement and the balance sheet together. Sole proprietorships, partnerships, and LLCs have statements of capital or capital accounts, while corporations have statements of stockholders' equity or statements of shareholders' equity. Whatever the title, the purpose and the general format is the same: to show the beginning and ending equity balance and explain the increases or decreases in the related accounts. The basic format for statements of capital accounts and stockholders' equity is as follows:

MOM'S COMPANY

Statement of Capital
For the Year Ending December 31, 2002

CHART 16-3

Owner's capital, beginning balance	$2,235
Add: net income	36,245
	38,480
Less: drawings	(30,000)
Owner's capital, ending balance	$8,480

CHART 16-3

(continued)

MOM AND POP, INC.

Statement of Stockholders' Equity
For the Year Ended December 31, 2002

	COMMON STOCK	ADD'L PAID-IN	RETAINED EARNINGS	TOTAL EQUITY
Beginning balance, 1/1/02	$10,000.00	$20,000.00	$18,350	$48,350
Net income	—	—	$55,000	$55,000
Dividends paid	—	—	($20,000)	($20,000)
Ending balance, 12/31/02	$10,000.00	$20,000.00	$53,350	$83,350

The statement of owners' equity can tell you a lot about a company, especially in a closely held company, even though it doesn't look like it contains much information. First, you can see how much of her own money the owner has invested in the company. In other words, did she put her "money where her mouth is" or is she relying on bank and other financing to grow the business? With this information, you can form an opinion about whether the company is adequately capitalized. You can also see if the owner has put additional capital into the company. If so, this could be an indication of cash flow problems or an inability for the company to get credit; otherwise, the company may have used a bank loan to fund normal growth or seasonal needs.

What can you learn from seeing distributions to owners in the statement of owners' equity? In the case of proprietorships and partnerships, owner draws are the principal way that owners get paid, both for rendering services to the company and for investing their capital. These owners do not receive salaries because of the tax and accounting rules related to proprietorships and partnerships, so you may find it difficult to determine what portion of draws or withdrawals is related to return on investment. However, all draws will reduce the owners' equity in the business but will not reduce the taxable income of the entity.

Corporate distributions to owners are in the form of dividends, and they do represent a return on the owners' investment. Corporations can pay dividends if the company has retained earnings and enough cash to make the payments. Dividends are paid on a pro rata basis of the number of shares held by each owner. Even if the company has plenty of retained earnings and a lot of cash, management may decide to reinvest the net income rather than pay it to the owners. Just as with proprietorships and partnerships, making distributions to owners reduces the equity in the company that can be used to fund future growth.

Many closely held companies don't have much activity in their common stock accounts after the initial purchase of stock to set up the company. Consequently, they can prepare an annual Statement of Retained Earnings instead of the Statement of Stockholders' Equity. This statement shows the beginning balance in retained earnings; net earnings are added and dividends are subtracted to arrive at the ending balance in retained earnings. The Sweet Treats and Good Eats, Inc. income statement incorporates a statement of retained earnings at the bottom of the page.

Valuation Issues

The statements of income, cash flows, and owners' equity provide much important information to the valuator of a business. When you are valuing a company, you want to know what its net income is but, more importantly, you want to know what portion of the net earnings are from the ongoing operations of the business. If you are going to make projections or assumptions about earnings and growth, you don't want to include anything that won't continue to occur.

> The statements of income, cash flows, and owners' equity provide much important information to the valuator of a business.

Consequently, expenditures are classified into three categories: operating, financing, and investing. Operating expenses are those that are related to producing the income of the current period, whereas investing expenditures are related to producing income or benefits in the future. Financing expenses, such as interest expense, relate to debt used to grow the business. You can see from the Sweet Treats and Good Eats, Inc. statements of income and cash flow that expenses and sources of cash are classified accordingly to aid with analysis. Depreciation and amortization are also broken out separately. These are accounting conventions that arbitrarily reduce the value of assets on an annual basis under the theory that their value is reduced by wear and tear with the passage of time. This theory and these conventions may not fit the assets you are valuing, so you can

Notes to the Financial Statements

The notes to the financial statements are an indispensable part of a company's financial statements, both for reporting purposes and understanding purposes. GAAP requires that notes be included with the other financial statements in order to "present fairly" the financial position of a company (though many small companies do not prepare their financial statements in accordance with GAAP and may not have the notes to the financial statements). The first basic type of note relates to accounting methods; it tells which inventory convention the company is using, if it has made major accounting policy or other changes, how it accounts for any long-term contracts, etc. The second type involves additional disclosures and gives specific information about debt, retirement plans, leases, etc. If you are valuing a company that does not have published notes to its financial statements, ask management to provide the same information. If you are management, be prepared to answer these questions.

easily make adjustments if you know what the accounting depreciation or amortization is.

Some important expenses or uses of cash may not be broken out, so you might need to consult the notes to the financial statements, source documents, or management. For example, the information technology department may have developed an important computer program to track inventory, or scientists in the lab may have discovered a miracle drug. The expenditures associated with these types of activities are generally included in operating expenses, but the unrecorded assets created will have future benefits. In situations like this, you may want to make an adjustment to reduce operating expenses and increase intangible assets.

➤ **Chapter 17**

"Normalizing" the Financial Statements

Part One

Part Two

Part Three

Part Four

Part Five

Part Six

"Why Be Normal?"

You might have seen the bumper sticker in the mid-1980s that read "Why Be Normal?" The connotation was that not being normal was something good, extraordinary, better than normal. Many small companies have either wittingly or unwittingly incorporated this mantra into their financial statements. Of course, most large companies purposefully present financial statements that make the company look as good as possible to the investing public. But what about the rules? Can companies really "manipulate" their financial statements to produce a desired result? The rules are Generally Accepted Accounting Principles (see Chapter 10 for a discussion of GAAP), and most large companies, especially publicly traded ones, must rigorously apply GAAP to their financial statements. However, they still have a lot of room for interpretation and judgement. Naturally, they will use the interpretation that puts their company in the most favorable light.

Small companies, on the other hand, have much more leeway in applying GAAP because they don't have outside or public investors and, therefore, do not usually have audited financial statements. In fact, small companies do not always use GAAP to prepare their financial statements for these reasons. In contrast to large companies, the small company bias is to portray a negative picture, thereby reducing income taxes. For example, most closely held companies use the cash basis of accounting, where income and expenses are reported only when cash is received or spent. You can see that these companies could easily influence their reportable income by delaying the creation of invoices or depositing receipts while accelerating the payment of expenses.

"Normalizing" financial statements is a process of making adjustments to the balance sheet and income statement to better approximate true economic income or financial position. Normalized statements are especially important when you want to compare one company to another company or the industry as a whole. Although you may further depart from GAAP by making normalizing adjustments to the financial statements, you must be diligent about using the double entry system of accounting for any of your changes. This means that for any adjustment you make, you will have a corresponding adjustment to another account. Sometimes you will make an income statement adjustment that will require a related balance sheet adjustment or vice versa.

Reasonable Compensation

The most common income statement adjustment involves owner's compensation. The owner's salary in a closely held business often has more to do with the availability of cash and the owner's personal lifestyle than the value of the services the owner performs for the business. For example, if the owner of a dry cleaning business is making $100,000 per year and he or she could hire a competent manager to run the business for $60,000, then the owner's reasonable compensation for services is $60,000. What happens to the remaining $40,000 of the owner's salary? You add the "excess compensation" of $40,000 to net income to reflect a truer picture of the company's profitability. The good news for the owner is that the value of the company will not be decreased because he or she pursued an aggressive tax reduction strategy. The normalizing adjustments add aggressive deductions back to the income number that is a major factor in the ultimate valuation of the company.

> The most common income statement adjustment involves owner's compensation.

You may also need to adjust compensation if the company "employs" any relatives or friends of the owners who do not perform services commensurate with their pay. For example, a dentist pays her spouse $40,000 and full benefits to perform banking duties, pick up the mail, and run errands even though she has a full-time office manager. This arrangement provides for segregation of duties in the office, which is a good management practice to prevent embezzling or fraud. However, she could probably achieve the same goal by rearranging duties within the office or hiring a part-time employee at less than half her husband's current salary. Consequently, you would add back the husband's salary and related benefits to the net profit to get a more accurate picture of the economic reality of this practice.

Segregation of Duties and Internal Control

Employees can be a company's greatest asset, but also its greatest risk. You can reduce the risk of employee fraud as well as errors and irregularities by setting up a system of internal control. Segregation of duties is the most important component of an internal control system because it sets up a series of checks and balances that makes it difficult for any one person to embezzle funds or otherwise perpetrate a fraud against the company. The four basic functions you need to segregate are the authorization of transactions, recordkeeping, asset custody, and reconciliation. For example, the person who deposits receipts should not also be posting the receipts to the accounts receivable ledgers. Or the person who authorizes purchases should not post the payments to the accounts payable ledgers.

This sounds great in theory, but what if you don't have enough employees to segregate all of these duties? Separate critical tasks as much as possible and use a supervisory-level person or yourself to perform the reconciliation function. You should compare collections to deposits on a regular basis, you can implement surprise asset or inventory "audits," and review accounts payable and receivable balances, etc. One of the important things about segregation of duties is letting your people know that this is good business practice, not a sign that you don't trust them. In fact, the first thing an outside auditor of your company's financial statements will determine is if you have a system of internal control that he or she can rely upon. If you have a good system, the auditor can use statistical sampling techniques to review transactions. If you don't, the auditor will have to review almost all of your transactions—which, of course, makes for a more time consuming and, therefore, more costly audit.

> Separate critical tasks as much as possible and use a supervisory-level person or yourself to perform the reconciliation function.

Researching What Is Reasonable

Making adjustments for reasonable compensation sounds easy enough, but how do you determine what is reasonable? The following list of databases and other resources is a good starting point:

1. Robert Morris Associates' *Annual Statement Studies*
2. *Almanac of Business and Industrial Financial Ratios* by Leo Troy
3. Financial Research Associates' *Financial Studies of the Small Business*
4. The IRS's *Sourcebook Statistics of Income*
5. Panel Publishers' *Officer Compensation Report*
6. *Executive Compensation Survey Analysis* by the National Institute of Business Management
7. Industry and Professional Associations
8. Employment Agencies and Executive Recruiters

Many of these resources will show information that is based on companies that are much larger than the company you are trying to value. In addition, the information is often categorized into ranges based on dollar amounts for sales or assets and then shown as a percentage of the total. For example, a database may show that officers' compensation represents 20% of sales for a particular service industry with sales of $5–10 million. Does this mean that one person earned between $1 million and $2 million? Maybe, but it might indicate that more than one owner received that level of compensation. Consequently, you will need to use your judgment to determine whether the relative percentage of compensation expenses to total income is comparable across size for a particular industry. You will also need to determine whether the published information includes the compensation of all owners and officers, or just one primary owner. One of the advantages of getting your information from industry and professional associations, employment agencies, or executive recruiters is that you will get a specific dollar amount for one person to perform a specific job.

Owners' Fringe Benefits

When adjusting the owner's compensation, you should also look at related accounts such as retirement plans and fringe benefits and make appropriate adjustments. For example, if the company made a retirement contribution in the amount of 25% of each eligible employee's salary, an owner making $150,000 would receive a $37,500 contribution that the company deducted from its net income. What should you do if you determine that the reasonable compensation for the owner is only $80,000? In addition to adding $70,000 to net income, you must recalculate the appropriate retirement contribution based on this amount of compensation. The appropriate retirement contribution would be $80,000 x 25%, or $20,000. Consequently, you would increase net income by $17,500, the difference between the original contribution and the recalculated one.

Other fringe benefits may not be based on a percentage of compensation, so you will need to determine if the owner's benefits exceed those available to other employees at a similar compensation or experience level. Some examples of these fringe benefits would be health, life, and disability insurance. In addition, you should look beyond the usual fringe benefits to automobile, travel, and entertainment expenses on the income statement and fixed assets such as cars, boats, and condos on the balance sheet that may be used for personal purposes. Similarly, you would add back to income any excess fringe benefit costs and especially any "beyond the fringe" expenses that were deducted.

Doubtful Accounts and Notes Receivable

Determining whether accounts receivable and notes receivable are collectible can be either really important or totally unimportant when analyzing financial statements for the purpose of a business valuation. The value of receivables is not important if the owner is selling the business and planning to collect his or her own receivables rather than transfer them to the buyer. In this case, you would adjust the balance sheet to remove the receivables altogether. In other situations, such as valuations for divorce or estate tax purposes where the business is not going to be sold, the accounts and notes receivable may constitute a large part of the assets being valued and, therefore, are important to value accurately. Many companies, and most professional practices, are on the cash basis and, therefore, don't report any receivables on their financial statements. In this case, you would adjust the balance sheet to add the receivables.

> If you decide that the value of the receivables is important, you must analyze them to determine their appropriate value.

If you decide that the value of the receivables is important, you must analyze them to determine their appropriate value. Most businesses on the accrual basis make their own estimate of what will not be collectible and reflect that amount as an allowance for doubtful accounts, which is a negative adjustment to accounts receivable. Estimates for doubtful accounts range from very aggressive to overly conservative because GAAP does not specify a set percentage or method of determining the proper allowance. So, what factors should you consider when evaluating the allowance for doubtful accounts and overall collectibility of receivables?

1. The credit terms the company offers
2. The aged accounts receivable schedule
3. The company's past collection history
4. The current and anticipated economic climate
5. The financial health of the customers, especially the largest ones

You need to know the credit terms of the company you are valuing to understand whether its customers are paying late or on time. Two similar companies may have different credit policies. For example, one may give its customers a 10% discount if they pay the invoice within 10 days and require final payment within thirty days (2% 10, NET 30), while the other one requires payment in sixty days. This difference in credit policy can make a difference when you look at the number of times the receivables "turn" and when you look at the aged accounts receivable schedule. In the first case, a receivable that is forty-five days old would be past due, whereas in the second case, this same receivable would be considered current.

The **aged accounts receivable schedule** will give you the most insight into whether the receivables will be able to be collected. This schedule lists the company's customers and categorizes the amounts according to how many days their invoices have been outstanding. Anything less than thirty days old is considered current and the rest of the schedule is self-explanatory. Generally, the older the receivable, the less likely the company will be able to collect it. Look at the aged account receivable schedule for Avery's Antiques:

CHART 17-1

Account Name	Total	Current	30–60	60–90	90–120	Over 120
Brown, Mary	1,500		1,500			
Brewer, Edna	555	555				
Coble, Henry	2,850			2,850		
Drew, Nancy	5,400	1,500	1,900			2,000
Hardy, Thomas	3,500				2,000	1,500
Smith, Russell	495	495				
Ward, Stella	2,500		2,500			
Total	16,800	2,550	5,900	2,850	2,000	3,500
	100%	15%	35%	17%	12%	21%

Avery reports on his balance sheet that his receivables are $16,800 with no allowance for doubtful accounts. You should analyze each of the above accounts, or at a minimum the larger accounts and the ones that are most past due, to determine if you need to make any adjustments. Questions to ask include: How has this customer paid in the past? Do you know anything about the customer that would indicate whether he or she will or won't pay? Has the customer made any special payment arrangements? What is the customary collection period for this business? What is the normal collection period for this industry?

As with accounts receivable, you may not even need to consider notes receivable if you are doing a valuation for the sale of a company and the notes receivable are not being transferred. However, you will need to analyze notes receivable for most other valuation purposes. Determining the origin of the note receivable will often give you an indication of its future collectibility. For example, if a customer had a long-standing account receivable, the company may have asked them to convert it into a note to increase the probability of collection. Or, the owner of the company "borrowed" some funds when he wanted to build a beach house and has never paid the company back. Both of these situations may produce receivables of questionable value. Some other items to consider in determining whether to adjust the value of notes receivable include:

> Determining the origin of the note receivable will often give you an indication of its future collectibility.

- Is there a loan document?
- What are the terms?
- Has the borrower paid as promised up to this point?
- Is there any collateral?
- Who is the borrower and are they financially sound?
- Is this the result of a related party transaction?

Inventory Method Adjustments

Businesses can choose from several different inventory valuation methods and still be in conformity with GAAP. Consequently, you often need to adjust the value of inventory on the balance sheet to be able to make useful comparisons to other companies or the industry as a whole. The four common inventory valuation methods are:

Specific Identification—You track each item at its purchase price.

First-In, First Out—You treat the first items purchased as being sold first.

Last-In, First-Out—You treat the last items purchased as being sold first.

Average Cost Method—You calculate an average cost using all the items purchased and their collective purchase price.

When companies choose the specific identification method, FIFO, or the average cost method, your analysis is usually limited to determining whether the physical inventory count ties back to what is shown on the books and whether any obsolete inventory is included in the number. The company should have already made any adjustments related to the physical inventory count, but they have a lot of leeway in how to treat obsolete inventory. You should review the company's write-down/writeoff policy for inventory—one person's "obsolete" inventory may be another person's "absolute" inventory. Use your judgment to determine if the inventory on the books should either be adjusted up or down.

If a company is using the LIFO method, you generally make an additional adjustment to inventory to essentially report inventory on the FIFO method. Business valuators adjust LIFO inventories to FIFO rather than the other way around because the FIFO method reflects the current fair market value of the inventory. In addition, you can easily adjust LIFO to FIFO with readily available information—the adjustment is the amount of the "LIFO reserve."

Advantages of LIFO

Back in the "old days"—that is, the late 1970s and early 1980s—inflation was rampant in the United States. In the United States, rampant inflation generally means more than 10 percent, which is nothing compared to other countries, such as Argentina, where annual inflation is from 20 to 30%. Wherever you are, inflation erodes the value of your money, so you try to find ways to preserve your purchasing power. Thus, LIFO became a way of life for many businesses to reduce taxes. This is how it works: Say you have a beginning inventory of *Simplify Your LIFO* books of 100 books purchased at $20 each and you add 200 books purchased at $25, then you sell 150 books during the accounting period. Let's compare your cost of goods sold and inventory numbers under the LIFO and FIFO methods.

CHART 17-2

	FIFO			LIFO	
Beginning inventory	100 @ $20 =	$2000		100 @ $20 =	$2000
Purchases	200 @ $25 =	$5000		200 @ $25 =	$5000
Total		$7000			$7000
Cost of goods sold	100 @ $20 =	$2000		150 @ $25 =	$3750
	50 @ $25 =	$1250			
Total CGS		$3250			$3750
Inventory	150 @ $25 =	$3750		100 @ $20 =	$2000
				50 @ $25 =	$1250
Total inventory		$3750			$3250

You can see that in times of inflation and rising prices, LIFO produces a higher cost of goods sold number, which reduces income and, more importantly, reduces income tax. Because cost of goods sold and inventory are inversely related, the LIFO calculation produces a lower cost for the remaining inventory. The value of the inventory becomes more skewed over time because the oldest, and presumably the least expensive items, continue to be the bulk of the inventory showing on the books.

Depreciation Adjustments

Depreciation is another one of those accounting constructs, like inventory valuation methods, where companies can choose from a variety of methods. See Chapter 4 for a discussion of various depreciation methods. Theoretically, companies should prepare their financial statements using an allowable method of depreciation that most closely reflects the actual wear and tear or obsolescence of its assets. This does not preclude them from using an accelerated method to report depreciation for tax purposes, thereby reducing their taxes.

Most large companies do keep separate depreciation schedules for book and tax purposes, but the reality for many closely held businesses is that only one depreciation schedule is kept and that is the tax depreciation schedule with the most accelerated methods. Consequently, you may want to adjust depreciation to an amount more in line with the actual useful life of the assets or consistent with depreciation practices in the industry. However, if you are normalizing the income statements to arrive at cash flow rather than net income, you should add back all of the depreciation taken and subtract an annual amount that would represent the replacement cost of the assets.

Other Adjustments

If your company owns real estate, you can approach the normalization process in several ways, depending on the purpose of the valuation. Usually, owners of small businesses that own real estate will consider, or even prefer, selling the business and retaining the real estate. In these cases, you would remove the asset and related accumulated depreciation from the balance sheet. In addition, you would need to adjust the income statement to take out related expenses such as property tax, insurance, interest, repairs, etc., and add in a fair market rent expense. Even if you plan to sell the real estate with the company, you may want to remove it from the business balance sheet and value it separately. Most small businesses and professional practices do not own their business real estate, or they may have a separate entity, such as a Limited Liability Company, which owns the property and leases it to the operating company. Consequently, you will be able to more effectively compare your company to others in the same industry if you take the real estate and related expenses off of the financial statements for valuation purposes.

Another reason to separate the real estate from the ongoing business for valuation purposes is that appraisers use different methods to value real estate than you would use to value a company. Appraisers use three primary methods to value real estate: the income capitalization approach, the sales comparison approach, and the cost approach. If you do want to adjust the balance sheet to reflect the fair market value of company real estate, you—or a qualified real estate appraiser—should use these methods to determine the appropriate value.

Limited Liability Companies (LLCs)

LLCs have some of the best characteristics of the other forms of business organization. LLCs have the liability protection of a corporation, the "flow-through" tax treatment of a partnership or sole proprietor, the capability of having one or many owners of all types, and operating flexibility to ignore the corporate baggage of minutes, resolutions, and board meetings. If you have decided for operating or tax purposes that the partnership or sole proprietorship makes the most sense for your business, you should consider getting some additional liability protection by forming an LLC. The primary benefit of an LLC, in contrast to a general partnership, is that members are not personally liable for company debts, unless they have personally guaranteed them. See your attorney to determine if your company can benefit from the legal protection of an LLC. However, forming an LLC does not preclude the need to insure against all of your insurable liabilities.

The **income capitalization approach** is very similar to the capitalization of earnings method of business valuation. The underlying premise is that the value today is based on the income or cash flow you anticipate receiving in the future from ongoing rental income and the ultimate sale of the property. Even if you are not actually renting the real estate, you would calculate the amount of rent you could expect to receive if the building were rented at fair rental value. You then convert these anticipated future cash flows to present value by capitalizing a measure of income or cash flow or by performing a discounted cash flow analysis. As with any of the business valuation methods that use capitalization or discount rates, you must be diligent about choosing an appropriate rate that will take into account the risk of the investment. Appraisers generally use this method to value commercial real estate of all kinds and rental properties.

The **sales comparison approach** is a straightforward valuation method that is based on an analysis of the market in order to find actual sales or listings of comparable properties. You can use this method to value all types of properties as long as you can find enough market information to determine that a sale or sales are indeed comparable to the property you are valuing. However, this method is most commonly used to value residential real estate and vacant land and is the basis for the Uniform Residential Appraisal Report (URAR). Although "location, location, location" is a major consideration for this approach, you also need to look at other factors including the date of any comparable sales, physical characteristics of the property, highest and best use of the property, market conditions, and any special financing terms.

The **cost method** is based on the economic principle of substitution, which means that a knowledgeable buyer will not pay more for a property than he or she would have to spend to acquire a similar piece of land and construct a similar building. The cost approach breaks real estate into its two component parts—land and improvements. You first determine the value of the land component at its highest and best use as vacant property. Then, you calculate the value of the improvements by determining their replacement cost and reducing this amount for depreciation and other types of obsolescence. You would primarily use the cost method for new buildings and special use buildings such as schools, churches, museums, etc.

Small businesses usually depreciate their business personal property, i.e., furniture, fixtures, and equipment, as rapidly as possible for tax purposes. Consequently, they show very little value for this property on the balance sheet unless they keep a separate set of books to record nontax depreciation. In any case, you should make an adjustment to the balance sheet to reflect the fair market value of the tangible personal property.

How do you determine the fair market value of these depreciated assets? One of the best methods is to calculate the depreciated replacement cost value, which is the cost to replace the assets in today's dollars reduced by depreciation that is based on the anticipated useful life of the asset and the length of time it has been in service. If you have machinery and equipment that is either very specialized or represents a significant portion of the value of the business, you should engage a professional equipment appraiser to value these items.

You will generally not need to make adjustments for notes payable and other liability accounts unless you are valuing a company for sale and these items will not be included in the sale. In that case, you simply make an adjustment to take them off the balance sheet. One exception to this rule would be in the case of a sale where a note at a very favorable interest rate was going to be assumed by the buyer. You can make an adjustment to the balance sheet to reflect the present value of the note payments, which will be lower than the face amount of the debt. If you have a large loan, this can make a significant difference in what someone would be willing to pay to acquire the assets and liabilities of a company.

You will need to make adjustments to the balance sheet for any contingent liabilities such as legal claims, regulatory compliance costs, environmental cleanup costs, employment-related obligations, etc. When these items are not on the balance sheet to begin with, it probably means that the company did not have a good way to value them. Consequently, you just have to do the best you can to determine the probable value by estimating an after-tax cost and weighing the probability of payment over time. If you can't do this with any level of comfort, don't make an adjustment on the balance sheet, but do make a note of the situation so it can be considered in the overall valuation of the company.

You may want to make some additional adjustments to the income statement to more accurately reflect the income from normal operations that

Small businesses usually depreciate their business personal property, i.e., furniture, fixtures, and equipment, as rapidly as possible for tax purposes.

can be expected to continue in the future. If you see that the company has recorded some unusual, nonrecurring items, you should consider adjusting them off the income statements. For example, you should eliminate the positive effect of receiving funds from insurance proceeds and legal settlements if they are not part of the normal operating activity of the company. Similarly, you should disregard the gain or loss on the sale of significant assets that will not be recurring. Analyze the income statement and compare it to previous years' statements to determine if the company has any of these "extraordinary" items to be adjusted off the income statement.

What about the tax effect of all of these adjustments? Sometimes you should take the tax effect into account and make appropriate adjustments, and other times you do not need to make any adjustments for taxes. If some or all of the underlying property being valued is going to be imminently sold, it may make sense to determine the fair market value less related taxes. However, when you are valuing a business for divorce or estate tax purposes, the basic premise is that the company or underlying assets are not going to be sold. If you decide that an adjustment for taxes is warranted, you may make it by creating a deferred tax account in the liability section of the balance sheet.

Now that you have totally reconstructed the financial statements, you are ready to analyze them further by using ratio analysis and other analytical techniques.

▶ **Chapter 18**

Financial Analysis

Part One

Part Two

Part Three

Part Four

Part Five

Part Six

Analyzing Financial Analysis

The word "analysis" conjures up visions of leather couches and Freudian figures helping you sift through layers of your subconscious to arrive at an understanding of your true personality. Financial analysis is a similar process: you dig beneath the superficial layers of numbers, make comparisons, draw analogies, and arrive at an understanding of the true financial position of the company. However, the goal of financial statement analysis is not "knowledge for the sake of knowledge alone"; rather, it is to make business and investment decisions. By using financial statement analysis, you can discover the strengths and weaknesses of the company and answer the basic question "how is the company doing?" However, if you are analyzing a company other than your own, you will probably raise more questions than you can answer by looking at the numbers alone. You will incorporate these questions into the dialog you have with the management or owners of the company to get to the heart of the business.

Where do you start the process of financial analysis? You begin by reviewing the following financial data and documents. Putting the information into a spreadsheet format will enable you to analyze it more effectively because the important information will be on one page. This will also make it easier to spot both differences and trends.

> By using financial statement analysis, you can discover the strengths and weaknesses of the company.

1. Historical and normalized financial statements for at least three to five years
2. Historical and normalized common-size income statements and balance sheets for at least three to five years
3. Financial ratios for at least three to five years
4. Comparisons between the company being valued and industry averages
5. Comparisons between the company being valued and other specific businesses, if available

Common-Size Financial Statements

What are common-size financial statements? Just as the name implies, they are the accounting world's version of the "one-size-fits-all" tee shirt. You can create common-size financial statements by converting income statement and balance sheet line items into percentages of a total. The total for income statements is gross revenue or net sales, while the total for balance sheets is total assets. You are essentially using a series of ratios to create a standardized income statement and balance sheet. Creating these standardized statements will allow you to compare your company to companies of different sizes in the same industry and to compare it to published industry averages. You will also find common-size statements particularly useful when you want to identify trends or spot differences from year to year because the numbers, i.e., percentages, are already reduced to their lowest common denominator; therefore, they are much easier to comprehend. In addition, you will also use common-size statements as the foundation for ratio analysis, which is the next step in the financial statement analysis process. Using common-size statements to spot trends and make comparisons will save you time and effort at a minimum, and probably will make your analysis more effective as well. Even if you wanted to do all the calculations and analysis using dollar amounts, as a practical matter, you would have difficulty finding comparative information, especially industry averages, in absolute dollars.

How do you create a common-size statement? Looking at the income statement first, you would calculate a series of ratios where each line item was the numerator and net sales was the constant denominator. For example, if net sales are $150,000 and cost of goods sold is $90,000, then you calculate the ratio as follows:

$$\text{Common-size ratio} = \frac{\text{Cost of goods sold}}{\text{Net sales}}$$

$$60\% = \frac{\$90,000}{\$150,000}$$

You construct the common-size balance sheet in a similar way, but the constant denominator is total assets. Assume that accounts receivable are $50,000 and total assets are $200,000, you would calculate the ratio as follows:

$$\text{Common-size ratio} = \frac{\text{Accounts receivable}}{\text{Total assets}}$$

$$25\% = \frac{\$50,000}{\$200,000}$$

Then you put all the ratios together to create the common-size income statement and balance sheet. Look at the common-size statements for Riley's Gift Shop for the last three years:

CHART 18-1

RILEY'S GIFT SHOP
Common-Size Income Statements

DOLLARS, IN THOUSANDS				COMMON-SIZE PERCENTAGES		
YEAR 1	YEAR 2	YEAR 3	YEARS	YEAR 1	YEAR 2	YEAR 3
100	150	200	Revenue	100%	100%	100%
65	75	125	Cost of goods sold	65%	50%	63%
35	75	75	Gross profit	35%	50%	38%
18	17	20	Selling expense	18%	11%	10%
10	10	12	General and admin	10%	7%	6%
7	48	43	Operating income	7%	32%	22%
3	1	1	Interest expense	3%	1%	1%
4	47	42	Income before tax	4%	31%	21%
1	11.75	10.5	Provision for taxes	1%	8%	5%
3	35.25	31.5	Net income	3%	24%	16%

RILEY'S GIFT SHOP
Common-Size Balance Sheets

DOLLARS, IN THOUSANDS				COMMON-SIZE PERCENTAGES		
YEAR 1	YEAR 2	YEAR 3	YEARS	YEAR 1	YEAR 2	YEAR 3
10	15	20	Cash	14%	24%	33%
20	15	12	Accounts receivable	29%	24%	20%
25	20	18	Inventory	36%	32%	30%
55	50	50	Total current assets	79%	81%	83%
15	12	10	Property, plant, equipment	21%	19%	17%
70	62	60	Total assets	100%	100%	100%
25	20	30	Accounts payable	36%	32%	50%
10	8	5	Other current liabilities	14%	13%	8%
35	28	35	Total current liabilities	50%	45%	58%
20	17	15	Long-Term debt	29%	27%	25%
55	45	50	Total liabilities	79%	73%	83%
15	17	10	Shareholder's equity	21%	27%	17%
70	62	60	Total liabilities and equity	100%	100%	100%

When you look at Riley's historical income statements, you immediately notice that revenues are consistently increasing along with cash. These are of course both positive indications that the company is growing and has the cash to fund additional growth or payments to the owner. However, when you look at the common-size statements, you can see more easily that after an initial increase in gross profit and operating income, these important variables have fallen off significantly. Gross profit remained the same at $75,000 in years two and three, but as you can see in the common-size statement, this represents a 12% decline in the gross profit percentage.

Benchmarking and Best Practices

Just as you can use common-size statements to compare a company with itself, over time, you can also use it to compare with other companies. When you make the comparison with the best-performing company in your industry, that process is called benchmarking, and it can be used to model and improve your own company's performance. You can also compare your company to industry averages to get an understanding of your strengths and weaknesses in the marketplace. See Chapter 19 for a more detailed discussion of industry comparisons and trends.

Benchmarking is the process of identifying the companies that are the best at what they do and figuring out a way to measure the processes and strategies that have made them successful. The theory behind benchmarking is that by comparing your performance to the standards set by your most successful competitors, you can set appropriate goals and work to achieve those goals. If you wanted to not only run in the Boston Marathon, but have a chance at winning it, what would you do? First you would need to determine what time you would have to run to win the race. Since the late 1970s, the winning times have been consistently under two hours and ten minutes, so you set your sights on this goal and create a training program to help you achieve it. You would probably research the methods that other winners used to achieve this same goal or you might hire a coach who is familiar with these best practices to help you set appropriate goals and stay on track.

This is what benchmarking is all about—defining standards and best practices in order to develop a plan for improvement. Chris Bogan of Best

> When you make the comparison with the best-performing company in your industry, that process is called benchmarking.

Practices, LLC (✑*www.best-in-class.com*) reports that "benchmarking can yield great benefits in the education of executives and the realized performance improvements of operations. In addition, benchmarking can be used to determine strategic areas of opportunity."

Financial Ratios

> A ratio is a mathematical term that describes the relationship of two quantities as the result of one number divided by the other.

You can also analyze financial statements using ratio analysis. A ratio is a mathematical term that describes the relationship of two quantities as the result of one number divided by the other. You use a series of ratios when you create a common-size statement—e.g., you show the relationship of all of the line items on the income statement to total income, by dividing the line item quantity by the total income number. Theoretically, you could create ratios by dividing every income statement and balance sheet number by each other, but every number does not have a meaningful relationship with every other number. Although this may sound like free dating advice rather than financial advice, you need to look for numbers that do have meaningful relationships with each other. Fortunately, financial analysts and accountants of the past have winnowed down all the possible combinations and permutations to a relatively few key financial ratios. These key financial ratios fall into five basic categories:

- **Liquidity ratios**—These ratios indicate the financial health of the company and how easily it can pay its bills.
- **Growth ratios**—These ratios indicate whether the company is growing.
- **Efficiency ratios**—These ratios show how effectively a company uses its resources.
- **Profitability ratios**—These ratios indicate the relative ability of the company to make money.
- **Risk ratios**—These ratios indicate the level of risk inherent in the capital structure of the business.

Calculating ratio after ratio can become a mesmerizing activity, but remember that deriving the ratio is only the beginning. You can really gain insight into a company by understanding the meaningful relationships you've just described mathematically and using these ratios to:

- Compare to the same ratios, for the same company, over time
- Compare to industry standards or benchmarks
- Compare to the same ratios for other specific companies
- Compare to ratios produced by industry averages

Liquidity Ratios

Liquidity ratios indicate whether a company has adequate working capital. Consequently, bankers, investors, vendors, and other interested parties look closely and look often at the liquidity ratios of companies in which they have an interest. They want to know "are we going to get our money?" If you determine that the company does not have adequate working capital, that is obviously a weakness. You may also uncover, using liquidity ratios, that a company has excessive working capital, which can also be a weakness. How can a company have too much cash? If a company has too much cash on hand, it may not be employing their resources effectively to enhance growth or profitability. The two primary liquidity ratios are the current ratio and the quick ratio.

You calculate the current ratio by dividing current assets by current liabilities on the balance sheet. Current assets include accounts that are currently liquid or that the company could convert to cash within a year; e.g., cash, marketable securities, accounts receivable, and inventory. Current liabilities represent debts the company will have to pay within a year including accounts payable, current portion of long-term debt, deposits, accrued expenses, etc. Using Riley's Gift Shop as an example, you would calculate the current ratio for each of the three years as follows:

YEAR 1	$\dfrac{\text{Current assets}}{\text{Current liabilities}}$	=	$\dfrac{55}{35}$	=	1.57	**CHART 18-2**
YEAR 2	$\dfrac{\text{Current assets}}{\text{Current liabilities}}$	=	$\dfrac{50}{28}$	=	1.79	
YEAR 3	$\dfrac{\text{Current assets}}{\text{Current liabilities}}$	=	$\dfrac{50}{35}$	=	1.43	

The current ratios for Riley's Gift Shop indicate that the company has between $1.43 and $1.79 of current assets for each dollar of current liabilities. The traditional benchmark for the current ratio is 2:1, meaning that a company should have twice as many current assets as current liabilities.

The quick ratio is a more severe test of liquidity. You calculate the quick ratio by excluding inventory from current assets and dividing the remaining current assets by the current liabilities. The theory here is that the company won't be able to immediately convert inventory into cash, so it is not available to pay current liabilities; therefore, inventory should be excluded from the calculation. The traditional benchmark for the quick ratio is 1:1, meaning that the company should have liquid funds totaling the amount of outstanding payables and short-term debt. You would calculate the quick ratio for Riley's Gift Shop as follows:

CHART 18-3

$$\text{YEAR 1} \qquad \frac{\text{Current assets-inventory}}{\text{Current liabilities}} \quad = \quad \frac{55\text{-}25}{35} \quad = \quad .86$$

$$\text{YEAR 2} \qquad \frac{\text{Current assets-inventory}}{\text{Current liabilities}} \quad = \quad \frac{50\text{-}20}{28} \quad = \quad 1.07$$

$$\text{YEAR 3} \qquad \frac{\text{Current assets-inventory}}{\text{Current liabilities}} \quad = \quad \frac{50\text{-}18}{35} \quad = \quad .91$$

What do these liquidity ratios tell you about Riley's Gift Shop? Although the current ratio and quick ratio are below the benchmarks of 2:1 and 1:1 respectively, Riley's Gift Shop appears to have adequate working capital to meet its short-term needs. In this case, looking at the quick ratio is especially helpful in making this determination because the ratios for the three years indicate that Riley's has enough cash to just about pay all of the short-term debt without relying on the conversion of any inventory to cash. If, on the other hand, the company had the same current ratios, which average 1.6, and quick ratios of .5, this might indicate some pending cash flow problems. Although the liquidity ratios indicate that Riley's Gift Shop has enough cash flow to pay the bills, you need to also look at how the ratios change over time. In this case, the ratios improve significantly in year two, only to drop off in year three. This decline in liquidity in year three may be the beginning of a trend or a one-time phenomenon due to an unusual transaction. In either case, you need to look beyond the ratios to determine what is happening within the company.

You can see on the balance sheet that cash is increasing while accounts receivable are decreasing. Since revenue is also increasing, this means that the company is doing a good job collecting accounts receivable and converting them to cash—a positive indicator. However, you also can see that despite increasing sales, inventory is declining, yet accounts payable are increasing. The inventory decline could mean that the company has found the right mix of items so that greater sales can be maintained with less inventory—this would be a positive indicator. On the other hand, the company may not be able to sustain increased sales without increased inventory, so this becomes a question for management—"Why is inventory decreasing when sales are increasing?" Another question for management would be "Why are accounts payable increasing when inventory is decreasing while at the same time, cash on hand is growing?" This trend could just indicate poor management of the payables, which is not a major problem, but you might wonder if poor management or not paying attention to details in one area of the business may manifest itself in another area. Keep your eyes open.

Managing Accounts Receivables and Accounts Payable

You create accounts receivable each time you sell a product or service and the customer does not pay for it immediately. Accounting for accounts receivable is a multipart process that is the backbone of a company's cash flow management. Initially, you create an accounts receivable ledger to record each customer's charges and payment, which can double as a customer statement. You can do this manually or on the computer with an accounts receivable software package. When you sell something on credit, you record the sale as a credit to your sales account and a debit to accounts receivable. When customers pay their accounts, you post a credit to cash and a debit to accounts receivable.

You should develop a system to monitor and collect accounts receivable and follow it consistently. For example, you might send a second notice thirty days after the invoice, a third notice after sixty days, and at that time

You create accounts receivable each time you sell a product or service and the customer does not pay for it immediately.

turn these past due accounts over to someone to follow up with a phone call. After ninety days, you would pass along all of the documentation related to collection attempts to management so they (you) can determine whether to write off the amounts as bad debts. Or you may pursue further collection actions such as lawyers' letters, collection agencies, or filing a lien against the property of the nonpayer. Although implementing collection actions is an important component of managing accounts receivable, creating fair pricing and collection policies is just as important because people feel better about paying for something for which they received value.

Accounts payable are your company's unpaid bills for goods and services. Just as you keep accounts receivable ledgers for each customer, you should keep an accounts payable ledger for each vender. When you buy something on credit, you debit the expense or the asset account and credit accounts payable. When you make a payment, you debit the accounts payable account and credit cash. By keeping accurate and contemporaneous payables ledgers, you can easily verify the bills you receive and their due dates, which will help you manage your cash flow. You can monitor your accounts payable by preparing an aged accounts payable schedule, which is the same concept in reverse as the aged accounts receivable schedule you saw in Chapter 17. As with receivables, good accounts payable management starts with good policy. An authorization policy designates who can approve purchases of a certain amount and type. For example, managers must sign off on purchases over $100, the controller must authorize purchases over $5,000, and the president must sign off on all purchases greater than $10,000. The accounts payable department writes checks to pay invoices and an officer, other than the person who authorized the expenditure, signs the check after reviewing the amounts and the authorization to order.

> Accounts payable are your company's unpaid bills for goods and services.

Growth Ratios

Growth ratios indicate whether a company is growing or contracting. You will want to focus on the two most important growth indicators: sales growth and earnings growth. You calculate sales growth by subtracting the sales of the first period from the sales in the second period and dividing the total by the sales of the first period. Looking at the income statements for Riley's Gift Shop, you would calculate the sales growth ratio as follows:

$$\frac{\text{Year 2 revenue} - \text{Year 1 revenue}}{\text{Year 1 revenue}} \quad = \quad \frac{150 - 100}{100} \quad = \quad .50$$

CHART 18-4

$$\frac{\text{Year 3 revenue} - \text{Year 2 revenue}}{\text{Year 2 Revenue}} \quad = \quad \frac{200 - 150}{150} \quad = \quad .33$$

The sales growth ratio is most useful when you can look at multiple years to see the growth trend. In the Riley's Gift Shop example, sales grew a very healthy 50% between years one and two. However, even though sales grew by the same $50,000 between years two and three, you can see that this represents a decrease in the rate of growth from 50% to 33%. In an absolute sense, sales growth is good, whether it is 50% or 33%, but you will have a difficult time making a projection of future sales with just these two reference points. If possible, you should try to get at least five years of financial statements so you can have more data to make a determination regarding the growth trend.

Although sales growth is an important indicator of how well a company is doing, earnings growth is perhaps more important. It doesn't matter how much of something a company sells if it isn't making a profit on those sales. You calculate the earnings growth ratio by subtracting the earnings of the first period from the earnings of the second period and dividing the total by the earnings of the first period. Looking again at the income statement of Riley's Gift Shop, you would calculate the earnings growth ratio as follows:

$$\frac{\text{Year 2 earnings} - \text{Year 1 earnings}}{\text{Year 1 earnings}} \quad = \quad \frac{35.25 - 3}{3} \quad = \quad 10.75$$

CHART 18-5

$$\frac{\text{Year 3 earnings} - \text{Year 2 earnings}}{\text{Year 2 earnings}} \quad = \quad \frac{31.5 - 35.25}{35.25} \quad = \quad (.11)$$

You can see that Riley's Gift Shop had phenomenal earnings growth of more than 1,000% between years one and two to coincide with the 50% growth in sales. However, although sales growth continued into year three, albeit at a lower rate, earnings growth turned negative. What happened? The biggest percentage changes in sales and earnings occurred between the first start-up year and the second year, mainly because the first year numbers were extremely modest. Consequently, you magnify the increase by dividing by a smaller number. The more troubling change, however, is the decrease in earnings growth occurring in a period in which sales grew by 33%. You can see the primary reason for this if you focus on the *cost of goods sold* line item. Looking at the common-size income statements, you can see that the cost of goods sold was 63% of sales compared to 50% the year before, leaving a profit margin of 38% compared to 50% the previous year.

You may not have noticed this negative trend so easily if you just looked at the income statement with dollar amounts because the gross profit stayed exactly the same between years two and three at $75,000. If you look more closely, you will see that the cost of goods sold increased $50,000, which is the same amount that sales increased over the same period. This indicates that the company made absolutely no profit on these new sales, which indicates a problem. You may want to investigate pricing policy and verify that the inventory was properly counted, properly priced, and that the figures were extended properly. If the company made errors either in pricing items for sale or managing inventory, that could explain the negative earnings growth in light of sales growth. Otherwise, you have another question for management: "Why are earnings decreasing while sales are increasing?"

Efficiency Ratios

Efficiency ratios show how effectively a company manages its resources to generate revenue. Efficiency ratios are also known as activity ratios or turnover ratios. The **inventory turnover ratio** measures how quickly the company converts inventory into sales. You calculate the inventory turnover ratio by dividing the cost of goods sold by the average inventory. A high ratio indicates that purchases or other components of inventory, such as work in progress or finished goods, spend a relatively shorter time in inventory. In addition, you can convert the inventory turnover ratio to days sales in inventory by dividing 365 days by the inventory turnover ratio. This is especially helpful when comparing to other companies and industry standards. Looking at Riley's Gift Shop you calculate the inventory turnover ratio as follows:

> Efficiency ratios are also known as activity ratios or turnover ratios.

YEAR 2 $\dfrac{\text{Cost of goods sold}}{(\text{Beginning inventory + ending inventory}) / 2}$ = $\dfrac{75}{(25 + 20) / 2}$ = 3.33   **CHART 18-6**

YEAR 3 $\dfrac{\text{Cost of goods sold}}{(\text{Beginning inventory + ending inventory}) / 2}$ = $\dfrac{125}{(20 + 18) / 2}$ = 6.58

The year two turnover ratio of 3.33 means that the inventory turns over more than three times a year, while the year three inventory turnover ratio of 6.58 indicates a significant improvement to over six and a half times per year. You can convert the above calculations into days sales in inventory as follows:

YEAR 2 $\dfrac{365}{\text{Inventory turnover ratio}}$ = $\dfrac{365}{3.33}$ = 109.6 days   **CHART 18-7**

YEAR 3 $\dfrac{365}{\text{Inventory turnover ratio}}$ = $\dfrac{365}{6.58}$ = 55.47 days

Riley's gift shop improved its inventory turnover by cutting the days in inventory almost in half. This indicates that the company is operating more efficiently as far as inventory is concerned, thereby reducing the amount of money the company has to tie up in inventory. In addition, a higher turnover rate helps prevent inventory from becoming obsolete. Riley's Gift shop has improved its inventory turnover ratio, but is 6.58 a good rate? How does it compare to other companies or the industry as a whole? You can consult an Internet database such as BizStats.com to determine what the average turnover ratio or days sales in inventory is for companies in your industry. BizStats.com shows an inventory turnover ratio of 2.4 for gift, novelty, and souvenir shops that are organized as sole proprietors. They don't show any data for gift shops that are organized as corporations, so the default comparison becomes "other retail stores," which have an inventory turnover ratio of 4.3 and days sales in inventory of 89. Based on these industry averages, you can conclude that Riley's Gift Shop has gone from being a company that underperformed the industry in the area of inventory management to one that is outperforming the industry.

The **accounts receivable turnover ratio** measures how fast a company is turning its sales into cash. The receivables turnover should be compared to the credit policy of the company to determine whether collections are on target or lagging. You calculate the accounts receivable turnover by dividing credit sales by the average accounts receivable. If you can't determine the percentage of sales that are on credit, you would use net sales in the calculation. In either case, you will need to pay attention to how industry standards or averages are calculated so you can make appropriate comparisons with the ratios you calculate. The accounts receivable turnover ratio can also be converted to days sales in accounts receivable by dividing 365 by the accounts receivable turnover ratio. Looking at the balance sheet and income statement of Riley's Gift Shop, you would calculate the accounts receivable turnover as follows:

CHART 18-8

$$\text{YEAR 2} \quad \frac{\text{Net sales}}{\text{(Beginning A/R + ending A/R) / 2}} = \frac{150}{(20 + 15) / 2} = 8.57$$

$$\text{YEAR 3} \quad \frac{\text{Net sales}}{\text{(Beginning A/R + ending A/R) / 2}} = \frac{200}{(15 + 12) / 2} = 14.81$$

The year two turnover ratio of 8.57 means that the accounts receivable turn over about eight and a half times a year, while the year three turnover ratio of 14.81 indicates that the company has increased its collections significantly to almost fifteen times a year. Rather than thinking in terms of turns, you will probably find it more "user friendly" to convert these turnover ratios into days in accounts receivable as follows:

CHART 18-9

$$\text{YEAR 2} \quad \frac{365}{\text{Receivable turnover ratio}} = \frac{365}{8.57} = 42.59$$

$$\text{YEAR 3} \quad \frac{365}{\text{Receivable turnover ratio}} = \frac{365}{14.81} = 24.64$$

If you assume that Riley's Gift Shop has credit terms of thirty days, and over half of their business is cash rather than credit, then the forty plus days in accounts receivable for year two indicate a very poor collection efficiency.

The year three number of around twenty-five days in receivables is more reasonable because it reflects the fact that a number of the sales were made in cash, thereby bringing the number down below the number of days in the stated credit policy.

Profitability Ratios

Profitability ratios measure the most important aspect of a business—its ability to earn income. You can learn a lot about a company by reviewing its profitability ratios over time, and you can use this information to make projections of future income. Projecting future income is a cornerstone of many valuation methods and is also an important management tool for budgeting and strategic planning within the company.

You calculate the profit margin, also known as gross profit or return on sales, by subtracting cost of goods sold from sales, and if you want to express this number as a percentage, you divide it by the total sales. The higher the profit margin, the more income the company has available to pay other expenses and give a return to the investors. The profit margin measures the company's ability to contain expenses related to sales and to appropriately price the goods for sale.

If you look at the common-size income statement for Riley's Gift Shop, you can see that the gross profit is already calculated and incorporated into the financial statements. Riley's gross profit is 35%, 50%, and 38% for years one through three, which compares to a 43.8% average gross profit for small gift, novelty, and souvenir shops businesses that BizStats.com reports. Riley's percentages aren't completely out of line unless the downward trend between years two and three continue.

Return on assets reflects how well the company can generate sales with their current asset mix. You can compare the return on the investment you make in a company's assets to the return you could receive by investing in a safe investment such as Treasury bills or CDs. Since investing in a company is riskier than investing in T-bills, you should expect a higher return. You calculate return on assets by dividing net income by average assets. Ideally you should use net income before interest expense since interest represents the cost of acquiring assets. Looking at Riley's Gift Shop again, you can calculate the return on assets as follows:

> Projecting future income is a cornerstone of many valuation methods.

CHART 18-10

YEAR 2 $$\frac{\text{Net income + interest expense}}{\text{(Average assets)}} = \frac{36.25}{(70 + 62) / 2} = .55$$

YEAR 3 $$\frac{\text{Net income + interest expense}}{\text{(Average assets)}} = \frac{32.5}{(62 + 60) / 2} = .53$$

You can see that Riley's Gift Shop return on assets of more than 50% is well above the return on assets that an investor could hope to receive in the marketplace of safe investments. Another measure of management performance is return on investment or shareholders' equity (ROE). This ratio reflects the income produced by the amount of the shareholders' investment. You calculate this ratio by dividing net income by the average shareholders' equity. Using the information for Riley's Gift Shop, you would calculate the return on investment as follows:

CHART 18-11

YEAR 2 $$\frac{\text{Net income}}{\text{Average shareholders' equity}} = \frac{35.25}{(15 + 17) / 2} = 2.20$$

YEAR 3 $$\frac{\text{Net income}}{\text{Average shareholders' equity}} = \frac{31.5}{(17 + 10) / 2} = 2.33$$

The high return on investment for Riley's Gift Shop indicates that management is doing a good job creating earnings on a relatively small shareholder investment. Although income decreased between years two and three, the ROE increased because shareholders' equity decreased, probably due to payment of dividends. Overall, the basic profitability ratios indicate that Riley's Gift Shop is very profitable.

Risk Ratios

Risk ratios reflect the percentage of debt a company has in its capital structure. Debt is synonymous with risk because it creates an obligation to pay interest in addition to principle, and creditors usually have recourse if the company doesn't pay. Equity financing on the other hand is less risky because the company does not have a legal obligation to pay its investors. With closely held businesses, especially start-up companies, bankers or other lenders like to see the owners "put their money where their mouth is" and have a substantial capital investment before the lending institution will commit its funds. On the other hand, entrepreneurs usually want to capitalize their businesses with as little of their own money as possible. These opposing perspectives play out in the risk and return ratios. As you saw in the return on equity calculations for Riley's Gift Shop, the ROE was very high, due in large part to the fact that the shareholders' investment was low.

The first risk ratio is the **debt to asset ratio,** which you calculate by simply dividing the total debt by the total assets. This ratio reflects the amount of debt the company is using to finance its assets. The second risk ratio is the **debt to equity ratio,** which you calculate by dividing total debt by total equity. This ratio reflects the relative risk of the creditors versus the investors. The higher the ratio, the more risk is being born by creditors and the less remaining debt capacity, which means that the company may not be able to borrow in the future. Both these situations indicate that the company is riskier than a similar company with a lower debt to equity ratio.

What do the risk ratios indicate for Riley's Gift Shop?

YEAR 1	$\dfrac{\text{Total debt}}{\text{Total assets}}$	=	$\dfrac{55}{70}$	=	.79	**CHART 18-12**
YEAR 2	$\dfrac{\text{Total debt}}{\text{Total assets}}$	=	$\dfrac{45}{62}$	=	.73	
YEAR 3	$\dfrac{\text{Total debt}}{\text{Total assets}}$	=	$\dfrac{50}{60}$	=	.83	
YEAR 1	$\dfrac{\text{Total debt}}{\text{Total equity}}$	=	$\dfrac{55}{15}$	=	3.67	
YEAR 2	$\dfrac{\text{Total debt}}{\text{Total equity}}$	=	$\dfrac{45}{17}$	=	2.65	
YEAR 3	$\dfrac{\text{Total debt}}{\text{Total equity}}$	=	$\dfrac{50}{10}$	=	5	

The risk ratios indicate that Riley's finances about 80% of its assets with debt and that debt exceeds equity by a five-to-one ratio in year three. Both of these risk ratios highlight that Riley's Gift Shop is highly risky, which correlates with the high positive return on equity that the investors are receiving.

Ratio analysis is a good tool to analyze financial statements because you can highlight strengths and weaknesses, assess management performance, and see trends over time. With ratios you can compare companies of different sizes and make comparisons with industry averages and benchmark standards. You can also use ratio analysis, especially over time, to help you formulate projections for the future. In the next chapter you will build on the concept of ratio analysis to look at various economic trends.

➤ Chapter 19

Comparative Analysis

Part One

Part Two

Part Three

Part Four

Part Five

Part Six

<table>
<tr><td>262</td><td>What Is Comparative Analysis?</td></tr>
<tr><td>262</td><td>Database Information</td></tr>
<tr><td>263</td><td>Using a Database to Make a Comparative Analysis</td></tr>
<tr><td>267</td><td>Industry Trends</td></tr>
<tr><td>269</td><td>Industry Consolidation and Change</td></tr>
<tr><td>271</td><td>Industry Regulation and License Requirements</td></tr>
<tr><td>272</td><td>Effects of Competition</td></tr>
<tr><td>273</td><td>Economic Trends</td></tr>
<tr><td>274</td><td>Forecasting the Economic Future</td></tr>
<tr><td>275</td><td>Local and Regional Economic Issues</td></tr>
</table>

PART FIVE: BASIC BUSINESS VALUATION CALCULATIONS AND ANALYSIS

■ CHAPTER 15 Analyzing the Balance Sheet ■ CHAPTER 16 Analyzing the Other Financial Statements ■ CHAPTER 17 "Normalizing" the Financial Statements ■ CHAPTER 18 Financial Analysis ■ CHAPTER 19 Comparative Analysis ■ CHAPTER 20 Qualitative Analysis

What Is Comparative Analysis?

Comparative analysis is what you do with all the normalized statements and ratios you learned to create in Chapters 17 and 18. Your obvious goal in using comparative analysis is to see how the company you are valuing compares to its peers and/or the best companies in the industry. This information is very useful in the valuation process—at a minimum you can use it to help you choose appropriate capitalization and discount rates, and, if you are fortunate, you can use it to compare to actual sales of similar companies. Of course, the more "similar" the similar company, the better. Some of the points of similarity you should consider include:

- Are the companies in the same industry?
- Are the companies in the same line of business within the industry?
- Do they have similar products or services?
- Are the companies relatively the same size?
- Do the companies use the same accounting methods?
- Do the companies have the same form of organization and similar capital structure?

Comparative analysis can also help you improve your business from an operating standpoint, even if you are not planning to sell it, by identifying problem areas and providing reasonable targets to aim for as you adjust your business policies and practices.

Database Information

How do you find all this information about other similar companies so you can make these insightful comparisons? The easy answer, in one word, is "databases." However, you will find a lot of different databases, so you will need to choose the one(s) that you think are most appropriate to the company you are valuing.

RMA *Annual Statement Studies* is the Bible of comparative industry data. According to the RMA Web site, at *www.rmahq.org*, "the *Statement Studies* captures financial statement data on commercial loan customers and prospects for more than 600 industries. It also provides composite ratios and financial statement benchmarks. A complete time series of data is available in an electronic format that spans the last twenty years. Custom uses of the database include scorecard development, risk grading, marketing identification, and portfolio management." RMA derives their benchmarks from the financial statements of more than 150,000 businesses that have submitted loan applications to banks and other lenders. The *Annual Statement Studies* include the following information for each industry:

- Common-size balance sheets and income statements
- Sixteen key financial statement ratios based on year-end statement data
- Information is grouped into six different size categories
- Industries are categorized according to SIC codes (Standard Industrial Classification) and cross-referenced to the NAICS codes (North American Industry Classification System.)
- Trend data is shown for four years

Using a Database to Make a Comparative Analysis

1. Prepare common-size income statements and balance sheets.
2. Calculate key financial ratios.
3. Determine the SIC code (Standard Industrial Classification) and/or the NAICS code (North American Industry Classification System).
4. Look up the RMA or other database financial statement study for the appropriate SIC or NAICS code.
5. Create a spreadsheet with columns for the company financial ratios, the industry ratios from the appropriate size category, the difference between the two, and comments.
6. Analyze the comparative information and draw conclusions.

Who or What Is RMA?

RMA was founded in 1914 as Robert Morris Associates and changed its name in 2000 to the Risk Management Association. RMA is a member-driven professional organization of banks and other lending institutions whose mission is to advance sound risk management principles in the financial services industry. The company was originally named for one of the founders of our country, Robert Morris (1733–1806). Morris was a respected businessperson and signer of the Declaration of Independence who spent several years in debtor's prison near the end of his life due to a failed land speculation. Allen Sanborn, president and CEO of RMA at the time of the name change, indicated in a press release that although Morris' tragic story illustrates the risks inherent in the financial services industry, the new name, Risk Management Association, better reflects the mission and work of the company.

You would use this same methodology to do a comparative analysis using any of the myriad of databases available in the marketplace and on the Internet. The following spreadsheet shows excerpts from a hypothetical comparative analysis of No Bones About It, Inc., a dog food manufacturer. Dog food manufacturers are classified as SIC code 2048, so you find the industry information corresponding to this SIC code. (Starting with the 2003/2004 *Annual Statement Studies*, RMA will begin using NAICS codes but will reference SIC codes until 2005.) In a complete analysis, you would compare all of the basic categories on your common-size income statement and balance sheet to the respective industry numbers.

CHART 19-1

NO BONES ABOUT IT, INC.

Comparative Analysis

	NO BONES	INDUSTRY	DIFF	COMMENTS
Balance sheet items:				
Total assets (000's)	2,944	3,400	(456)	
Current assets/total assets	18.0	63.1	(45.1)	Negative
Inventory/total assets	4.45	27.6	(23.2)	Negative
Fixed assets/total assets	21.0	31.3	(10.3)	
Current liabilities/total assets	19.3	4.2	15.1	Negative
Total debt/total assets	85.1	92	(6.9)	Positive
Net worth/total assets	14.9	8	6.9	Positive
Income statement items:				
Annual sales (000's)	2,764	15,237	(12,473)	Negative
Gross profit/sales	59.3	36.2	23.1	Positive
Operating profit/sales	20.1	4	16.1	Positive
EBT/sales	21.0	2.7	18.3	Positive
Turnover ratios:				
Accounts receivable	12.4	15.4	(3.0)	Positive
Inventory	21.1	16.4	4.7	Positive
Fixed assets	4.5	14.4	(9.9)	Negative
Total assets	1.0	4.52	(3.52)	Negative

NO BONES ABOUT IT, INC.

CHART 19-1
(continued)

Comparative Analysis

	NO BONES	INDUSTRY	DIFF	COMMENTS
Profitability:				
Pretax ROA	29.3	6.6	22.7	very positive
Pretax ROE	159.0	153	6	positive
Risk:				
Current ratio	0.9	1.5	(.6)	Negative
Quick ratio	0.7	0.9	(.2)	Negative
Debt/equity	5.7	6.3	(.6)	Positive

You can see that some of the ratios compare favorably and some compare negatively. Consequently, you need to assess the relative importance of the various indicators in making a judgment about how this company compares to others in its industry. The profitability ratios indicate that No Bones About It, Inc. is more profitable than the industry averages. In addition, the total debt to equity ratio is positive despite the negative indications related to liquidity ratios and asset composition. These factors indicate that No Bones About It, Inc. is an industry leader; therefore, you would attribute more value to it than a similar, but less successful, company.

SIC and NAICS Codes

A now defunct committee established by the Central Statistical Board of the United States government developed the Standard Industrial Classification (SIC) system in the 1930s to provide uniform and comparable data about business and industry to all levels of government, trade associations, businesses, and researchers. As you might imagine, this classification system has not kept pace with the growth, diversity, and globalization of business over the last fifty years. A branch of the OMB (Office of Management and Budget), in conjunction with statistical agencies in Canada and Mexico, developed the new North American Industry Classification System (NAICS). Their goal was to provide international comparability and more useful information about a wider range of businesses including those in the growing service and technology sectors.

The OMB adopted NAICS in 1997, and the international committee, under their purview, will review the system every five years to ensure its continued relevance as economies and businesses change. Government agencies and other providers of statistical information about business are adopting NAICS, so SIC codes will become a relic of the past. However, since many databases are in transition, you can still use a SIC code to find comparative data, but you should start making the transition and check out a conversion table such as the one the U.S. Census Bureau provides on their Web site at ✍ *www.census.gov/epcd/www/naicstab.htm*. You can find SIC codes in the *Standard Industrial Classification Manual* and NAICS codes in the *North American Industry Classification System* at a library near you.

Where Can You Look for Other Databases?

In contrast to the RMA databases that use information gathered from banks and other lenders, several other useful databases incorporate information derived from corporate income tax returns. One of the benefits of these IRS-based databases is that their creators have a lot of data points to draw on, making their results more consistent. On the other hand, retrieving millions of data points from the IRS is a long process; consequently, these databases use information that may be three or more years old. *IRS Corporate Ratios,* published by John Wiley & Sons, includes data derived from more than 3.7 million tax returns that is categorized into 235 industries. You can easily use this software database to compare companies of similar size in the same industry because the information is further divided into six groups by total asset size. Leo Troy also compiles the *Almanac of Business and Industrial Financial Ratios* from Internal Revenue Service information about corporate tax returns. Although the *Almanac* does not cover as many industries as RMA, the information can provide valuable comparisons since similar statistics are derived from different sources. In addition, Troy includes information from start-up and unprofitable companies.

Dun & Bradstreet annually publish *Industry Norms and Key Business Ratios,* using information they derive from credit reports. Their information is current to the previous year and they include some industries that are not routinely covered in other databases. Financial Research Associates publish

Financial Studies of Small Business using financial statements of small companies, which they gather from certified public accountants across the country. This reference book is especially noteworthy because it provides data for much smaller firms than most of the other databases. Therefore, the information is more comparable to small closely held businesses.

Industry Trends

You just learned how to do a comparative industry analysis from a quantitative perspective, but qualitative factors are also important. Is the industry robust and growing, or has it crashed and burned like the dot-com sector did at the turn of the twenty-first century? How is technology influencing productivity and required investment in the industry? What is the regulatory climate of the industry? Some of the qualitative issues you should consider about the industry as a whole include:

- Is the market expanding, contracting, becoming global, or staying the same?
- Is the industry consolidating or franchising?
- What is the effect of technology?
- How will current or proposed regulations influence your business?
- What is your company's relative market position in the industry?

Market Changes and Trends

Understanding the market for the product or service provided by your business or one you are valuing is essential for arriving at a good valuation number. Up to this point, you have just looked at historical numbers or made projections based on these figures. If you were lucky, you were able to see some clear trends to help you make reasonable projections based on this data. However, no matter how profitable you have been in the past, that trend won't continue if you are making a product that will become obsolete or if your competitor can now produce the same thing at half the price by moving his operations to a developing nation.

How can a product become obsolete if it is a good product and you are manufacturing it efficiently? That is probably what the executives at

Understanding the market for the product or service provided by your business or one you are valuing is essential for arriving at a good valuation number.

Sony Corporation thought in the 1980s when they had the corner on the market of the Beta video format, which was arguably a better product than the VHS format that eclipsed it by the late 1980s. Sony finally adopted an "if you can't beat 'em, join 'em" attitude and started making VHS video recorders, but they never duplicated the brand recognition they had with the "Sony Betamax" product. When is the last time you saw a Beta videotape? You may be able to ask yourself the same question soon about VHS tapes—and get the same answer since DVDs began gobbling up shelf space at the video store at a rapid pace.

What if you are valuing a company that makes equipment for the textile industry? Even if nothing has changed regarding the production of the equipment, the factories, and employees—the market has changed. Since the implementation of the North American Free Trade Act (NAFTA) in 1994, many U.S. textile companies have either folded or moved their operations to Mexico or other foreign countries where they can employ cheap labor. This changing market may increase the demand for new machines as new plants are established, but perhaps the company will have to manufacture to new specifications and certainly will need to offer instructions and training in other languages. The client relationships that the company has built over time may be nullified overnight. Does the company need a new sales and marketing team to sell their product in a new environment or can the current team be retrained? What will all of these changes cost? Can the company adapt? You must factor the answers to these questions into your projection for the future and your ultimate valuation of the company.

> Since the implementation of NAFTA in 1994, many U.S. textile companies have either folded or moved their operations to Mexico or other foreign countries.

Discovering Market Trends Before They Overtake the Industry

If you are not already in the type of business you are valuing, the best place to start is with the owner of the company. Ask him or her "What are the market trends you see affecting this industry in the next three- to five- and five- to ten-year periods?" and "What are you doing to position your company to take advantage of opportunities or withstand the challenges of these changes?" Beyond that, ask them about any industry associations or publications they use for information and guidance. You can also consult the Gale Research publications *Encyclopedia of Associations* and the

Encyclopedia of Business Information for extensive information about different industries and professions.

In addition, online services such as the annual *BusinessWeek Industry Outlook* and *Hoover's Industry Snapshot* give very current analysis on the market trends of selected businesses and industries. *Standard & Poor's Industry Surveys* provides a basic analysis of about thirty to forty industries and the *US Industry and Trade Outlook* examines national and international market trends and the factors affecting them. This publication utilizes a unique combination of public and private sector experts from U.S. government agencies and McGraw-Hill's Standard & Poor's financial services to provide both information and ideas for business development. IndustryLink.com is a product of Kuhn Technology Marketing, one of Canada's leading industry-to-industry marketing agencies. This Web site provides information about foreign and U.S. industries and market segments with an orientation toward technology companies. The Research Bank Web at *www.Investext.com* is another Web-based resource that you can use to access research reports from more than 600 investment and research firms about market and industry trends in specific industries and global emerging markets. The Research Bank Web is being integrated into Thomson Research at *http//:research.thomsonib.com*. The international consulting firm, McKinsey & Co., publishes the *McKinsey Quarterly* online, which provides in-depth articles about major industries and their leaders.

Industry Consolidation and Change

In addition to understanding market trends, do you know if your industry is consolidating or franchising? These industry trends are very important to the value of your company. The trend toward consolidation in many industries produces both winners and losers within the industry. The obvious winners in a consolidating industry are the industry giants who can attain economies of scale and undercut their competition on the basis of price. Consolidation not only increases the barriers to entry in an industry, but also usually causes a "shake-out" when the medium-size businesses in the industry can't make the necessary investment to stay competitive with the consolidators. Sometimes this provides an opportunity for the medium or small industry participants to be purchased by the consolidators. At the beginning of a consolidation phase, the values of the target companies are generally higher than they will be after the initial round of purchases. This is the case for two reasons: The consolidators usually will initially pay a premium to attract unwilling sellers, and they will try to find the best companies in the field or the geographic region. If the major industry consolidators have made their purchases and are now concentrating on eliminating competition, the values of some of the medium or small members of the industry may decline in the face of narrowing profit margins caused by greater competition and fewer exit strategy options.

This is what happened when the accounting industry started consolidating in the late 1990s and early 2000s. Financial services companies such as American Express, Century Business Services, and H & R Block started to buy individual certified public accounting firms. In addition to economies of scale, these companies wanted a captive market to which they could sell financial products and services using a "most trusted advisor," the CPA. Initially, these companies were paying well over the industry standard of 100% of annual gross revenue to purchase accounting firms. Now, the consolidators are not in a buying frenzy, and the value of accounting firms has decreased to historical or below normal levels.

However, consolidation does provide the opportunity for smaller businesses in an industry to specialize. You need to assess the potential impact of consolidation on your business or the business you are valuing. Is the company going to be an early adapter and sell out? Will the company refocus on a profitable niche? Should you consider becoming a franchisee of a larger company? What are the costs and benefits of each of these strategies?

What effect will changing technology have on the industry? Will technology completely pass you by, or will the cost of adopting new technology be prohibitive? Will new technology make your company more productive? You won't always find it easy to address the issue of technology, but it is important you do so and estimate the costs and benefits that will affect the value of the company. You will find a lot of information about technological change in industry publications and from trade associations. Look at the advertisements for new products, software, etc., and review the course listings for continuing professional education related to technology. Contact the speakers who are giving the seminars and courses on technology in a particular industry. They may be able to refer you to some other sources of information about the anticipated effects of technology in their industry or

> You won't always find it easy to address the issue of technology, but it is important you do so.

give you all the information you need to factor in the costs and benefits of technology to the company you are valuing.

Industry Regulation and License Requirements

Industry regulation is another external factor that can have a profound effect on the value of a business. Government regulations, in particular, can be almost impossible to understand, difficult and expensive to implement, and can have either a positive or negative effect on a particular company. The tax laws are a good example of this—nobody can completely understand them; businesses pay thousands of dollars in professional fees and in-house salaries to comply; and sometimes an industry or a company may preferentially benefit from a particular credit, such as the low income housing credit. The Environmental Protection Agency (EPA) and the Occupational Safety and Health Administration (OSHA) also have a myriad of complex and changing regulations affecting industry, which were instituted to help individuals or society at large. When you are valuing a company, you should try to extract the costs a company spends for compliance with these regulations and track these numbers to better assess the costs and trends of regulation.

In addition to complying with government regulations, many industries, and especially professions, also need licenses and must adhere to trade or professional rules of conduct. The theory behind licenses and professional regulation is that of protecting the public interest and safety. For example, you would want to know that a doctor who is operating on you passed all the necessary tests to become a licensed physician and is staying current by attending continuing professional education classes. Other professions such as architects and engineers are protecting the public's physical safety by having strict licensure and continuing education requirements.

You have probably heard of the bar exam and the CPA exam, which are parts of the licensure requirements for lawyers and CPAs. In addition to passing these grueling exams, lawyers and CPAs must adhere to professional codes of ethics and must take a certain number of hours each year of continuing professional education. In each state, the state bar and the state board of CPA examiners regulate the professions from a licensure perspective. The state bar association and state CPA association, along with their national counterparts the American Bar Association and American Institute of CPAs, are professional membership organizations that help self-regulate these professions from a professional conduct and ethics standpoint.

In addition to protecting the public interest, licenses also serve to regulate the number of practitioners or operators in a business. The laws of supply and demand indicate that the price for a product or service will be higher if the demand is more than the supply. For example, if anyone could sell liquor without a license, the price of the licenses and the price of liquor would be lower. Conversely, liquor licenses are very expensive because they are not readily available, and bar owners can build a high profit margin into the sales price of alcoholic beverages because regulation has reduced the competition.

Usually, professional regulations don't change drastically in a short period of time, but they can, and when this happens, the value of the regulated businesses can change drastically as well. Witness the Sarbanes-Oxley bill passed by Congress in 2002, which places severe restrictions on CPA firms who audit clients listed with the SEC (Securities and Exchange Commission). This bill effectively prohibits accountants who are auditing SEC clients from performing nonaudit services. Most large CPA firms are also consulting firms. Why? Consulting is where the money is. Compliance services like audits usually are awarded to the low bidder and, therefore, are priced as commodities, not value-added services. In the past, CPA firms could leverage the information and contacts they acquired performing the lower margin audits by having their consulting arm provide value-added tax and business planning services at premium rates. Even before this legislation, accounting firms started spinning off their consulting divisions to address independence issues and prepare for anticipated legislation. Although this legislation currently affects only large accounting firms who audit large publicly traded companies, smaller accounting firms are expecting a "trickle-down" effect and are taking similar actions. Needless to say, spinning off the most profitable part of a business due to regulation or anticipated regulation can have a dramatic effect on the value of a company.

Effects of Competition

Deregulation can have similar consequences. Deregulation of industries such as airlines and telecommunications have negatively affected the former industry leaders who previously operated in a quasi-monopoly environment. The lowered stock prices of these publicly traded companies reflect that the market has efficiently and effectively devalued them. However, many new competitors have been able to enter the field, often with artificially lowered barriers to entry. If you are valuing one of these companies that had been operating in a small niche or is just forming to take advantage of the increased opportunities provided by deregulation, you may be able to factor in more rapid growth than you otherwise would have considered in your valuation.

If you are valuing your own company, you most certainly know who your competitors are. On the other hand, if you are valuing another company, especially if you are planning to purchase it, you need to find out about the competition. In either case you should create a chart showing the names, locations, size, estimated market share, market focus, and assessment of the competitive advantages and disadvantages of the various companies. In addition, you need to factor in the effects of new or potential competition. For example, has the city council approved any new shopping centers on the outskirts of town that will have a large grocery store as an anchor tenant? If so, this may significantly reduce the value of an otherwise profitable mom-and-pop grocery in town.

Economic Trends

How is your company affected by actual or anticipated changes in the economy? Some companies can be devastated by an extended downturn in the economy and others can benefit from it. For example, fine dining restaurants usually experience a decrease in patrons during recessions, while fast food or other "low-end" establishments may actually see an increase in customers. Generally, economic factors play a greater role in industries where consumers or businesses are purchasing goods and services that they consider luxuries rather than necessities. However, the economy does not always affect industries in a logical way. For instance, companies or industries that market high-end goods and services to the very rich may not see a decline in business during recessions because their customers may not experience the same decreased cash flow as the rest of the society.

Consequently, before you start analyzing the economy, you should understand how the industry and the company you are valuing behave

> Some companies can be devastated by an extended downturn in the economy and others can benefit from it.

under different economic conditions. You can get this information by reading the industry analyses referenced above, reviewing the historical financial trends in the industry, and by reviewing the historical financial experience of the company you are valuing. Once you have the industry and company financial information for a period of years, you can easily create a graph or chart by plotting key numbers such as gross sales or net profit against a general measure of the economy such as the Dow Jones Industrial Average. This type of graph will allow you to readily visualize whether the company and industry you are investigating move with the economy, lag behind it, or run counter to it.

Forecasting the Economic Future

Now that you know how the industry and company you are valuing behave in economic downturns or upsurges, you can join the economists, prognosticators, astrologers, and everyone else who is trying to predict what the economy will do. Where should you begin? You can start by taking advantage of the experts' number crunching and thoughtful analysis that is communicated in an understandable, even interesting, manner in the popular business press. The *Wall Street Journal, Fortune, Barron's,* and *BusinessWeek* are the leading publications that report statistical data about the economy and also analyze and synthesize the information. All of these publications make general economic forecasts on a regular basis and often have specific forecasts for a number of industries. The economic statistics that the staff economists and writers of these publications use in their analysis is directly available to you, so you can verify their analyses or form your own opinion that may be very different.

The U.S. government and banks compile most of the information that economists, or you, can use to make informed opinions of where the economy is going. The Board of Governors of the Federal Reserve System in Washington, D.C. publishes the *Federal Reserve Bulletin* on a monthly basis. The *Bulletin* includes information about key interest rates and other monetary statistics, employment statistics, consumer prices, housing starts, and other leading economic indicators. The U.S. Department of Commerce publishes the *Survey of Current Business* on a monthly basis, which includes statistics on all phases of the economy with an emphasis on statistics effecting business. In addition, the *Survey* includes an analysis of business and economic developments that makes the raw statistics more accessible. The *Statistical Abstract of the United States* is another Department of Commerce publication that includes comprehensive statistics on all aspects of the U.S. economy. The *Statistical Abstract* is an annual publication that also includes some international statistics for comparison purposes. Several of the Federal Reserve Banks publish information and statistics about economic trends on a quarterly, monthly, or even weekly basis. You can find these publications in libraries or on the Web sites for the various federal reserve banks.

Local and Regional Economic Issues

Even if you can assimilate all of this economic information and you feel comfortable with where the national economy is going, you need to give some thought to the local and regional economy. Obviously, the national economy will have a major impact on the local economy, but often that impact can be felt at a later time or it could be exacerbated or softened by factors present in the local economy. For example, if the business you are valuing is located in a region that is heavily dependent on manufacturing, this area will probably experience a deeper and longer recession in a severe economic downturn than an area with a more balanced economic base. Manufacturing companies often reduce their work force when business declines, so this creates an area of high unemployment, which negatively affects the demand for goods and services of all kinds. Another example would be a service business or retail store that is located in a region near a military base. If the government deploys a large number of the soldiers at the base to fight a war, the local economy will suffer because the consumers of the goods and services will not be there. Again, this has a ripple effect throughout the economy. On the other hand, if the business you are valuing is located in an area near a large defense contractor, you might expect the economy to preferentially pick up as production at the plant picks up in anticipation of war.

How do you find out about local and regional economies? Most state governments have useful statistics on their Web sites about population, employment, and income. In addition, you can often find state and regional economic forecasts there as well. State and local chambers of commerce

> The national economy will have a major impact on the local economy, but often that impact can be felt at a later time.

and economic development agencies also collect and publish similar information on a county-by-county basis. You can access their information by calling or writing them directly or often you can find the relevant information posted on their Web site. The best way to get information about state and regional economies is to conduct a search on the Internet. In addition to finding links to the statistics provided by governmental and business organizations, you will usually find references to articles and forecasts about the economy. As with any Internet search, you need to be careful to do your own due diligence because information found on the Internet is not necessarily corroborated or correct. Usually you can be comfortable with your findings if the analyses and forecasts are consistent with the raw data you have found and several sources seem to be saying similar things.

If the Internet is not for you, you can use reference books such as *Regional Economies and Markets*, which is published by a division of the Conference Board. Woods & Poole Economics, an independent firm that specializes in county economics and demographics, publishes several good resources: *The Complete Economic and Demographic Data Source, State Profiles*, and *MSA Profiles*. You can also contact state and local economic agencies directly for a wealth of information as well as chambers of commerce. Don't forget to read the local or regional newspaper to get a sense of the general economic trend—are the articles optimistic or pessimistic about the economy?

Now that you have considered some of the external qualitative factors that will influence the value of a company, you should next look at some of the qualitative factors that are particular to the business you are valuing.

► Chapter 20

Qualitative Analysis

Part One

Part Two

Part Three

Part Four

Part Five

Part Six

PART FIVE: BASIC BUSINESS VALUATION CALCULATIONS AND ANALYSIS

■ CHAPTER 15 Analyzing the Balance Sheet ■ CHAPTER 16 Analyzing the Other Financial Statements

■ CHAPTER 17 "Normalizing" the Financial Statements ■ CHAPTER 18 Financial Analysis

■ CHAPTER 19 Comparative Analysis ■ CHAPTER 20 Qualitative Analysis

What Is Qualitative Analysis?

When you paraphrase the common expression, "quality, not quantity" to "qualitative, not quantitative," you get the sense of what qualitative analysis is about. It is not row after row of numbers or calculations. Rather, qualitative analysis involves examining the nonfinancial aspects of a company or industry that influenced its performance in the past and may affect its future success. Some of the elements of comparative analysis discussed in Chapter 19, such as economic trend analysis, are included in the broad category of qualitative analysis. In Chapter 20, the focus will be on the qualitative analysis of factors internal to a company, such as the history of the company, the products and services, suppliers and customers, the work force, and the tangible assets of the company.

Qualitative analysis will give you information about whether additional investments may need to be made in human or physical resources to maintain productivity. In addition, this type of analysis will help you determine the relative risk of the company, which is crucial to choosing the correct discount or capitalization rate you will ultimately use in your valuation calculation. Qualitative analysis helps you go beyond what a company looks like on paper to what it looks like in real life. Qualitative analysis of a company is just like kicking the tires of a used car before you buy it. When you kick the tires of the used car, you have to actually go and look at the car and speak to the person selling it. This first impression can make a huge difference in your decision to purchase the car, no matter how good it looks on paper. Do you like or dislike the style and/or color of the car? Is it clean? Is the owner a little old lady or a sixteen-year-old boy? Did they maintain it? Similarly, the qualitative factors you examine in the course of valuing a business can make or break the deal, or materially affect the price.

> Qualitative analysis helps you go beyond what a company looks like on paper to what it looks like in real life.

History of the Company

How can the history of the company possibly affect the current value of the company? You can gain many insights into the present health of the company, sustainability of earnings, and relative risk of the company by learning about the history of the company. Some things to look for:

Corporate culture—Does the business environment promote creativity, giving back to society, loyalty of employees and customers, etc.? Or is it an authoritarian environment? Can you get a sense of the company's ethics?

Longevity—Has the company been around for 100 years or five?

Dealing with adversity—How has the company met the challenges of the past? Does management fire employees at the first sign of an economic downturn; or do they go without a paycheck themselves? If it is an old and established company, how did it survive the Great Depression?

Vision—Do the founders and/or current leaders have the vision to lead the company into the future? Who are these people?

Reputation—Does the company have the reputation of being a good company to work for and a good corporate citizen, or is it a company known for taking advantage of both customers and employees?

Adaptability to change—Is the company an early adapter or a late adapter?

The numbers may speak for themselves, but these qualitative factors may either corroborate or contradict what the numbers are saying. How do you get at this qualitative information? Or, even more important than getting information, how do you get a "sense" of the company's corporate culture and where they are heading? You have to "kick the tires." You need to visit the business location or locations and talk with people. Of course, you can get a lot of information without leaving your office or your computer. You can look on the company's Web site, or have them send you their historical narrative, so you will know who founded the company, when they started it, how many employees they have, what business they are in, etc.

Although many companies do a good job of capturing more than just the facts on their Web sites, you can get a better overall feel for the company by going for a visit. When you talk to the owners, managers, and regular employees you can judge whether you are dealing with people of integrity, passion, loyalty, with respect for the history of the company along with a willingness to change. Understanding the history and traditions of a company is important in any valuation situation, but if you are planning to purchase a company, this knowledge is crucial to your decision. If the company has been successful, in part because of its history and the corporate culture that arose from it, what is going to happen if you change all that? Is this a family business and you are an outsider? Is the corporate culture a family-like environment, and you are planning to institute a number of systems to make everyone more efficient and personally accountable? Does the company make significant contributions of time and money to the community in an effort to "give back"? Do you plan to cut those expenditures to become more profitable? Do you know what is important to the employees? Is it making top dollar or is it flexibility with their schedule? If you are comparing several companies that look similar on paper, the qualitative factors that emerge from the company history and a site visit can be the difference in choosing one company over another.

Products or Services

A company's product line or service offerings can give you a lot of information that you can use to form your opinion of the value of the company. How many product lines does the company support? How long have they had each of them? Have they discontinued any major product lines and why? Do they make or carry any brand-name items? You can get basic information about a company's current product line from their sales literature and their Web site; however, you will need to visit the operation and talk to management to learn more about changes over time and the relative importance of different products.

Let's look at a hypothetical example of how product lines might affect the value of a company, especially in a purchase situation. Hector's Pro Shop is an independently owned golf shop in central Pennsylvania that carries a variety of golf equipment and apparel for the middle class, weekend golfer. Hector went to school with Dr. Johnny Scott, who designed the "Great Scott" line of woods and putters, which are the current national best-selling line of golf clubs. Because of his personal relationship with Dr. Scott, Hector has an exclusive right to distribute the Great Scott line in central Pennsylvania. However, most of Hector's clientele can only dream of owning a set of Great Scott clubs because they are so expensive. Consequently, Hector divides his display space equally among the five brands he currently sells.

As a potential buyer, Hector's Pro Shop may have more value to you

> A company's product line or service offerings can give you a lot of information that you can use to form your opinion of the value of the company.

than the financial results indicate, if you could capitalize on this exclusive distribution contract for Great Scott clubs. For example, if you had other outlets in the region, you could immediately expand the market. Or if you were set up to do Web-based marketing, you could reach a wider customer base. Maybe all you would need to do is invest in some advertising and reallocate the display space. Beyond capitalizing on the underutilized brand relationship, you may see opportunities to expand sales by dropping slow-selling lines and increasing the inventory and display space of the best sellers.

Another thing you will want to investigate is the relative profitability of the various product lines. Hector paid more attention to the sales volume of his various lines than he did to their relative profitability. Consequently, he was surprised to learn that the line producing the most sales was the least profitable overall. If low-margin sales make up a high percentage of the total revenues or earnings, you may need to make adjustments in your valuation calculations. You have to be particularly careful if you are using any type of rule of thumb method that uses a multiple of revenue because the value would be overstated. Discovering low-margin product lines can also indicate some hidden value for a purchaser because of the opportunity to make changes in the product mix that will have an immediate positive impact.

Pricing Policies

Profitability is also related to pricing policy. When you are analyzing a company's financial statements, you can determine the overall profitability of the firm and the gross profit on sales. However, you can't always determine the profitability of individual products or services. Even if the company literature or Web site states the pricing policy, you don't know whether the company applies the policy without exception to all product or service lines. Has the sales force offered discounts to promote sales, at the expense of profit? Do professionals who bill on an hourly rate basis always bill 100% of their time or do they "write off" unproductive time? If a product or service is priced as a "loss leader," is it doing the job of attracting more lucrative business or has it turned into a loss loser? You will need to talk to management to get the answers to these and other pricing policy questions.

What Is a Loss Leader?

A *loss leader* is a product or service that a company deliberately underprices in order to attract future business. The idea is to attract new customers to your business with a bargain price, usually on a new product or service. What good are new customers and more sales if you aren't making a profit? That is where the second part of the equation, the back end product, comes in. The back end product is a highly profitable product you sell to the person who came to you because of the loss leader bargain. The strategy is very similar to the "bait and switch" tactic flimflam artists use.

To Discount or Not to Discount?

If you are a salesperson whose compensation depends on your total sales or a mom-and-pop grocer threatened by the competition of national discount chains, you might consider discounting. Psychologically, discounting looks like the way to generate more sales and/or stay in business, but deep discounting could actually be the precursor of a company's demise. The best way to determine whether discounting makes sense is to run the numbers. Let's say you are selling gourmet coffee beans at $10.00 per one pound bag and your margin is 50%. If you reduce your price by 10% to $9.00 per bag, you would need to sell 25% more coffee. That means that if you currently sell 100 bags per day, you would have to sell 125 bags to maintain the same profit. Assume the same facts, except that your profit margin is 35% instead of 50%. If you reduce your price 10% to $9.00 per bag in this case, you would need to increase your sales by 40% to maintain the same profit. That means that you would need to sell 140 bags a day to stay even, which might be a little too much caffeine for one day.

Commodity Pricing

When a company tries to beat the competition on the basis of price alone, they are putting their fate in the hands of the marketplace and the economic laws of supply and demand. This strategy is called **commodity**

pricing. Commodity pricing is the norm for bulk goods such as grains, livestock, metals, oil, and other raw materials. Companies selling commodities rely on "buying low and selling high" to make their profit. In order to buy low, they usually have to buy in volume and rely on economies of scale in the storage and distribution phase of operations to make a profit. The same theory applies if the company is producing, mining, or otherwise originating the product—they have to do it as inexpensively and efficiently as possible. Since companies selling true commodities can't differentiate their products, they sell them on a commodities exchange or on the spot market.

Why would a business price a product or service that is not a true commodity as if it were? Usually only large companies can replicate the commodity operational model of buying low in bulk and relying on cost-effective economies of scale for storage and distribution. These companies can make up for lost margins by selling in volume. Sometimes part of their strategy is to undercut the price of the competition to force them out of business. When no direct competition exists, they can raise their price and increase their margins. The business strategy of commodity pricing is very risky, especially for the small producer, distributor, retailer, or service provider. Most small businesses cannot hope to compete on the basis of price alone for a sustained period because they can't achieve the volumes that make the economics work. Consequently, you would deeply discount the value of a small company using a commodity pricing structure to reflect the extreme risk of this strategy.

Premium Pricing

The opposite of a commodity pricing policy would be a premium pricing strategy. Companies can successfully pursue a premium pricing strategy when they have a clearly superior product or service or can otherwise distinguish their offering

How Do Commodity Markets Work?

Commodity markets are the exchanges where buyers and sellers make contracts for the transfer of a specified amount of product at a specific price and a specific date. In the spot markets, buyers purchase commodities for cash and the sellers deliver them immediately. In the futures markets, the buyers and sellers are dealing in futures contracts, not the actual commodities themselves. Consequently, you can trade in the futures market without ever owning or taking delivery of a commodity. How would you explain that truckload of pork bellies to your spouse? All commodity markets are based solely on the economic laws of supply and demand—prices go up when demand exceeds supply and prices go down when supply exceeds demand. Commodity markets are very volatile, which reflects the inherent risk of the commodity pricing system where the marketplace controls the price rather than the producer.

from the competition. For example, a specialty audio equipment store may be able to sell speakers at a much higher price than the large discount retailers for several reasons:

- The specialty store sells top of the line speakers that aren't generally available.
- The specialty store has more knowledgeable sales people.
- The specialty store offers delivery and set up services.
- The specialty store provides individual service and follow-up.
- The specialty store provides maintenance and repair services.

Service businesses can use this same strategy when they offer specialized services, have experienced professionals, and provide awesome customer service. Businesses using a premium pricing strategy can usually maintain higher profit margins and better returns. Consequently, you would value them more highly than a similar company that was not pricing at a premium. Of course, you need to look at the big picture. Perhaps a law firm priced its estate planning services at a premium because one of the partners is the most highly regarded estate planning attorney in the area. But what if the firm always ended up writing off or not billing all of their time? Or maybe the estate planning department of the firm was indeed highly profitable, but the rest of the lawyers worked in low-profit residential real estate? When you are valuing a company you need to learn more about the pricing policy to see if the gross margin reflects the policy. Often the pricing policy will give you insight into whether the company is more or less risky, making it more or less valuable than the gross numbers would indicate. You can incorporate what you learn here in your choice of discount or capitalization rates.

Suppliers and Customers

A company's relationship with its suppliers can be an important factor weighing on the ultimate value of a company. If the business relies on only one or two suppliers, the level of risk increases because of the potential devastating effect of the loss of a supplier. If you are a potential buyer for the company, you will also need to assess whether you will be able to continue the supplier relationships developed by the current owner over a long period of time. Even if you will be able to maintain these relationships, you may not receive the same beneficial pricing structures that were based on long standing business and personal relationships. Consequently, you may need to factor in the effect of reduced margins on the value of the business. On the other hand, you may already have supplier relationships in place that will enable you to increase the margins of the target company after you purchase it.

One situation in which having a single supplier can be a positive rather than negative factor is when the company has an exclusive right to sell or distribute the supplier's product within a specified territory. As long as the territory is sufficiently large, the company should be able to maintain good profit margins on the product since they will have a "mini-monopoly" on the product. As an example, Harrison's Farm Equipment Company has the exclusive distribution rights for Workhorse Tractors for eastern Illinois. Harrison can make a profit even with the costs of advertising and selling because he does not need to keep his price in line with any competition. He is the only game in town as long as Workhorse Tractors continue to offer superior products or have superior brand recognition and as long as Workhorse does not award another distributorship nearby. This type of favorable supplier relationship can add to the value of a company because it promotes the stability of earnings and enables the company to maintain high profit margins. However, you need to assess the strength and value of exclusive relationships—sometimes suppliers reduce the territory originally granted in order to open more outlets for their products, and sometimes the supplier's product loses popularity or market share.

Customer Relationships

Companies that rely on a few big customers are in a similar risk position to companies relying on a few main suppliers. When the effect of losing one big customer would be devastating, the risk is great, and the value of the company is less. In contrast, if the customer base is so diverse that losing any one customer would not affect the bottom line, you have a reduced risk and higher value situation. To some extent, concentration of a customer base is a good thing, so the business can adequately serve its

> You may need to factor in the effect of reduced margins on the value of the business.

Pareto's Law

Vilfredo Pareto was a nineteenth-century Italian economist who developed the 80/20 rule that is a mainstay of twenty-first century management strategy. His original work determined that 80% of the land was owned by 20% of the people, but his theory took on broader meaning when he noticed that 20% of the pea pods in his garden produced 80% of the peas. He went on to prove that 80% of the income is distributed to 20% of the people regardless of taxation and welfare policies. Today, people apply this principle to time management, advertising, personnel problems, etc. Our common sense tells us that about 20% of our efforts usually account for about 80% of the results and about 80% of the time spent dealing with problems is caused by only 20% of the problems. You can use this principle to improve productivity by concentrating your efforts on the most important priorities.

most profitable customers. A derivation of Pareto's Law is that a company will derive 80% of its profit from 20% of its customers.

In any case, you must analyze the quality of the customer base and the probability that the customers will stay with the business under new ownership. In companies where the customers have a personal relationship with the owner, especially in personal service companies, the risk of losing customers is very great. You can mitigate this risk by negotiating incentives for the owner to encourage client loyalty to the firm or even require the owner to continue to work in the business for a period of time.

Human Resources

Key people are often the key to the success of a small business, so you need to determine who the key people are in the organization. You can gain some insight into this question by looking at an employee census that shows the birth date, hire date, number of hours worked, and compensation information for all the employees. If the company has a retirement plan, they should already be preparing this information on an annual basis for the plan administrator to determine who is eligible to participate and to calculate the retirement contributions. If the company does not have this information available for another reason, you should ask them to prepare it. The standard census information will give you a good idea about whether the company has retained long-term employees or whether they have a lot of turnover. You can also determine whether the company pays at the top, bottom, or middle of the pay scale, which can have implications for employee retention.

After you identify probable key people based on their salary and/or longevity with the company, you need to get some more information about this group. You will want to know more about their education, qualifications, experience, the role they play with the company, and under what circumstances they would be at risk for leaving. Beyond these objective measures of key employees, you should ask the owner or other management leaders who they think are the key employees and why. You might be surprised to find that someone with a relatively low-level job may be a key employee. When you are valuing the company, you need to assess the added value that key employees bring to a company, and you also need to assess the risk of what would happen if they were to leave or die. Depending on the risk you perceive regarding losing key employees, you can make employment agreements and/or noncompete agreements part of the total transaction. In addition, you may want to take out key person insurance on some of these people so that the company would have a financial cushion while it was recovering from the loss of a key person.

What about the rest of the work force? You need to determine whether the company is appropriately staffed, both in terms of numbers of people and their relative skill levels. You will be able to make some judgment about this by looking at the financial statements and analyzing the relationship between payroll and earnings. However, you can learn more by talking to management about their assessment of human resources. Ask them about their compensation philosophy. Do they pay top dollar to attract highly skilled long-term employees, or do they pay as little as possible because they mostly use unskilled workers who are plentiful? Do they hire plenty of people for busy seasons and lay them off as soon as business slows, or do they have a small core of full-time employees who work year-round and put in overtime when it is busy?

All things being equal, you will value a company with a stable work force more highly than you would a company with a lot of turnover. High turnover is a good thing when it relates to inventory or accounts receivable, but high employee turnover reduces value because of retraining costs and decreased productivity.

Physical Plant

Although you can determine how old the buildings and equipment are by analyzing the depreciation schedule, you can learn a lot about the company as a whole by visiting the facility. You can determine whether the company adequately maintains and repairs the facilities and see if they keep a clean workplace. You can see whether safety precautions, if needed, are taken seriously or ignored. You can determine whether the buildings are too small for the level of business activity or whether the company has room to expand. When the owner or manager gives you a tour of the facilities, you will learn a lot about how the business functions, not only from a physical standpoint, but also from a human resource perspective. You will have the opportunity to see workers interacting with each other and with the boss as you visit each department.

If the company owns the facility and it makes up a significant portion of the value of a business, you should have the real estate and perhaps the equipment appraised separately by qualified real estate and equipment appraisers. Even if you have the facilities professionally appraised, you should pay particular attention to the infrastructure of the buildings. This includes the basic operating systems such as electricity, heating and air, and plumbing. If any of these systems are old or not in good repair, you will need to come up with an estimate of how much you will need to invest to cure these problems. In general, you will reduce the value of the business by this amount unless you will be creating efficiencies that will produce off-setting earnings gains.

Summary of Qualitative Analysis

Qualitative analysis explores the myriad of factors that can affect the value of a business without necessarily being quantitative. This chapter touched on several of these factors, but one of the characteristics of qualitative analysis is that it is different for each company. Therefore, it is impossible to come up with a comprehensive list or even a ranking of the level of importance of various factors. When you are valuing a company, just as when you are buying a car, you need to form your first impression, kick the tires, and do your homework. Your qualitative analysis may make or break a deal, even though it is one of the aspects of the business valuation process that is more art than science.

The next section of the book discusses complex business valuation calculations and analyses, which are some of the most scientific aspects of the business valuation process. At the same time, you must use a lot of judgment and experience to choose the appropriate methods and inputs.

Chapter 21

Projecting Future Income

Defining Income or Earnings

Projecting future income or earnings is the backbone of the discounted cash flow method of valuation discussed in Chapter 13. That chapter introduced the basic types of earning you can use when projecting future income as part of valuing a company. Establishing the proper earnings type is also instrumental in a capitalization of earnings calculation. To recap:

- Financial statement operating income based on GAAP
- Operating cash flow
- Operating cash flow after taxes
- Discretionary cash flow
- EBIT—earnings before interest and taxes
- EBITDA—earnings before interest, taxes, depreciation, and amortization

> The type of earnings you use in a projection of future income may depend on the purpose of the valuation.

The type of earnings you use in a projection of future income may depend on the purpose of the valuation. Some business analysts prefer to use GAAP operating income because the company calculates it using standardized and objective methods that make it comparable to other companies' reported earnings. Even if you use GAAP income, you would still make normalizing adjustments (see Chapter 17) in order to more accurately reflect the income of the operation. For example, if the owner of Julian's Quick Shoppe earns $200,000 for managing his convenience store, you might make a normalizing adjustment to reflect a lower salary of $75,000 (or whatever he would have to pay someone else to do the job) and add back $125,000 to earnings. So, if GAAP income from operations were $25,000, you would use normalized earnings of $150,000 ($25,000 + $125,000) to make future projections.

GAAP income has the advantage that it is accessible and easily comparable to other companies and industry averages. However, most valuation analysts use some type of cash flow to represent earnings because cash is more tangible and more meaningful. You can do something with cash, like spend it. Cash is directly related to value. If you had a company with one asset and no liabilities, a $100,000 checking account for instance, your company would be worth about $100,000.

Cash flow and earnings are closely related, but the same accounting constructs that produce consistency in GAAP numbers often cause earnings and cash flow numbers to diverge. For example, although a company with a lot of debt may have the same accounting earnings as a similar firm with no debt, their cash flow will be different. When the company with debt makes principal payments on the debt, they reduce the cash flow without affecting earnings. The interest portion of the payment would already be reflected in the net earnings.

Simple Average Method

After you choose the type of earnings you are going to use and make the appropriate normalizing adjustments, you can start the process of projecting future earnings. (See Chapter 13 for guidance on choosing the type of earnings and Chapter 17 for guidance on making normalizing adjustments.) You calculate the simple average, also known as the unweighted average, by adding the earnings for the years for which you have information and dividing by that number of years. You should have at least three to five years of earnings information to make this calculation meaningful. Assume that you have the following earnings information for Julian's Quick Shoppe:

YEAR	EARNINGS
2003	$150,000
2002	$75,000
2001	$120,000
2000	$45,000
1999	$100,000
Total	$490,000

CHART 21-1

$$\text{Simple Average Earnings} = \frac{\$490,000}{5} = \$98,000$$

You calculate the simple average earnings in this case by totaling five years of earnings information and dividing that number by five to arrive at a projected value of future earnings of $98,000. The simple average method is most appropriate in situations like this where the earnings do not appear to have any type of pattern.

One reason that you would use five years of information instead of three is that you cannot easily spot a trend in three years or you may think you have a trend that does not exist. In this case, if you make the same simple average calculation using the three most recent years, you come up with a significantly different number: $115,000. If you just look at the last three years of earnings for Julian's Quick Shoppe, you may be tempted to think that a trend of growing earnings in the mid-$100,000 range exists and that 2002 was just an aberration. However, if you look at the full five years of information, you can see that a distinct pattern does not exist. At this point you would rely on the information you gathered from your other research into the company to determine whether a five-year or three-year simple average will be more indicative of future earnings.

Weighted Average Earnings

Like the simple average method, the weighted average method of projecting future earnings is based on the arithmetic mean. However, you use the weighted average method when you do see a discernable pattern in the historic earnings. By "weighting" the most recent years, you are saying that those years are more indicative of the future because of the trend you see. The trend can be positive or negative. The following calculation for Mitch's Cigar Shop shows how the weighted average calculation works:

CHART 21-2

YEAR	EARNINGS		WEIGHTING FACTOR		
2003	100,000	X	5	=	$500,000
2002	90,000	X	4	=	$360,000
2001	85,000	X	3	=	$255,000
2000	75,000	X	2	=	$150,000
1999	20,000	X	1	=	$20,000
Total			15		$1,285,000

$$\text{Weighted Average Earnings} = \frac{\$1,285,000}{15} = \$85,667$$

Trend Line Methods

Trend line methods forecast the future by looking at the trend of past data and projecting future data points or tendencies. As the name implies, you chart your data points on a graph and construct a line that "fits" or describes the trend of the data that moves beyond the historical data. The historical earnings for the C&H Organic Café are as follows:

CHART 21-3

YEAR	EARNINGS
1996	$10,000
1997	$15,000
1998	$22,500
1999	$33,750
2000	$50,625
2001	$75,938
2002	$113,907

You can use spreadsheet software such as Excel to plot the earnings over time to get an idea of the trend. By using the least squares method of statistical analysis, you can develop a trend line that best "fits" the data, meaning that there is minimal variance between the data points and the trend line. C&H's earnings have a positive trend, and the least squares method predicts future earnings to continue at about $95,000. Computer software makes this calculation look easy, but you should remember that trend line analysis is a statistical calculation. Consequently, you should have as many data points as possible to make the analysis more meaningful. A trend line analysis with less than five data points would not be reliable.

If you want to dust off your statistics book and get out your calculator, you can work through the least squares method for estimating future earnings. The formula used here is from the National Association of Certified Valuation Analysts' *Business Valuations: Fundamentals, Techniques and Theory* (Black & Isom Associates, 1995).

CHART 21-4   Least squares formula: $Y = a_0 + bx$

Where: $a_0 = \dfrac{\Sigma Y - b(\Sigma X)}{N}$ = intercept of Y axis

And: $b = \dfrac{N(\Sigma\, X \cdot Y) - (\Sigma X)\, (\Sigma Y)}{N(\Sigma X^2) - (\Sigma X)^2}$ = slope

Where: x = Total number of observed years

X = The ith year, and weighting to be accorded in the ith year (x^2)

Y = Earnings in the ith year

N = Number of observations

Σ = Sum of the variables

Using the earnings information for C&H Organic Café you would calculate the trend line as follows:

X	Y	X^2	$X \cdot Y$
1	10,000	1	10,000
2	15,000	4	30,000
3	22,500	9	67,500
4	33,750	16	135,000
5	50,625	25	253,125
6	75,938	36	455,628
7	113,907	49	797,349

$\Sigma X = 28$ $\Sigma Y = 321,720$ $\Sigma X^2 = 140$ $\Sigma\, X \cdot Y = 1,748,602$

Using this information you determine the value of the slope, i.e., solve for b:

CHART 21-4
(continued)

$$b = \frac{7(1,748,602) - [28(321,720)]}{7(140) - 28^2}$$

$$b = \frac{12,240,214 - 9,008,160}{980 - 784}$$

$$b = \frac{3,232,054}{196}$$

$$b = 16,490$$

Next, you determine the value of intercept of the Y axis, a_0

$$a_0 = \frac{321,720 - [16,490(28)]}{7}$$

$$a_0 = \frac{(140,002)}{7}$$

$$a_0 = (20,000)$$

Next, you project the future earnings:

$$Y = a_0 + bx$$

$$Y = (20,000) + 16,490(7)$$

$$Y = 95,430$$

The Three M's—Mean, Median, and Mode

If Joe says "the average price of a bottle of beer at the Green Room Pool Hall is $3.00," what does he mean? If he adds up the price of all of the beer sold and divides it by the number of bottles and comes up with $3.00, then he means the "arithmetical mean." If he prices bottles of beer as follows: $2.00/domestic, $3.00/premium domestic, and $3.50/imports, then the $3.00 premium domestic bottles would be the median or middle point. On the other hand, if he is referring to the fact that he sells more premium domestics than anything else, he would be referring to the mode, which is the number that occurs most frequently.

You can see that the mathematical calculation of the least squares method predicts future earnings at $95,430. The trend line static method predicts the level at which earnings will continue without growth, and it is therefore most appropriate when you are capitalizing earnings rather than discounting them.

The trend line projected method assumes that earnings will continue to grow, but at a declining rate. You use the same formulas to develop the trend line and then you project future earnings for the next five years by increasing the earnings of the latest year by the value of 'b,' the slope of the trend line. This method is most appropriate when a company's earnings are consistently increasing or decreasing. You also use this method when you don't expect future earnings to be similar to the most recent year's results.

Starting with the earnings of $95,430 you projected for C&H Organic Café using the least squares method, you can project earnings through 2008 as follows:

CHART 21-5

Year	Earnings	+	b	=	Future Earnings
2004	95,430	+	16,490	=	111,920
2005	111,920	+	16,490	=	128,410
2006	128.410	+	16,490	=	144,900
2007	144,900	+	16,490	=	161,390
2008	161,390	+	16,490	=	177,880

Projected Growth Rate Methods

You can use the projected growth rate method to project future earnings when the growth rate is constant. Unlike the projected trend line method, where the data is linear, the data points form an upward sloping curve called an exponential curve. You would only use this method if your analysis of the company indicates that earnings will continue to grow at this rate for the foreseeable future. You start by determining the annual compound growth rate of the last five years of earnings. Using a financial calculator, you enter the base earnings as a negative number for the present value (PV), you enter the number of years of the calculation as 'n,' you enter the final year's earnings as the future value (FV), and you solve for the interest rate (i). Then you apply this growth rate to the most recent year's earnings and continue sequentially over the remaining years.

Using the last five years of earnings from Nancy's Atelier you would make the calculations as follows:

CHART 21-6

YEAR	EARNINGS	ANNUAL GROWTH RATE
1999	75,800	Base
2000	81,200	7%
2001	87,500	8%
2002	96,000	10%
2003	105,000	9%

Average growth rate = 8.5%
Compound growth rate = 8.49%
Future earnings projections:

YEAR	EARNINGS	x	RATE =	FUTURE EARNINGS
2004	105,000	x	1.0849 =	113,915
2005	113,915	x	1.0849 =	123,586
2006	123,586	x	1.0849 =	134,078
2007	134,078	x	1.0849 =	145,462
2008	145,462	x	1.0849 =	157,811

Gompertz Curves

Benjamin Gompertz was an English actuary and mathematician who developed a formula to describe the process of birth, growth, maturity, and death for actuarial purposes. His formula, which produces a growth curve that resembles the shape of the letter *S*, can be used to model the growth of human populations, the development of organisms and organizations, and the substitution of new technology for old technology. This curve provides a good characterization of the earnings movements in a mature company.

Other Projection Methods

Other growth rate projection methods include the geometric method, which produces an upward sloping curve called the power curve when earnings increase at an increasing rate. The logarithmic method reflects earnings increasing at an increasingly declining rate. This curve rises rapidly and then levels off. Earnings that grow slowly in the beginning, then grow rapidly, then slow down and finally grow only at a declining rate produce the Gompertz Curve, which looks like a loose 'S' curve. You can use any of these projected growth rate methods or the projected trend line method to forecast future earnings for a discounted earnings calculation. They would not be appropriate for a capitalization of earnings valuation method.

When Will Your Investment Double?

The "Rule of 70" is a nifty little math trick that allows you to approximate when an investment, or anything else growing at a constant rate, will double. How does it work? Just divide the number 70 by the annual growth rate to get the number of years it will take for the initial amount to double. Using the example of the $1,000 investment earning 6 percent, you can expect to double your investment in about eleven and a half years (70/6% = 11.6667). Why does it work? The Rule of 70 is based on the mathematical concepts of logarithms and exponential growth. Is it exact? No, "rule" in this case is short for "rule of thumb," which means that this is a quick, easy way to approximate something that would be time consuming and complicated to calculate exactly. The mathematical underpinning of the Rule of 70 is based on daily, rather than yearly, compounding, so you will derive a number that is a little bit fast if you are using annual compounding.

How Do You Choose the Most Appropriate Method?

One of the first things you should do is create a graph reflecting the earnings of the company. (Remember that the earnings you are analyzing and projecting are the earnings that you have already normalized to arrive at a truer economic picture of the company.) When you see the earnings plotted on a graph, you should be able to visually determine which of the growth curves or trend lines is most similar to your data.

If you prefer number crunching and statistics, you can use correlation analysis to help you determine which method to use to project future earnings in your specific case. Correlation analysis uses the correlation coefficient (r) and the coefficient of determination (r^2) to measure the degree to which two variables are related. The formula that describes the coefficient of determination, r^2, is:

$$r^2 = 1 - \frac{\text{Unexplained variance}}{\text{Total variance}}$$

CHART 21-7

Other variables include:

N = Number of observations
X = the ith year
Y = earnings for a particular year

$$r^2 = \frac{[(N\Sigma XY) - (\Sigma X)(\Sigma Y)]^2}{[N\Sigma X^2 - (\Sigma X)^2][N\Sigma Y^2 - (\Sigma Y)^2]}$$

You can use r^2 to create a time series analysis so that you can determine how much of the change in earnings between years is related to the passage of time. Using the 1999–2003 earnings from Nancy's Atelier, the calculation is as follows:

CHART 21-8

YEAR	X	Y
1999	1	75,800
2000	2	81,200
2001	3	87,500
2002	4	96,000
2003	5	105,000

X	Y	X·Y	X^2	Y^2
1	75,800	75,800	1	5,745,640,000
2	81,200	162,400	4	6,593,440,000
3	87,500	262,500	9	7,656,250,000
4	96,000	384,000	16	9,216,000,000
5	105,000	525,000	25	11,025,000,000

(In 000s):

$\Sigma X = .015 \quad \Sigma Y = 446 \quad \Sigma(X \cdot Y) = 1{,}409 \quad \Sigma X^2 = .055 \quad \Sigma Y^2 = 40{,}236{,}330$

$$r^2 = \frac{[(5 \times 1{,}409) - (.015 \times 446)]^2}{[(5 \times .055) - .015^2][(5 \times 40{,}236{,}330) - (446)^2]}$$

$$r^2 = \frac{(7{,}045 - 6.69)^2}{.275\,(201{,}181{,}650 - 198{,}916)} = \frac{49{,}537{,}667}{55{,}270{,}252} = 90\%$$

The coefficient of determination for Nancy's Atelier is slightly less than 100 percent, which means that there is a good correlation between earnings increases and the passage of time. Consequently, you can use the projected growth rate method of estimating future earnings with a high degree of confidence. When you use correlation analysis to help you choose the proper method of estimating future earnings, the closer your r^2 number is to one, the more you can rely on a projected growth rate method. The further away your r^2 number is from one, the less you can rely on any method that incorporates an element of growth. The following list represents the hierarchy of methods for projecting future income ranked by r^2 numbers from lowest to highest:

1. **Unweighted average**—All earnings carry the same weight.
2. **Weighted average**—The most recent earnings carry more weight.
3. **Trend-line static**—Earnings are projected for the last year based on the historical trend and expected to continue at this level.
4. **Trend-line projected**—Earnings are projected on a straight-line basis into the future.
5. **Projected growth rate**—Earnings are projected on a nonlinear basis into the future.

Based on this hierarchy, you would use the unweighted average method when you calculate a very low r^2, which means that you have a very low correlation between the way earnings change and the passage of time. The higher the correlation between earnings changes and the passage of time, the more you can rely on past trends to predict the future. As with Nancy's Atelier, when you have a high r^2, you can project earnings into the future that continue to grow.

And you thought that coming up with your earnings figure was going to be the easy part? You were right. The mathematics gets more complicated in the next chapter, which discusses how to calculate capitalization and discount rates. You can either resharpen your pencil or relax and skip over all the calculations that you would rather pay someone else to make.

Chapter 22

Capitalization and Discount Rates

Part One

Part Two

Part Three

Part Four

Part Five

Part Six

Appropriate Rate of Return

Determining the appropriate capitalization or discount rate to apply to your chosen measure of economic income is the most difficult and the most important component of valuing a business. The capitalization or discount rate is like alchemy—you multiply or divide your earnings by this "magic number" to get the value of the company. And just as medieval philosophers and scientists found that the process of turning base metals into gold was not so easy, you will find that converting a company's earnings into its value requires more than the flick of a magic wand. If you choose an appropriate valuation method but choose an inappropriate capitalization or discount rate, you will invalidate the entire calculation.

Learning how to determine appropriate discount and capitalization rates is a long-term process, even for professional business valuators. Entire books and professional development courses are devoted to the subject. Consequently, this chapter will serve as an introduction to the complex topic, not the unabridged final word on the subject.

> Learning how to determine appropriate discount and capitalization rates is a long-term process, even for professional business valuators.

Distinguishing Capitalization Rates from Discount Rates

Although you calculate capitalization rates and discount rates in a similar manner, they have important differences. The basic difference between discount rates and capitalization rates relates to whether you are trying to determine the present value of future income streams (discounting) or converting a single income stream into a projected value (capitalizing). As the names suggest, you use a discount rate to do a discounted cash flow valuation, and you use a capitalization rate to do a capitalization of earnings valuation. See Chapter 13 for a full discussion of the discounted cash flow method and Chapter 11 for the details of the capitalization of earnings method.

The discounting process answers the question: "How much do I have to invest today, assuming a certain compound rate of return, in order to receive a certain lump sum amount in the future?" In other words, you are converting a future projected cash flow or series of cash flows into a present value using a present value discount rate. The present value discount rate is the total rate of return for the investment over its life, indicated as an annual percentage rate. The mathematical formula for discounting is expressed as follows:

$$PV = \frac{FV}{(1 + k)^i}$$

CHART 22-1

Where: PV = Present value
FV = Future value
k = Rate of return
i = the number of years

If you want to receive $10,000 five years from now and you can earn 8% interest, how much do you need to invest? You can use the formula to make the calculation as follows:

$$PV = \frac{\$10,000}{(1 + .08)^5} = \frac{\$10,000}{1.47} = \$6,803$$

CHART 22-2

What if you want to calculate the present value of a series of future income streams? In order to calculate the present value of a series of inflows, you use the same formula, but you sum the calculation for the number of years involved. The formula is simply modified by adding the symbol for summation, "Σ":

$$PV = \frac{\Sigma \, FVi}{(1 + k)^i}$$

CHART 22-3

A classic example of discounting a series of future income streams is determining the yield to maturity, or present value, of a bond. How would you calculate the present value of a $10,000 Airport Authority bond with a 4% coupon rate that will mature in three years? Using the formula and assuming that the current market rate of interest on these type bonds is 5 percent, the calculation is as follows:

CHART 22-4

$$PV = \frac{\$400}{1.05} + \frac{\$400}{1.05 \times 1.05} + \frac{\$400}{1.05 \times 1.05 \times 1.05} + \frac{\$10,000}{1.05 \times 1.05 \times 1.05}$$

$$= \$381 + \$363 + \$346 + \$8,638$$

$$= \$9,728$$

If you try some more examples or "what ifs" in this formula, you will find that as the discount rate increases, the present value decreases. Why would the discount rate increase? The main component of increasing discount rates is risk. The rate must increase to compensate investors for taking risks, so the higher the risk, the higher the return that the market will demand. And, as you see with this formula, the higher the rate, the lower the present value.

In contrast, a capitalization rate converts a single measure of earnings into a value of the total investment. The capitalization formula is very simple: You merely divide the expected earnings by the capitalization rate to get the present value.

CHART 22-5

$$PV = \frac{E}{c}$$

Where PV = Present value
E = Earnings
c = Capitalization rate

If you are valuing a company with $50,000 in earnings and you have determined that the capitalization rate is 25%, then the value of the company using a capitalization of earnings approach is $200,000 ($50,000 / 25%). You can see that the formula for the capitalization process is very different from the formula for the discounted cash flow calculation. You may want to refer back to these formulas whenever you need to distinguish between capitalization and discount rates.

Now that you know that capitalization rates and discount rates are not completely interchangeable, what *is* their relationship? The basic relationship between the two types of rates is that the capitalization rate equals the discount rate minus the expected sustainable long-term growth rate. In essence, capitalization is a streamlined version of discounting. The underlying assumption of capitalization is that the earnings of the company will continue to grow evenly forever. Does this sound like a realistic assumption? Maybe not, but this is what you are left with when you do not have confidence in projecting more realistic year-by-year earnings that you can use in the discounting process. The capitalization rate and discount rate would be the same when you project no earnings growth.

Components of Capitalization and Discount Rates

The capitalization rate or discount rate is the "yield rate" on an investment in the business you are valuing. The yield rate is the rate of return an investor expects or requires in order to make an investment. Another way of thinking about the yield rate is that it represents the total return an investor hopes to achieve with an investment. Total return incorporates not only earnings such as interest or dividends, but also any capital appreciation or depreciation of the investment. In other words, total return is all the cash or other property the investor will ultimately take out of the investment.

> The yield rate is the rate of return an investor expects or requires in order to make an investment.

You calculate the total return by adding the cash distributions to the capital appreciation and dividing that sum by the amount you originally paid for the investment. For example, assume that you bought 100 shares of Total Return, Inc. stock for $1,000, you received $100 in dividends, and the stock price went up to $12 per share by the end of the year. Your total return would be $100 + $200 ($2 x 100 shares), or $300. You divide this total numerical return by your investment of $1,000 to get a 30% total return percentage. Make sure that you take into account the time period over which you receive this total return so that your percentage rate of return is comparable to other rates of return that are calculated on an annual basis. If you earned this same total return over three years, you would divide the 30% return by three years, which would produce a much more modest 10% annual rate. When you are valuing a business, the total return also represents the cost of capital. The cost of capital is the expected rate of return that a particular type of investment must provide in order to entice investors to put money in it. This means that the same total rate of return is available in the marketplace for other investments with similar levels of risk and

Opportunity Cost

The notion of opportunity cost is the concept we use in our everyday lives to recognize that all of the choices we make have a cost. For example, if you choose to spend your time writing a book, you may have to give up playing golf with your friends. Or if you buy a vacation home, you may not be able to afford to take a trip to Europe. The fundamental economic concept of scarcity is at the heart of the idea of opportunity cost. Scarcity means that we have limited resources, such as time or money, with which to fulfill our needs and desires. Consequently, we make choices about how to spend these resources efficiently. The opportunity cost of choosing one alternative is the cost of not choosing the next best option.

marketability. Another way to look at the cost of capital is as an opportunity cost—the cost of foregoing the opportunity to invest in something else.

The yield rate for a Treasury bond is usually the starting point for determining the yield rate for any other investment. Treasury bond rates represent a risk-free rate of return because the "full faith and credit" of the United States government secures this investment. What kind of return can you expect on this "safe" investment? The short answer is "not much." This is because the yield rate on an investment compensates investors for the risk they are willing to take with their money. Since investors are practically guaranteed that they will get back the principal they invested, the government does not need to compensate them for the risk that they might not get their money back. In addition to the certainty of getting their principal back at maturity, investors also have the benefit of being able to cash in their investment at any time, i.e., they have liquidity and marketability. Therefore, the real rate of return on Treasury bills is usually around 2 percent, which represents the cost of borrowing money at a risk-free rate. The nominal rate of return on Treasury bills is higher than 2% to reflect the rate of inflation. This relatively low risk-free rate is the baseline you use to determine the appropriate rate of return for other investments.

The second component of the yield rate reflects the additional compensation an investor requires or expects when his or her money is put in an investment that does not have the same level of safety as an investment in government bonds. In other words, when an investor takes on more risk, he expects more return. What are some of the elements that make up the overall risk of a particular investment? First, the general economic and industry environments in which the company operates influence the risk inherent in a particular company. Secondly, the characteristics of the business itself naturally play a major role in the risk level of the company and, finally, factors relating to the investment itself have risk implications.

Risk Premiums

A risk premium is the additional return that the market requires in order to entice investors to put their money in investments other than risk-free vehicles such as Treasury bills. The following list gives specific examples of some of these elements of risk:

1. Current and projected economic situation
2. Current industry conditions and projected trends
3. Current and projected regulatory environment
4. Historical profitability and financial position of the company
5. Projected profitability and financial position of the company
6. The volatility of earnings
7. The size of the business
8. Qualitative factors, such as human resources, physical plant, suppliers, and customers
9. Liquidity and marketability of the investment
10. Projected capital appreciation of the investment

Although business valuation analysts agree that the above factors are important in assessing the risk of an investment in a closely held company, a simple formula does not exist to translate each of these factors into percentages of a discount rate. However, several organizations and databases including Ibbotson Associates, Price Waterhouse, Bizcomps, and Pratt's Stats have published research about the relationship between size, risk, and required rates of return. See Chapter 9 for a full discussion about how the size of a company affects its value. The results of this research indicate that size alone accounts for a large part of the risk inherent in a business investment. In addition, the research shows that the smaller the size of the company, the greater the risk and, therefore, the greater the required rate of return. Consequently, you should add a significant risk premium to the risk-free rate to obtain an appropriate discount rate for a small business.

Another characteristic most closely held businesses have that makes them riskier than Treasury bills is that they are not liquid. Unlike highly marketable government securities, you cannot just sell an investment in a small business when you want to, nor can you expect to pocket proceeds totalling the fair market value. Usually a business owner must incur significant costs in terms of commissions, effort expended in marketing, lost productivity, and direct selling expenses. In addition, it may take months or even years to find the right buyer. Even then, the seller will rarely get a 100-percent cash deal. One important caveat: If you add a risk premium to the discount rate to account for illiquidity, you should not take an additional discount for lack of marketability. See Chapter 23 for a discussion of valuation discounts.

After that, you will spend time meeting prospective buyers and potentially providing additional information to them. If the process takes only a few months, you will probably spend about 500 hours. If you do it all yourself, you should probably figure that you will use about twice that much time. Brokers usually charge around 10% of the sales price, so you can judge how much your time is worth compared to the broker's time, expertise, connections, and commission.

Build-Up Methods

How do you quantify all of these risk factors to determine the appropriate capitalization or discount rate for a particular investment? Several individuals and organizations have published their research, which you can use as a guide to "build-up" the capitalization or discount rate from the risk-free rate. The primary methods are the Ibbotson Build-Up Method, the Schilt's Risk Premium Method, and the Black/Green Summation Method. See Chapter 13 for examples of the Ibbotson Build-Up Method and the Schilt's Risk Premium Method.

The Ibbotson Method uses sophisticated database information that they update annually and publish in their *Stocks, Bonds, Bills and Inflation Yearbook* (Ibbotson Associates, 2003). The method starts with the risk-free long-term government bond rate, adds a risk premium for a long-term equity investment, adds an additional risk premium for small companies, and adds a final premium for any additional specific company risk they identify. The Ibbotson Build-Up Method is the most theoretically sound of the popular methods because it is based on extensive and updated research on actual stock performance. However, because the Ibbotson research is based on publicly traded companies, the smallest size premium relates to companies under approximately $200 million. Although the Ibbotson organization considers this level of equity to be in the micro-capitalization category, this is a big company compared to most closely held businesses. Consequently, you would need to add an additional risk premium if you are valuing a much smaller company.

The Schilt's Risk Premium Method is a more accessible, but less precise, method of constructing an appropriate discount or capitalization rate for a small company. James H. Schilt categorizes companies according to their business characteristics and size and assigns risk premiums accordingly. On the low end are established, well financed businesses with stable earnings, good management, and a predictable future. For these companies you would add a risk premium of 6–10% to the risk-free rate. At the high end would be the "one-man" shop where the seller may not be able to transfer the customers or earnings to a new buyer. You would add a premium to the risk-free rate for this riskiest type of business in the 26–30% range. The discount or capitalization rate you compute with this method is on a pretax basis; therefore, you should only apply it to pretax measures of income.

Parnell Black and Robert L. Green, of Black, Green, Yeanopls & Company, Salt Lake City, Utah, developed their method using the basic theory of the Capital Asset Pricing Model, which incorporates the fundamental idea that investors in risky investments require a greater return. This method also is a pretax method that starts with a risk-free rate such as the intermediate-term government bond rate, and then adds an additional premium for each of the following risk factors:

The Reality of Selling a Business

How much time, effort, and money does it take to sell your business if you are using a business broker? One of the primary reasons you would use a business broker is to significantly reduce the time you spend personally marketing the business. Even so, you will need to spend some time describing your company and discussing your objectives with the broker. Then you will need to gather a significant amount of financial information. The better shape your records are in, the less time this will take. Then you will fill out extensive questionnaires to get information beyond the numbers about your personnel, facilities, commitments, company history, competitors, etc.

1. Competition
2. Financial strength
3. Management ability and depth
4. Profitability and stability of earnings
5. National economic effects
6. Local economic effects

You calculate the premiums for each of the first four categories based on a weighted average of additional factors under each category by assigning numbers to each factor ranging from ten, which corresponds to high risk, to one, which corresponds to low risk. The economic factors contribute one to two points if the economy is weak or reduce the total by one to two points if the economy is particularly robust. See the following chart for a hypothetical example of the Black/Green Summation Method:

CHART 22-6

RISK FACTOR	RISK	WEIGHT	WEIGHTED RISK
Competition			
Proprietary content	5	1	5
Size of company	8	1	8
Product/service quality	3	1	3
Product/service differentiation	4	1	4
Market strength	4	1	4
Market size/share	6	1	6
Pricing competition	6	1	6
Ease of market entry	2	1	2
Patent/copyright protection	6	<u>1</u>	<u>6</u>
Total weight factors		9	44
Total weighted average			4.89%
Financial strength			
Total debt to assets	3	1	3
Long-term debt to equity	2	1	2
Current ratio	3	1	3
Quick ratio	3	1	3
Interest coverage	2	<u>1</u>	<u>2</u>

RISK FACTOR	RISK	WEIGHT	WEIGHTED RISK
Total weight factors		5	13
Total weighted average			2.6%
Management ability and depth			
Accounts receivable turnover	2	1	2
Inventory turnover	2	1	2
Fixed asset turnover	4	1	4
Total asset turnover	4	1	4
Employee turnover	2	1	2
Management depth	8	1	8
Facilities condition	5	1	5
Family involvement	8	1	8
Accounting records quality	8	1	8
Contracts	6	1	6
Gross margin	3	1	3
Operating margin	5	1	5
Total weight factors		12	57
Total weighted average			4.75%
Profitability/stability of earnings			
Years in business	2	1	2
Industry life cycle	7	1	7
Return on sales	4	1	4
Return on assets	4	1	4
Return on equity	4	1	4
Total weight factors	5	21	
Total weighted average			4.2%
Total risk premium factor			16.44%
Assumed risk-free rate			6.00%
National economic trends			0.00%
Local economic trends			1.00%
CAPITALIZATION RATE			23.44%

CHART 22-6
(continued)

The Capital Asset Pricing Model

The Capital Asset Pricing Model (CAPM) is a sophisticated method for determining an appropriate capitalization or discount rate. The CAPM posits that every investment has two risks: the risk of being in the market, and the risk related to a specific company's performance. Another name for market risk is systematic risk, which is represented by the term "beta." According to this theory, investors cannot reduce their systematic risk by diversifying; however, they can reduce the risk inherent in any individual investment by diversification. Therefore, a portfolio's expected return depends on its risk relative to the market, or its beta. A corollary to this theory is that investors can't expect a greater return just because they are willing to take any kind of risk. They can only expect a greater return for the risk they can't mitigate.

The essence of the CAPM is the formula stating that the expected return on an investment equals the risk-free rate, plus beta times the net of the expected return on a market portfolio, less the risk-free rate. In mathematical notation this is:

CHART 22-7

$$ER_i = R_f + B (ER_m - R_f)$$

Where: ER_i = Expected return of the investment

R_f = Risk-free rate (30-day Treasury bill rate)

B = Beta

ER_m = Expected return of the market (S&P 500 Index appreciation)

What is beta? Beta represents the volatility of an individual investment compared to the market. In statistical terms it is the co-variance of a security in relation to the rest of the stock market. "Co-variance" is the statistical measure of the interrelationship between two things. Normally, you would compute beta using the return on investment of the stock you are analyzing, which implies that you know the price of the stock. However, in a valuation situation, you would not need to go through all of the gyrations of the CAPM if you knew the price of the stock. Consequently, you have to modify the variables in the CAPM equation to be able to calculate beta without already knowing the price of the stock you are trying to value.

You can do this by changing some of the variables to reflect return on equity numbers for the company and the industry, which will allow you to calculate a beta that represents the risk of the company relative to the industry. This still involves getting good industry information, calculating the co-variance of the pretax return on equity of the company with the return on equity for specific companies or industry averages, and calculating the variance of the return on equity of the industry. The benefit of going through all of these complicated calculations is that you can determine whether the investment you are valuing is more or less risky, i.e., volatile, than the industry. A beta of one indicates that the expected return of the stock is exactly the same as the market. If a security had a beta of zero, its rate of return would be the risk-free rate. Stocks with betas higher than one would have expected returns greater than the market or the industry. Consequently, you would add a risk premium greater than the industry average return.

The CAPM is theoretically appealing and economists have created many even more sophisticated variations of it. However, in practice you will often have a difficult time getting the good comparable industry or specific company data that make it viable.

The Weighted Average Cost of Capital

The weighted average cost of capital (WACC) method of determining a capitalization or discount rate incorporates factors for both the cost of debt and the cost of equity in a company's capital structure. The theory is very straightforward: The cost of capital equals the after-tax cost of debt weighted according to its percentage of the capital structure, plus the weighted cost of equity. Calculating the cost of debt is very easy once you know the current or expected interest rate on debt. However, calculating the equity portion of the equation is not so easy.

Traditionally you would use the Gordon Growth Model to calculate the equity component of the WACC. You divide next year's dividends by the current stock price and add the anticipated growth rate in earnings, then you multiply this result by the equity weighting percentage. This may work well for large publicly traded companies, but it is almost impossible for closely held companies since in these situations the stock price is not a given; it is what you are trying to determine.

In practice, business valuators will use either a derivation of the CAPM or an average of the company's return on equity over the last several years. As with any dilutions of rigorous theories, these numbers would have less integrity and less precision than the illusive numbers derived from years of research and mathematical modeling. You can see how the WACC method works for a company with a debt/equity ratio of 60/40; a cost of debt of 10%; an income tax rate of 45%; expected dividends of $2 per share; current stock price of $25 per share; and expected earnings per share growth of 10%:

CHART 22-8

DEBT COMPONENT

Weight	x	Cost of debt	x	(1-tax rate)	=	Cost of debt
.6	x	.1	x	.55	=	3%

EQUITY COMPONENT

Weight	x	Dividend next year / Current stock price	+	Growth rate in earnings	=	Cost of equity
.4	x	$\dfrac{2}{25}$	+	.1	=	Cost of equity
.4	x	.08	+	.1	=	13%

WEIGHTED COST OF CAPITAL

Cost of debt	3%
Cost of equity	13%
Total cost of capital	16%

The WACC produces a blended rate that you can use when you are capitalizing or discounting income that is available to both debt and equity holders. The corresponding rate of return you would calculate would be return on invested capital, ROI. Be careful not to confuse this with calculations of return on equity (ROE), which refer only to the returns received by owners.

Converting Pretax Rates to After-Tax Rates

One of the biggest mistakes that anyone valuing a business can make is applying a pretax capitalization or discount rate to after-tax earnings, or vice versa. Previous chapters have discussed the different types of earnings that you can capitalize or discount. Some of these categories are listed below with a notation regarding their pretax or after-tax status.

- Gross revenue—pretax
- Owner's discretionary cash flow—pretax
- EBITDA (earnings before interest, taxes, depreciation, and amortization)—pretax
- EBIT (earnings before interest and taxes)—pretax
- EBT (earnings before taxes)—pretax
- Net income—after tax
- Net cash flow—after tax

Likewise, the various methods of deriving capitalization and discount rates inherently have either a pretax or after-tax orientation as follows:

- Ibbotson Build-Up Method—pretax
- Schilt's Risk Premium Method—pretax
- Black/Green Summation Method—pretax
- Capital Asset Pricing Model—pretax
- Weighted Average Cost of Capital—after tax

You can see that most of the methods of deriving capitalization and discount rates are pretax methods. In contrast, the widely used earnings measure, net cash flow, is an after-tax measure. What do you do when the earnings measure you want to use is not consistent with your capitalization or discount rate? You can convert pretax rates to after-tax rates by multiplying the number by (1 – tax rate), and you can convert after-tax rates to pretax rates by dividing by (1 – tax rate). For example, if you have calculated a capitalization rate of 19% using the Black/Green Summation Method, and your tax rate is 35%, the after-tax rate would be .19 x (1 – .35), or 12%.

Professional business valuation analysts use many of the sophisticated methods discussed in this chapter to arrive at the all-important capitalization or discount rate. However, even if you love complicated mathematical formulas and lots of correlated statistical data derived from empirical research, you can't always use the most sophisticated techniques when you are valuing a small company. Although the theories are applicable, you can't always get all of the information you need to input into the formulas. Consequently, even professional analysts need to use professional judgment when they determine the appropriate capitalization or discount rate for valuation purposes.

Valuation Discounts and Premiums

Part One

Part Two

Part Three

Part Four

Part Five

Part Six

PART SIX: COMPLEX BUSINESS VALUATION CALCULATIONS AND ANALYSIS

■ CHAPTER 21 Projecting Future Income ■ CHAPTER 22 Capitalization and Discount Rates
■ CHAPTER 23 Valuation Discounts and Premiums ■ CHAPTER 24 Engaging a Valuation Professional

What Are Valuation Discounts and Premiums?

Valuation discounts are downward adjustments that you make to the value of an ownership share in a business after you have valued the company as a whole. You take valuation discounts when the ownership share is worth less than its pro rata percentage of the total value of the company. In contrast, a **valuation premium** is an addition to value when a particular ownership share is worth more than its pro rata percentage of the total value of the business.

If you own 40% of a business, why wouldn't your share be 40% of the total value of the company? Owners of less than 51% of a business suffer from two problems that reduce the value of their shares: They do not have control over the decision-making process of the firm, and they generally do not have a readily marketable investment. All closely held companies have issues with lack of marketability because they are not publicly traded. However, minority interests are even more difficult to sell because most buyers would want to purchase a controlling interest.

This chapter will focus on minority discounts and discounts for lack of marketability because they are the two most common discounts. In fact, you will use at least one of them in almost every valuation of a closely held company. You will also learn about other situations that call for specialized discounts such as reliance on a key person, restricted stock, and restrictive covenants.

When would an ownership share be worth more than its pro rata share of the total value of the company? Assume that you were interested in buying into a company that was worth $100,000. If you ignore any applicable discounts for the sake of this example, you could purchase 50% of the company for $50,000. How much would you pay for 51% of the business? Would you be willing to pay more than $51,000? Most buyers would pay more than $51,000 in this case because the extra 1% would give them control of the entire company. The extra amount a buyer would pay to get a controlling interest is called a control premium. You can apply a control premium to ownership interests less than 51%, if that percentage would give the buyer control. For example, say you already owned 40% of the company and had the opportunity to purchase another 11%. You can apply a control premium to that interest since it would "put you over the top" with respect to your total ownership in the company.

Although the concept of valuation discounts and premiums is relatively straightforward, determining the appropriate amount by which to increase or decrease the value of an ownership share is not so easy. This chapter will cover the basic methods you can use to calculate discounts and premiums. However, you will see that as with other valuation methodologies and techniques, a one-size-fits-all method does not exist. In every case, the valuator must use his or her judgment and experience to choose the appropriate discount or premium percentage.

If you determine that a discount or premium is justified, you apply it to the final value you have calculated for the company. Therefore, you would not make allowances for discounts or premiums during the valuation process when you are determining the appropriate earnings or discount or capitalization rate. In addition, you should apply discount rates sequentially rather than add them together. If you are valuing a 10% ownership share of a closely held company, you might apply a 20% lack of marketability discount to the total value of the business to reflect its illiquidity. Then you might apply a 30% minority interest discount to the 10% of the company after taking the lack of marketability discount. If you determined that the company was worth $100,000 the discounts would work as follows:

$100,000 value – 20% lack of marketability discount = $80,0000

CHART 23-1

$80,000 value x 10% ownership share = $8,000

$8,000 value of 10% share – 30% minority interest discount = $5,600

If you were to simply add the discounts together, you would get a different, incorrect result as follows: ($100,000 – 50% combined discounts) x 10% = $5,000. In valuation situations that may ultimately go to court or be challenged by the taxing authorities, taking your discounts separately better indicates the theory behind the discounts. In addition, if the court were to disallow one of your discounts, you would still have the other one. If you lump them together, as the court sometimes does, you may be completely out of luck.

Minority Interest Vs. Noncontrolling Interest

A *minority interest* is an ownership share of less than 50%. A *noncontrolling interest* is any ownership interest, regardless of size, which does not have the right or the power to control the business. For example, two 50% owners of a business each have noncontrolling interests even though neither one of them is a minority shareholder. In situations where a company issues nonvoting stock, the nonvoting shareholders may have a majority of the stock, but you would apply a lack of control discount to their stock because they cannot control the actions of the company.

Minority Interest Discounts

Minority interest discounts are a misnomer. Although you do take a minority interest discount for minority interests, you can also use this discount in other situations where the ownership interest has a lack of control. Consequently, the appropriate term is the more unwieldy "discount for lack of controlling interest." These terms are used interchangeably in valuation situations, even though they technically have different meanings.

What does having a controlling interest in a company get you besides a fancy title like "Chairperson of the Board"? In *Valuing Small Businesses & Professional Practices,* Third Edition (McGraw-Hill, 1998), Shannon Pratt, et al. list the following benefits and rights of ownership control:

1. Appoint management
2. Determine management compensation and perquisites
3. Set policy and change the course of business
4. Acquire or liquidate assets
5. Select people with whom to do business and award contracts
6. Make acquisitions
7. Liquidate, dissolve, sell out, or recapitalize the company
8. Sell or acquire treasury shares
9. Register the company's stock for a public offering
10. Declare and pay dividends
11. Change the articles of incorporation or bylaws

In closely held businesses, the owners often appoint themselves as the managers, so controlling owners control not only the big picture corporate activities but also the day-to-day business activities of the firm. This is why investors may pay a premium for a controlling ownership interest and why they expect a discount for a minority or noncontrolling interest.

Determining what constitutes a majority interest is not always so easy. At first glance, someone who owns a 51% share of a company would appear to be in control. This is generally true for most of the ownership prerogatives listed above, but some states have enacted legislation to protect minority shareholders in certain situations. For example, some states require a two-thirds supermajority to approve major actions such as mergers, liquidations, or sales. In those states, someone owning just over one-third of the stock could block those initiatives. Although that person would not be "in control," he or she could effectively prevent a 67% shareholder from having control.

Consequently, when you are determining whether to apply a discount for lack of control, you must look beyond the total percentage of ownership. In addition to looking at relevant state laws, you should review the articles of incorporation and bylaws to see if minority shareholders enjoy any special rights. You also have to understand how the total ownership of the company is distributed. For example, the minority shares you are valuing may constitute a "swing vote" in an otherwise evenly split ownership

What Is So Super About a Supermajority?

A *supermajority* is any specified percentage of votes, greater than 51%, which an organization or governmental unit can require for passage of certain types of measures. For instance, Congress must have a two-thirds majority to overturn a presidential veto. Some states require a supermajority of their legislators in order to raise taxes or make constitutional amendments. In governmental settings, the purpose of a supermajority requirement is to prevent undue control by a relatively small number of people and to encourage more discussion and inclusiveness in the process. In a corporate environment, supermajority requirements protect minority shareholders and deter hostile takeovers.

situation, which would give those shares a greater than pro rata value. On the other hand, a one-third interest may be worth less than the other two one-third interests if two of the shareholders always vote together as a block.

How to Value Minority Interests

Valuing the overall business, calculating the minority percentage, and then taking a discount for lack of control is the most common method of valuing a minority interest. You need to analyze the degree of control or lack of control the shareholder has and take into account special situations like those noted above. Other things to watch for include shareholder agreements, such as buy-sell agreements that might specify that minority shares will be valued on a pro rata basis. In addition, you may want to reconsider some of the normalizing adjustments discussed in Chapter 17. You may have added back "excess" owner compensation or other management perquisites to get a more realistic view of the income figure to use in your calculations. When you are valuing a minority interest, this shareholder would not benefit from the increased value represented by these adjustments unless management actually makes the identified changes. Taking all of these issues into consideration, discounts for lack of control range from 20 to 40% and usually fall in the 30 to 35% range.

Another method you can use to value minority interests is to compare the minority interest you are valuing to other minority interests. The best source for good comparative information would be any prior transactions of minority interests in the same company. Otherwise, you will find it very difficult to find good comparison information for minority interest sales of closely held companies. However, you can find a wealth of data regarding publicly traded minority sales because publicly traded stocks are virtually all minority interests. Of course, you will need to make adjustments for the differences in risk and marketability. Various studies show that discounts from 30 to 50% reasonably reflect the difference in marketability between otherwise similar publicly traded and closely held minority interests.

The third method for valuing a minority interest completely disregards the value you have calculated for the business as a whole. You project the expected earnings of the minority interest, i.e., dividends and sales proceeds, then you perform a discounted cash flow analysis to determine the

> Another method you can use to value minority interests is to compare the minority interest you are valuing to other minority interests.

value of the minority interest. This method works well in situations where a company pays competitive dividends to attract and keep minority capital, but the controlling ownership does not want any interference in management from minority shareholders.

A variation of the third method is the Quantitative Marketability Discount Model developed by Chris Mercer. In order to use this model, you must input the following information:

1. Expected growth rate in value from the marketable minority value today
2. Assumed dividends based on the yield of the marketable minority interest
3. Assumed growth rate of dividends
4. Assumed liquidation date
5. Required holding period return is the equity discount rate plus adjustments for specific risk

The theory behind this model makes sense, but, again, you may have difficulty determining the information that goes into the calculation. Therefore, you would normally only use this model when you believe that the discount for lack of marketability should be significantly different than that produced by using the restrictive stock studies or the pre-IPO studies.

Lack of Marketability Discounts

What is marketability? Marketability is synonymous with liquidity—it is the ability to sell an investment for cash, at its fair market value, in a short period of time, and with a minimum transaction cost. Marketability is what investors in the public securities market have—the ability to call their broker or get on the Internet and sell their investment in a matter of seconds at the going price. Owners of closely held company stock do not have the luxury of marketability. Not only can't they sell their shares in seconds, but they may be lucky to sell in several months' time and with steep transaction costs. Consequently, investors will only buy closely held stock at a significant discount. This means that almost all closely held shares, controlling and noncontrolling interests alike, are eligible for a lack of marketability discount.

Why Is Restricted Stock Restricted?

A company that sells restricted stock, also known as letter stock, outside of the public marketplace is not subject to the registration rules of the SEC, so they are prohibited from selling their stock to the public for a certain period of time. One source of restricted stock is stock held by the original owners of a company that has gone public. Another source is public companies that issue letter stock to make acquisitions or attract additional capital. The issuance of restricted stock is quicker and easier than going through the costly and laborious process of registering with the SEC. Generally, the restrictions on letter stock lapse in about two years so that the investors can eventually sell their shares in the public marketplace.

Determining a Reasonable Discount

As with so many concepts in the business valuation field, the idea is straightforward, but getting to the right number is not so easy. How do you determine what is a reasonable discount for lack of marketability? Fortunately, several individuals and organizations have done extensive research to help quantify appropriate discounts in this area. These studies are called restrictive stock studies and initial public offering studies.

Restrictive stock studies are based on observing the discounts on transactions of restricted shares of publicly traded companies compared to the freely traded shares of the same company. Restricted stock is the same as publicly traded stock except that it can't be traded for a certain period of time, so these transactions isolate the marketability factor. Over ten individuals and organizations have conducted major restrictive stock studies over the last thirty years. The average discounts that the researchers quantified ranged from 13 to 36%, with the majority in the 21 to 35% range. Even though holders of restricted stock can't sell their investment publicly for a period of time, they do have marketability in the future. This would imply that the restricted stock discounts would be less than the discounts applicable to closely held shares that do not have a guaranteed liquidity event in their future. So you still have to answer the question: How much more is the discount for lack of marketability for closely held shares than the lack of marketability discounts based on the restrictive stock studies?

The pre-IPO discount studies are based on analyzing the SEC registration statements that firms must complete before they can offer their shares to the public. The information in these public statements allows researchers to compare the prices of private transactions with the IPO price and the later market price. The pre-IPO studies indicate that the average price differential between public and private companies ranges from 40 to 63%. This is consistent with the data from the restrictive stock studies, and it answers the question posed above—the additional discount applicable to closely held shares compared to restrictive shares is in the 20–25% range.

Like the restrictive stock studies, the data for the pre-IPO studies has been analyzed for the last thirty years. Willamette Management Associates and John Emory Sr., ASA were the first two researchers to study pre-IPO information to quantify lack of marketability discounts. They have continued to update their information and their most recent research is showing discounts in the 40–45% range. Philip Saunders Jr., Ph.D. analyzed the Emory research and found: "Other things being equal, the minimum value for a discount on a pre-IPO transaction is 25%. The discount increases 15 to 20 basis points for every day that separates a pre-IPO transaction from the IPO. When the anticipated liquidity event is five months away, the discount, other things being equal, is estimated to be about 50–55% " ("Marketability Discounts and Risk in Transactions Prior to Initial Public Offerings," *Business Valuation Review*, Vol. 19, No.4, December 2000.)

What does this mean for shares of the typical closely held company that is never going to have an IPO? These stocks would be in the category of being at least five months away from a liquidity event, so the place to start for a lack of marketability discount would be in the 50% range.

Factors Affecting Marketability Discounts

- Uncertain prospects and time horizon for a sale
- Size of the company and the block of stock
- Restrictive provisions on the stock
- Availability and quality of financial information
- Shareholder "put" rights
- Payment of dividends
- Potential buyers

You will need to consider each of the above items when you are trying to determine an appropriate marketability discount. For example, if the company has interested buyers, you would take a lesser discount than if the company had not been able to identify any potential buyers. Likewise, if the company paid regular dividends, the discount would be less than if they paid no dividends because the potential buyer has some prospect of near-term return. Small companies are generally riskier than large companies, so you would apply a greater lack of marketability discount to these companies to reflect the risk aversion of investors. If you decide that some of these items affect the applicable discount, you will have to use your subjective judgment to pick an appropriate percentage. Despite all of the empirical research in this area, you will not find a formula or a percentage related to each of the factors. However, you should generally choose discounts that fall within the range of the empirical studies.

Other Discounts

Minority interest discounts and lack of marketability discounts are the two most common types of discounts you will see. In fact, you should consider whether a lack of marketability discount is warranted in virtually every closely held business valuation. Also, remember that minority interest discounts really are discounts for lack of control, so you should look beyond the percentage of stock you are valuing to the underlying issues of control, including voting rights, undivided interests, veto power, swing votes, relationships with other shareholders, etc.

Another specialized situation in which you can apply a discount is when you have a "key person" who would be difficult to replace. Often this is the owner, but it could be an employee who is responsible for a major part of the business or has some specialized knowledge that is integral to the success of the firm. The IRS refers to this situation in Revenue Ruling 59-60 by acknowledging that the loss of such a person could reduce the value of the stock, especially if the company does not have adequately trained people capable of replacing the key person. You could also take this risk into account by using a higher discount rate instead of taking a valuation discount after the whole business was valued.

A derivation of the lack of marketability discount is a discount for restrictive agreements. Sometimes the buy-sell agreements or other corporate documents will contain provisions relating to voting rights, limitations on the sale of the stock, income and dividend distribution policies, etc. The more restrictive these provisions are, the greater the discount. In cases like these, taking a special discount is more appropriate than increasing the discount rate you use to calculate the value of the company because these items don't affect the day-to-day running of the company. Also, they could be changed if a new owner took over the helm.

IRS discounts should not be a separate category, but sometimes they appear to be since they often are different than the discounts that professionals use. Even if you rigorously calculate a valuation discount using one of the theoretically sound methods discussed above, you need to know what the IRS usually accepts. When you are dealing with the IRS, the theoretical soundness of your methodology and calculations may be impeccable, but they can use different reasoning to come up with a different discount. Consequently, you need to review any Tax Court or other cases before you apply your final discount in a valuation that may go to Tax Court or otherwise be contested. Generally, the Tax Court accepts valuation discounts at significantly lower rates than the empirical studies and other methodologies indicate. This does not mean that you need to have your discount in a "safe-harbor" range, but you should be able to convincingly argue why you are taking a greater discount than the ones the IRS traditionally accepts. The NACVA publication, *Business Valuations: Fundamentals, Technique & Theory* (Black & Isom Associates, 1995), lists the following ranges of discounts that the IRS has historically accepted:

- Minority interest discounts: 30–35%
- Lack of marketability discounts: 20–25%
- Restrictive agreement discounts: 30–35%

What Are "Put" Rights?

"Put" rights are a type of option whereby the holder has a guaranteed contract to sell his or her stock to another person or organization at a specified time and price or at a time and price that will be determined based on the criteria specified in the contract. In other words, put rights create a market for the stock and thereby eliminate the need for a lack of marketability discount. You will most frequently see put rights when an ESOP is one of the owners of the company's stock.

Control Premiums

A control premium is the additional amount a buyer would pay to purchase a controlling interest in a company. You can refer back to the list at the beginning of this chapter to see why someone would want to have a controlling interest. However, you should only apply a control premium if you think that the potential buyer can increase the value of the business after the purchase. If, on the other hand, the potential buyer has the philosophy "if it ain't broke, don't fix it," you wouldn't apply a control premium because nothing is going to change.

One of the obvious ways a new buyer could increase the value of the company is by getting rid of owners with inflated salaries and perquisites and having that savings go straight to the bottom line. Be careful not to "double dip" if you have already adjusted the financial statements to add these inflated expenses back to income. However, a new owner could create additional value by having better management, systems, etc. Another possibility is that genuine synergy exists between the two companies, so the transaction will enhance productivity and profitability. And finally, the individual assets of the company may be more valuable than the ongoing business, so a purchaser may be willing to pay a premium with the idea of selling off the assets at a profit.

How are control premiums calculated? *Mergerstat Review*, published by Houlihan, Lokey, Howard, and Zukin, compiles statistics on mergers and acquisitions. The difference between the price per share before the announcement of a buy out and the price per share offered by the buyer is the control premium or acquisition premium. The average control premiums reported by *Mergerstat Review* are in the 30–40% range. *Mergerstat Review* lists transactions by SIC Codes, so you can perhaps find very relevant data from your same industry. Do not just blindly apply a control premium in the 30–40% range if you are valuing a controlling interest. Analyze the specific facts and circumstances of the company you are valuing to determine if a premium is warranted.

Determining the appropriate valuation discount or premium is one of the most difficult aspects of business valuation. It is also one of the most highly contested aspects of business valuations that go to court. Consequently, you should consult a professional business valuation analyst regarding any valuation that could go to court, e.g., gift and estate valuations, valuations for divorce purposes, and other litigation. The next chapter will focus on how you work with a valuation professional and what to expect.

> **Chapter 24**

Engaging a Valuation
Professional

Part One

Part Two

Part Three

Part Four

Part Five

Part Six

PART SIX: COMPLEX BUSINESS VALUATION CALCULATIONS AND ANALYSIS

■ CHAPTER 21 Projecting Future Income ■ CHAPTER 22 Capitalization and Discount Rates
■ CHAPTER 23 Valuation Discounts and Premiums ■ CHAPTER 24 Engaging a Valuation Professional

Why Do You Need a Professional?

The short answer to this question is that business valuation is a complex field and you may not have the skills and experience to do it yourself. Valuing a business is more complex than a company's annual tax return, so it makes sense that if you hire a CPA or other tax professional to prepare your company tax returns, you would hire a professional to value your business. In addition, depending on the purpose of the valuation, the outcome of the valuation may have financial consequences that will affect you for years to come. For example, if you are selling your company, this is your one chance to negotiate a good price. Or, if you are getting divorced, you may have to exchange most of your other assets in order to keep your business. If you are using the valuation to make gifts, the IRS can come back and challenge your valuation, which might cost more in taxes and definitely will cost some time and money to resolve the issue.

Chapters 3 through 6 discuss many of the business, tax, and other reasons for having your company valued. Many of the purposes for business valuation, such as buy-sell agreements, estate planning, property division for divorce, and litigation are inherently adversarial. This means that your valuation may be challenged, either in negotiations or in court. If your matter were to go to court, you would want to have a professional valuation that can withstand scrutiny. You may also need to have an expert, usually the person who prepared your valuation, go to court on your behalf and testify as an expert witness about the valuation. Sometimes you may be able to avoid litigation simply by having a professional valuation because the other party knows that you hired a qualified valuation analyst rather than coming up with a self-serving value on your own.

> The outcome of the valuation may have financial consequences that will affect you for years to come.

Business Valuation Service Offerings

Business valuation professionals offer a wide range of services in a variety of categories. All valuators do not offer all the services listed below, but most of them will offer a number of services that grow out of the business valuation engagement. Most services fall into one of these categories:

- Tax-related services
- Mergers and acquisitions

- Other corporate transactions
- Litigation support services
- Intangible asset valuations
- Financial statement reporting
- Employee stock ownership plans

Tax-related services generally include business valuations for estate and gift tax purposes of closely held stock, limited partnership, and LLC interests. An important aspect of these valuations is taking any appropriate discounts for minority interest or lack of control. In addition, most professional business valuators can help determine the built-in gains when a C corporation changes to an S corporation as well as valuing newly created nonvoting S-corporation stock for gifting purposes. Professional valuators can also value stock options on the upside of things and distressed companies on the downside for purposes of debt forgiveness and bankruptcy

Merger and acquisition services include performing valuations and providing advice for the purchase or sale of a closely held business or ownership interest, initial public offerings, recapitalizations, management buyouts, going private, allocating purchase price among asset classes, and leveraged buyouts. Business valuators give professional advice in the areas of proposed transactions, structuring deals, negotiations, providing fairness and solvency opinions, assisting with bank and other financing, and providing referrals to other professionals such as bankers, business brokers, qualified intermediaries, CPAs, and attorneys.

The valuator's role in other corporate transactions can include business valuations for dissenting minority shareholder issues, buy-sell agreements and other shareholder agreements, life insurance planning and funding, financial restructuring, and valuation of nonstandard classes of debt, equity, and preferred stock. Professional business valuators can go beyond calculating the value of the business for these purposes but can also advise management along the way as they implement any of these procedures. In addition, a professional valuator can serve as either a mediator or an arbitrator in valuation disputes that have not gotten to the litigation stage.

The litigation support area provides opportunities for an experienced business valuator. Valuing closely held businesses for equitable distribution purposes in a divorce matter can be one of the most stressful areas of practice.

What Is a Fraudulent Conveyance?

According to the Solvency.com Web site (✑ *www.solvency.com*), "any transfer of a debtor's assets made for the purpose of hindering, delaying, or defrauding actual or potential creditors may be determined to be a fraudulent conveyance." In order to be found guilty, the creditor must prove that the debtor *intended* to put the property out of reach of a creditor. How do you prove intent? Solvency.com lists the "badges of fraud," which the courts use to indicate fraud since intent is so difficult to prove. Business valuators can help uncover these factors including whether the transfer comprised all or most of the debtor's assets, whether the debtor became insolvent soon after the transfer, whether the transfer was made to insiders or family, and whether the transfer or assets were concealed.

The divorcing parties are emotionally involved, and they often hire attorneys to discredit the valuation experts. Of course, this opens up an avenue of opportunity for valuators who consult with attorneys to prepare them for trial and the brutal cross-examination of the opposing experts. Valuators can provide rebuttal testimony in a wide range of business valuation cases where someone else performed the valuation. Other litigation support services are in the areas of business damages, securities fraud, eminent domain, bankruptcy, and fraudulent conveyances.

How can a professional valuator help you and your attorney in a litigation situation? The knowledge and experience of most business valuators can provide benefits well beyond the expected benefits of having a good, supportable business valuation and a good expert witness. In addition to providing these usual services, professional business valuators can:

1. Help you and your attorney evaluate the case
2. Review the opposing valuation reports
3. Help the attorney depose other experts and witnesses
4. Provide research on technical subjects and case law relating to business valuations
5. Evaluate settlement offers and help the attorneys write and respond to briefs.

A professional business valuator can assist with the many forms of intangible asset valuations can take many forms including:

- Trademarks, copyrights, patents, and trade secrets
- Covenants not to compete
- Computer software and proprietary technology
- Customer lists, databases, subscription lists
- Assembled work force, supplier contracts, customer contracts
- Development rights, distribution rights, drilling rights

You might need to have intangibles such as these valued for a variety of purposes including sale of the asset, purchase of adequate insurance coverage, litigation or infringement of rights, etc.

Financial statement reporting services often overlap some of the other categories. You would hire a valuation professional to value intangible assets such as the ones listed above to enable the company to correctly reflect their value on the financial statements. Purchase price allocation is an important component of financial statement reporting as well as part of the services a valuator provides in a merger and acquisition engagement. The valuation of shareholder options and restricted stock options have important financial statement ramifications. Valuation professionals also provide goodwill impairment testing as required by FASB Statement 142, Goodwill and Other Intangible Assets. Financial statements prepared according to GAAP no longer amortize goodwill over a set time period. Instead, you must determine if the goodwill is impaired and adjust the financial statements at that time. (You still amortize acquired goodwill for tax purposes over fifteen years.)

The professional business valuator plays a major role when a company has an ESOP. First, the valuator values the company to get the plan started and helps with security

Goodwill Impairment Testing

Matthew S. Maudlin of Willamette Associates discusses goodwill impairment testing in the firm's Web publication, *Insights Quarterly Journal*. In a financial statement, goodwill is whatever is left over after you allocate the purchase price of a company to its financial assets, tangible assets, and identifiable intangible assets. Goodwill does not decrease ratably over time as it did when it was an amortizable asset. Now it decreases only if it is impaired. To test for goodwill impairment, company management must provide an estimate of the fair value of the reporting units and, potentially, the fair value of each of the assets and liabilities in a reporting unit, including the intangible assets. To tell if goodwill is impaired, compare the values of the reporting units and their respective assets and liabilities to the book value on the financial statements. If the goodwill on the balance sheet exceeds the fair value of goodwill, then you write off the excess.

design and equity allocation. Then the valuator generally stays involved by performing the annual appraisals that ESOP regulations require. Finally, professional valuators can provide fairness opinions in the ESOP context to aid the trustees of the plan, in their fiduciary role, in meeting the business judgment rule. The business judgment rule says that fiduciaries should act on an informed basis, in good faith, and in the best interests of the parties to whom they have a fiduciary responsibility.

Finding and Comparing Business Valuation Professionals

The first step in hiring a business appraiser is to get referrals from your trusted advisors such as your CPA, attorney, banker, insurance agent, or other financial advisor. These advisors probably have experience working with professional business valuators in other client situations, so they would be in a good position to recommend an appropriately qualified person or persons to value your business. If you can't get a good recommendation from someone you know, then you can turn to the professional organizations that represent professional business valuators:

- American Institute of Certified Public Accountants (AICPA) (212-596-6200), *www.aicpa.org*
- American Society of Appraisers (ASA) (703-478-2228), *www.appraisers.org*
- Institute of Business Appraisers (IBA) (954-584-1144), *www.instbusapp.org*
- National Association of Certified Valuation Analysts (NACVA) (801-486-0600), *www.nacva.com*

These are all national organizations, but they have databases with information about their members throughout the country. In addition, many of these organizations have state or local chapters that you could contact.

Once you have selected one or a few potential appraisers, you should inquire about their qualifications. Most valuators will give you brochures or resumes that highlight their credentials, education, experience, and qualifications. See Chapter 1 for an overview of the various credentials and designations in the business valuation field. Next, you should talk with the prospective appraiser in person or on the phone to discuss his or her experience and qualifications relevant to your engagement. You should consider involving your CPA or other trusted financial advisor in this process to help you evaluate the candidates. The more specific you can be about your needs, the more targeted responses you can get to your inquiries. If you expect that your matter will go to court, you will want to make sure that the valuator has experience testifying as an expert witness. On the other hand, if you are hiring an appraiser for a nonadversarial matter, you may not want to pay a premium for someone with extensive court experience.

How Much Will It Cost?

This may not be the $64,000 question, but you can expect to pay on an hourly rate basis what you would pay an attorney or CPA. Business valuators generally charge from $150 to $300 per hour for their professional services. Of course, the actual cost of the job will depend on many factors including the purpose of the valuation, the complexity of the business, the condition of your books and records, the level of valuation report you need, and the time frame in which you need a completed report. Business valuators usually will bill litigation support services, such as depositions and expert testimony, separately from performing the valuation at their hourly rate.

Business valuators generally charge from $150 to $300 per hour for their professional services.

The cost of a professional business valuation for a small closely held business will usually be in the $4,500 to $10,000 range, depending on the complexity and the purpose of the valuation. As you have seen from reading this book, a professional valuator analyzes a lot of quantitative and qualitative information before determining the capitalization or discount rates, valuation methods, economic earnings, and appropriate discounts or premiums that go into a valuation. The price can go up to $30,000 or more if you have a particularly complex situation that will go to litigation. Some firms charge strictly on an hourly rate basis and offer a range where they expect the price to fall. Other firms will charge a flat fee for a complete business valuation. Some valuators will charge a reduced fee, $2,500 to $3,500, for updating complete appraisals or giving an estimate of value letter.

When you are comparing proposals from different valuators, you will be looking at price, but resist the temptation to make your decision on price alone. If you need a comprehensive valuation for one of the many reasons mentioned in Chapters 4 through 6, you are making an investment with future implications. As with most things, you usually get what you pay for. Make sure you are comparing apples with apples—compare the appraisers' credentials, experience levels, references, litigation history, communication skills, commitment to a time frame, etc. Particularly if you anticipate litigation, an important component of your choice should be whether you and your other advisors feel comfortable working with this person. Then choose the person or firm that will best meet your needs at a fair price for the specific job at hand.

You can find business valuation services on the Web that charge less than the rates mentioned above for their services. For example, comprehensive business valuation reports are advertised at under $1,000 for businesses with sales of less than $3 million. Most of the low-cost, Web-based valuations take information that the owner has given them over the phone or via e-mail and input it into computer programs that generate valuation reports. At the lowest level, nobody would be analyzing the data, and you would not be able to use the valuator as a consultant or a witness in litigation. The benefit of these types of services is that you can get a low-cost estimate of the value of your company in a short period of time. You can use this information to get an idea of what your business may be worth for purposes of a divorce, estate planning, preliminary planning for a sale, etc. However, you should not get a "quickie valuation" and expect it to hold up to the scrutiny of the court, taxing authorities, or a determined adversary. Other business valuation firms that you can access on the Web perform comprehensive valuations with all of the due diligence of a local valuator. Consequently, the price of these valuations is usually in the $4,500 to $10,000 price range. One of the benefits of most of these firms is a quick turnaround time.

Process and Time Frame Expectations

You can see from reading this book that the process of performing a business valuation is a complex one. Consequently, you should expect that the process will normally take from several weeks to several months to complete. You can help speed up the process by having good records and being responsive to the appraiser's questions and requests for additional information. If for some reason you have a "rush job," most valuators will try to accommodate you, but they may charge a premium for their services because they have to put other clients' work on hold and work overtime to get your job done.

What is the process? Once you have selected the valuator and agreed on the scope of the engagement and the price, the next step is to formalize that agreement. The appraiser should send you a standard engagement letter that summarizes everything you have agreed upon. The engagement letter will specify, at a minimum, the purpose of the valuation, the property being valued, the valuation date, the fee arrangements, and any limiting conditions. You will need to sign and return it to start the engagement. See Appendix 2 for a sample engagement letter.

The valuation analyst will present you with a list of financial and other information that he or she will need to perform the valuation. After reading this book, you should already be able to anticipate the information they will request, which is summarized in the next section below.

Generally, the valuation analyst will want to see your financial statements and tax returns for the last five years. He or she will also want to see your budgets or projections for the next five years. Otherwise, the information you will need to provide is everything relative to the qualitative and quantitative aspects of the business valuation discussed in the previous chapters of this book. See Appendix 2 for a sample document request list. To the extent that you already have this information organized and in an understandable format, you will speed up the process and thereby potentially reduce the price.

What Are Limiting Conditions?

Limiting conditions are the assumptions that the appraiser is making or asking the users to make with regard to the valuation. One important assumption that you will see with every appraisal is that the valuation is only applicable for the stated purpose and for the stated appraisal date. Other assumptions or limiting conditions might include: that the company have good legal title to all of the assets, that the company is in full compliance with all government regulations and tax laws, that information received from other people or organizations is reliable, and that the valuator is not required to testify in court about the valuation unless prior arrangements were made.

The valuator will generally want to schedule a visit to your business after he or she has had a chance to review the information you have already provided. The appraiser will want to interview you and possibly some of your employees, and he or she will want to take a tour of the facilities and learn more about how your business works. One of the main purposes of the site visit is to assess some of the qualitative factors discussed in Chapter 20. In addition, the appraiser will be looking for any indications that the business may perform differently, either positively or negatively, from the historical financial statements.

Sometimes special situations can alter the normal field visit. First, if the owner does not want any of his employees to know he or she is contemplating a transaction, the appraiser may need to visit after normal working hours. This of course limits the valuator's ability to see everyone in action and to interview employees. If you can "sell" the valuator as a consultant or other visitor while maintaining the level of secrecy you desire, you will not limit the ability of the valuator to get good information. The second difficult situation is when the appraiser is working for your soon-to-be ex-spouse or other adversary. The important thing to remember in these situations is that although someone else is paying the appraiser, the appraiser's professional standards require him or her to perform independent valuations and not be an advocate for either side. In addition, this is your chance to tell your side of the story to the appraiser, so you may want to make the most of it. On the other hand, if you are acting like you have something to hide, the appraiser may dig deeper and find something or just make unfavorable assumptions and move on.

After the field visit, the valuator will work in his or her office to develop the valuation. The valuator may contact you periodically for additional information or questions. The valuator will prepare a preliminary draft of his or her valuation report for your review. Often you will have a face-to-face meeting at this point to discuss the report and any outstanding concerns or issues. After you have reviewed the preliminary report, the appraiser will ask you to sign a client representation letter, which indicates that all of the information you have provided is correct and complete. See Appendix 2 for a sample client representation letter.

The final stage is the delivery of the final appraisal report. If the report is an estimate of value, opinion report, or short-form report, you can expect from two to ten pages of narrative. A comprehensive business valuation report will usually be from twenty to over a hundred pages long and will include a number of exhibits and resource documentation. The purpose of the valuation dictates the type and length of report you need. If the valuation is for your internal use only, the report can be relatively brief, and relatively inexpensive. However, if you need the report for tax purposes or litigation, you will need a comprehensive report.

Once the appraiser delivers the valuation report, he or she can be of additional help by providing some of the auxiliary services discussed above such as litigation support, negotiation, deal structuring, assistance with drafting agreements, tax planning, allocating the purchase price to the assets, and general business consulting. The appraiser can be a valuable resource in these areas because in addition to his or her professional expertise and experience, the appraiser now has a lot of specialized knowledge about your company, your industry, your competitors, etc.

> The purpose of the valuation dictates the type and length of report you need.

Learning from the Process and Interpreting the Reports

Interpreting the valuation report should be pretty straightforward, especially if you have reviewed a preliminary draft with the valuation analyst and had a chance to ask questions and make comments. The report will be organized in a logical, readable manner. It usually starts with an identification or cover page, which identifies the company being valued and the person or firm doing the valuation. In addition, it states the effective date of the valuation and the date the report is issued. The table of contents comes next and lists all of the important sections of the report to make it easier for the user to negotiate all of the information. Next is the opinion letter, which goes further in identifying the property being valued and the purpose of the valuation. The opinion letter states the analyst's conclusion regarding the value of the interest being valued, any limitations on the use of the report, and the analyst's signature.

The body of the report restates the purpose of the valuation, discusses the methodology and information the analyst used, and communicates the reasoning behind the appraiser's conclusion of value. The appendix includes resources that the valuator used to draw his or her conclusion of value including historical and projected financial statements, financial statement adjustments, comparative analysis data, common size statements, ratio analysis, and the reports of any other appraisers regarding real estate or other tangible assets.

Now what? You have an expensive piece of paper that tells you how much your business is worth. Presumably, you needed this valuation for a particular purpose, but can you do anything else with it? Although you should only use the valuation report itself for the intended purpose stated in the report, you can learn a lot from the process. Some of the things you can learn from doing a business valuation include:

- What your company looks like from the outside in
- The strengths and weaknesses of your company
- The need for some sophisticated gift and estate planning
- The need for implementing a succession plan
- The need for implementing buy-sell agreements, noncompete agreements, etc.
- That your insurance coverage is inadequate
- The need to reduce your debt
- The need to build value, not just profits, if you want to sell in the future
- The need to improve your records, policies, and systematization of operations

The investment you have made in time and money for your business valuation can provide returns of many times that amount if you use what you have learned to improve the business. You can enlist the help of the business valuator, your CPA, other consultants, employees, or do it yourself. How you take advantage of this opportunity for insight and improvement is not the important thing, but *doing* it is.

Resources

Appendix 1

Appendix 2

Appendix 3

Overview

Business valuation is a complex and interesting subject, especially when you are dealing with the value of your own business. This chapter has a number of resources to help you find the right business valuator for your situation and sample correspondence so you will know what to expect in the process. The Books and Periodicals section lists some of the major resources that you or your appraiser may want to consult for technical information about how to perform a business valuation as well as data sources that you can use in the process. The Web Sites section lists a number of useful Web sites where you can learn about the business valuation process, access important databases, or find out about some related topics. The Additional References section includes specific articles and Web sites that the author consulted in writing this book, in addition to the resources mentioned above.

Directories of Business Valuation Professionals

The following directories, listed in alphabetical order, are the major professional organizations in the business valuation field. These organizations grant the credentials and develop and enforce the standards that business valuators use to distinguish themselves from other professionals who are not specialists in this field. You can contact each of the organizations by phone or through their Web sites to learn more about their organization as well as to access directories of local members.

American Society of Appraisers

555 Herndon Parkway, Suite 125
Herndon, Virginia 20170
(703) 478-2228
✍ *www.appraisers.org*

American Institute of Certified Public Accountants

1211 Avenue of the Americas
New York, New York 10036
(212) 596-6200
✍ *www.aicpa.org*

The Institute of Business Appraisers

6950 Cypress Rd.
Suite 209
Plantation, Florida 33318
(954) 584-1144
✑ *www.instbusapp.org*

National Association of Certified Valuation Analysts

1111 E. Brickyard Road, Suite 200
Salt Lake City, Utah 84106
 (801) 486-0600
✑ *www.nacva.com*

Books and Periodicals

The following books and periodical references are important resources for valuing a closely held business. They include some technical and not so technical "how-to" books as well as some of the statistical and database information you will need to actually do a valuation.

Dun & Bradstreet. *Industry Norms and Key Business Ratios.* (Murray Hill, NJ: Dun & Bradstreet). Financial Research Associates. *Financial Studies of the Small Business,* 25th ed. (Winter Haven, FL: Financial Research Associates, 2002).

Friedman, Jack P. *Dictionary of Business Terms*, 3d ed. (Hauppauge, NY: Barron's Educational Services, Inc., 2000).

Ibbotson, Roger G., and Rex A. Sinqufield. *Stocks, Bonds, Bills, and Inflation 2003 Yearbook.* (Chicago: Ibbotson Associates, 2003).

National Institute of Business Management. *Executive Compensation Survey Analysis.* (McLean, VA: National Institute of Business Management, 2001).

National Association of Certified Valuation Analysts. *Business Valuations: Fundamentals, Technique & Theory.* (Salt Lake City, UT: Black & Isom Associates, 1995).

Pratt, Shannon P., Robert F. Reilly, and Robert P. Schweihs. *Valuing Small Business and Professional Practices,* 3d ed. (New York: McGraw-Hill, 1998).

Schilt, James H. "Selection of Capitalization Rates-Revisited," *Business Valuation Review,* American Society of Appraisers, June 1991, p. 51.

Sibson Consulting. *2003 Officer Compensation Report*. (New York: Aspen Publishers, Inc., 2003).

Simmons, Chad. *Business Valuation Bluebook*. (Tempe, AZ: Facts on Demand Press, 2002).

Troy, Leo. *Almanac of Business and Industrial Financial Ratios*. (Englewood Cliffs, NJ: Prentice Hall, 2002).

West, Tom. *The Business Reference Guide*. (Niantic, CT: Business Book Press, 2003).

Yegge, Wilbur M. *A Basic Guide for Valuing a Company*. (New York: John Wiley & Sons, 1996).

Web Sites

The following Web sites have a wealth of information about business valuation and related topics. You can access "how-to" information, major statistical and database information, and learn more about a variety of business, economic, and finance topics.

✑ *www.appraisalfoundation.org*—This is the Web site of the Appraisal Foundation. The Appraisal Foundation is the parent organization for the Appraisal Standards Board and the Appraiser Qualifications Board. One of its missions is disseminating information about USPAP.

✑ *www.balancedscorecard.org*—This Web site explains the Balanced Scorecard approach to strategic management pioneered by Robert Kaplan and David Norton.

✑ *http://finance.yahoo.com*—A Web site that publishes timely news in the business and finance arenas.

✑ *www.BizStats.com*—This Web site contains useful business statistics.

✑ *www.bls.gov*—This is the Bureau of Labor Statistics Web site. You can access state and local information regarding unemployment in general and in some specific industry segments.

✑ *www.businesstown.com*—A comprehensive Web site dealing with all things business. A good resource for a variety of topics.

✍ *www.businessweek.com*—The *BusinessWeek* magazine Web site that includes the Industry Outlook.

✍ *www.bvlibrary.com*—A business valuation Web site with links to research, data directories, and other information and resources for business valuations.

✍ *www.cbiz-onesource.com/valuationgroup/*—This is a very informative Web site that discusses many important topics related to business valuation.

✍ *www.ceband.com/se/course/sbvpreview/*—This Web site contains a series of modules you can use to learn about many facets of business valuation.

✍ *www.collaborative-divorce.com/*—This Web site of the Collaborative Divorce Lawyers Association of Connecticut has a lot of good general information about collaborative divorce.

✍ *www.constructionequipment.com/economics/index.asp*—This Web site has good information and statistics about general economic indicators as well as industry-specific data.

✍ *www.cpa2biz.com*—A Web site sponsored by the AICPA, which includes the *CPA Letter* and other resources for business, accounting, and finance.

✍ *www.divorceinfo.com*—A Web site with information regarding all aspects of divorce, including business valuation.

✍ *www.dixonodom.com/bv_quickref.htm*—This is the Web site for Dixon Odom PLLC, Certified Public Accountants and Consultants. It gives a good overview of business valuation issues, concepts, and terms.

✍ *www.dol.gov*—This is the U.S. Department of Labor Web site, which reports economic information from the Bureau of Labor Statistics such as the Consumer Price Index, Producer Price Index, unemployment rates, etc.

✍ *www.equalityinmarriage.org*—This Web site of the Equity in Marriage Institute has a lot of good practical advice about prenuptial and postnuptial agreements and how to discuss business and financial issues with your partner.

✍ *www.familybusinessinstitute.com*—This is the Web site of the Family Business Institute, which is devoted to helping family businesses operate successfully and implement workable succession plans.

✍ *www.federalreserve.gov/releases/*—Selected interest rates updated daily.

✍ *www.finance.cch.com*—The Financial Planning Toolkit here includes articles, financial calculators, and planning tools related to personal finance issues.

✍ *www.hoovers.com*—The Hoovers Online Web site contains information and statistics about different industries and businesses.

✍ *www.ibba.org*—The Web site of the International Business Brokers Association, Inc. You can find resources related to selling or purchasing a business and finding a broker.

✍ *www.industrylink.com*—A Web site that links to industry databases.

✍ *www.investorwords.com*—A comprehensive glossary of business and finance words.

✍ *www.irs.gov*—The Internal Revenue Service Web site, which has many resources relating to tax issues and small businesses, including the *Corporate Sourcebook* of income statistics.

✍ *www.jsc.nasa.gov*—A Web site with inflation calculators using the CPI.

✍ *www.law.cornell.edu/uniform/vol9.html*—This Web site provides a Uniform Matrimonial, Family, and Health Laws Locator so you can check out the laws in different states.

✍ *www.mergerstat.com*—A Web site containing global mergers and acquisitions information and access to extensive databases on a fee basis.

✍ *www.nationalbizval.com*—This Web site gives a good overview of the business valuation process and important concepts.

✍ *www.rmahq.org*—The RMA Annual Statement Studies Online.

✍ *www.sba.gov*—This is the Small Business Administration Web site; it contains statistics about small business, news, laws and regulations, and links to other resources.

✍ *www.standardandpoors.com*—The Standard and Poor's Web site includes access to the *Standard & Poor's Industry Surveys* and the *US Industry and Trade Outlook*.

✍ *www.smartmoney.com*—This Web site has a variety of business, economic, and personal finance information and tools.

✍ *http://taxes.yahoo.com*—This Web site contains tax tools including rate schedules, tax tips, tax forms, tax calculators, and resources to help with planning, finding an accountant, and understanding tax and financial issues.

✍ *http://research.thomsonib.com*—The Thomson Research Web site includes reports on market and industry trends.

✍ *www.toolkit.cch.com*—The Business Owner's Toolkit includes articles and resources for the business owner.

✍ *www.ustreas.gov*—The Web site of the U.S. Treasury Department.

✍ *www.woodsandpoole.com*—The Woods & Poole Economics Web site that has links to county, state, and metropolitan area economic and demographic data.

Additional References

In addition to the resources listed previously, the following books, articles, and Web sites were consulted and incorporated into this book. Many of the topics referenced below were just touched on in the book, so you may want to check out these resources for more insight on particular themes. You may find some of these interesting reading and others reminiscent of being back in school.

American Heritage Dictionary of the English Language, 4th ed. (Boston: Houghton Mifflin, 2000).

Ask Dr. Math. "Compound Interest-Rule of 70," (✍ *http://mathforum.org/ library/drmath/view/54615.html*).

Allee, Verna. "The Art and Practice of Being a Revolutionary," *The Knowledge Management Journal*, June 1997.

Allee, Verna. "Intangible Assets and Value Creation," (✍ *www.vernaallee.com/ primary%20pages/Intangible%20Assets%20and%20Value%20Creation. html*).

Andrews, Scott. "Keys to Successful Mergers," (✍ *www.aspirenow.com/ leader_0302_successful_mergers.htm*).

Apostolou, Barbara, John M. Hassell, and Sally A. Webber. "Forensic Expert Classification of Management Fraud Risk Factors," *Journal of Forensic Accounting*, Vol.1 2000, pp. 181–192.

Berg, Adriane G. "Prenuptial Agreements Take Away the Financial Pain," *http://moneycentral.msn.com/articles/family/wed/1436.asp*.

Bernstein, Ronald. "The Basics of Stock Appreciation Rights and Phantom Stock," *www.fed.org/onlinemag/jan03/tips.htm*.

Best Practices, LLC. "What Is Benchmarking?" *www.best-in-class.com/site_tools/faq.htm*.

Borglum, Keith. "Value vs. Price in Medical Practice Appraisal," (*www.medicalpracticeappraisal.com/valuevsprice.html*).

Burton, Jonathan. "Revisiting the Capital Asset Pricing Model," *Dow Jones Asset Manager*, May/June 1998, pp. 20–28.

Carroll, Robert Todd. "Alchemy," (*http://skepdic.com/alchem.html*).

Colo, Michael. "IPO: Is It Appropriate?" (*www.ps-nc-law.com/infocenter/Merger_Acquisitions/IPOArticle_May_2000.as*p)

Del Vecchio, John. "The Dividend Discount Model," *www.fool.com/research/2000/features000406.htm*.

DiStefano, Paul J., and G. Edward Kalbaugh. "Equity-based Compensation Programs," *www.roughnotes.com/rnmag/february99/02p78.htm*.

Divorcemoney.com. "Alimony Recapture (Excessive Alimony Front Loading)," *www.divorcemoney.com/tax/Recapture.html*.

Dubin, Arlene G. *Prenups for Lovers: A Romantic Guide to Prenuptual Agreements*. (Villard Books, 2001).

Emory, John D., Sr. and John D. Emory, Jr. "Empirical Studies on Marketability Discounts," Presented to the 2002 NACVA Annual Business Valuation Conference, May 23, 2002 in San Diego, California.

Federal Reserve Bank of Minneapolis. "The History of Money," *http://minneapolisfed.org/econed/curric/history.cfm*.

Feldman, Stanley J. "Business Valuation 101: The Five Myths of Valuing a Private Business," *www.score.org/guest/feldman.html*.

Forecasts.org. "Real Gross National Product." *www.forecasts.org/data/data/GNP96.htm*.

Graduate Management Admission Council. "MBA Salaries and Bonuses," *www.gmac.com/gmac/SurveysandTrends/CorporateRecruitersSurvey 2002/MBASalaries*.

"Salary and Compensation," ✑ *www.gmac.com/gmac/SurveysandTrends/
CorporateRecruitersSurvey2002-03_related/SalaryandCompensation.htm*

Goldman, Michael. "Valuation Issues: Capitalization, Discounting and
Discounts," ✑ *www.michaelgoldman.com/valuation_-_discounting.htm.*

Greenspan, Alan. "Testimony of Chairman Alan Greenspan Before the Joint
Economic Committee, U.S. Congress, November 13, 2002." ✑ *www.
federalreserve.gov/boarddocs/testimony/2002/20021113/default.htm.*

Hamilton Capital Partners. "A Practical Guide for Preliminary Valuations in
the Merger and Acquisition Arena," ✑ *www.hamiltonllc.com/pract_
val_guide.htm.*

Hoovers Online. "IPO Scorecard Stats and Industry Breakdown."
✑ *www.hoovers.com/global/ipoc/index.xhtml.*

IPO Maven. "Given Imaging Breaks IPO Lull."
(✑ *www.123jump.com/ipomaven.htm*), March 1, 2003.

Johnson, Paul M. "Gross National Product (GNP)."
✑ *www.auburn.edu/~johnspm/gloss/GNP.html.*

Kerrigan, Karen. "Will Small Business Regulatory Costs Bottom Out in 2003?"
✑ *www.sbsc.org/LatestNews_Action.asp?FormMode=SmallBusBriefs&ID=140.*

LaPray, Joseph, and William C. Herber. "Business Control Premiums:
Apply with Caution," ✑ *www.shenehon.com/Library/valuation_
viewpoint/business2.htm.*

Legal Café. "Frequently Asked Questions about Prenuptial Agreements,"
✑ *www.courttv.com/legalcafe/family/preup/prenup_background.html.*

Lemberg, Paul. "Next Year's Planning: The Critical Factors for Success,"
✑ *www.lemberg.com/nextyearsplanning-criticalfactors.html.*

Lerner, Robert L "The Mechanics of the Commodity Futures Market,"
✑ *www.mtlucas.com.*

Lewis, Jone Johnson. "Married Women's Property Act New York State, 1849,"
✑ *http://womenshistory.about.com/library/ency/blwh_married_women_
property_1848.ht.*

Limited Liability Company Web site. "The Basics: What is It?—Who Needs
It?—Why Should I Care?" ✑ *www.llcweb.com/Basics.htm.*

Lowe, Keith. "Why You Need Key Man Insurance,"
✑ *www.entrepreneur.com/article/0,4621,303635,00.html.*

Marketscreen.com. "Correlation Analysis," ✑ *www.marketscreen.com/help/
atoz/default.asp?Num=37.*

Maudlin, Matthew S. "Goodwill Impairment Testing," ✐ *www.willamettein sights.com/02/goodwill.html.*

McKenzie, Robert E. "Reasonable Compensation," ✐ *www.mckenzielaw.com/reasonable.htm.*

Mercer, Christopher Z. "The Quantitative Marketability Discount Model Revisited," ✐ *www.bizval.com/publications.*

Miller, Warren D. "Unsystematic Risk and Valuation," *The CPA Letter,* ✐ *www.cpa2biz.com/ResourceCenters/Business+Performance+ Management/Controllership/2000_11_pubs_cpaltr_nov_supps_busind_ unsystematic_ri_04074.htm.*

Mintmark.com "Money Past and Present," ✐ *www.mintmark.com/moneyhistory.htm.*

Mitchell, Matthew. "Technological Change and the Scale of Production." ✐ *http://ideas.repec.org/a/red/issued.*

Moneychimp.com. "Capital Asset Pricing Model," ✐ *www.moneychimp.com/articles/risk/classes.htm.*

Moore, Chris. "Unraveling the Size Effect," ✐ *www.elon.edu/ipe/moore.pdf.*

Moorhead Management Services. "Behind the Scenes of In-depth Financial Statement Analysis," ✐ *www.moorheadmgmt.com/scene/income statement.htm.*

Nasdaq Stock Market, Inc. "Form 10-K, Annual Report Pursuant to Section 13 or 15(d) of the Securities and Exchange Act of 1934 for Fiscal Year End December 31, 2001."

National Center for Policy Analysis. "Technology Spurred Productivity Growth." ✐ *www.ncpa.org/iss/eco/2002/pd031202f.html.*

Obringer, Lee Ann. "How Franchising Works." ✐ *http://money.howstuff works.com/franchising.*

Ohio State University Department of History. "Temperance & Prohibition," ✐ *http://prohibition.history.ohio-state.edu/.*

Peed, Koross, Finkelstein & Crain, P.A. "Should Fair Value Include a Strategic Premium?" *Valuations Concepts Newsletter,* Fall 1999, ✐ *www.pkfccpa.com/ pkfc/home.nsf/public/C744551EEE8A1CC685256A6300613A93*

Peter, Laurence J., and Raymond Hull. *The Peter Principle: Why things always go wrong.* (New York: William Morrow & Company, Inc., 1969).

Pike, Steve and Anna Rylander and Goran Roos. "Intellectual Capital Management and Disclosure," *The Strategic Management of Intellectual*

Capital and Organizational Knowledge: A Selection of Readings. (New York: Oxford University Press, 2001).

Quickmba.com. "Terminal Value,"
 ℮*www.quickmba.com/finance/terminal-value/*.

Rushforth, Layne T. "Postnuptial Property Agreements,"
 ℮*http://rushforth.net/answers5.html*.

Saunders, Philip, Jr. "Control Premiums and Minority Discounts,"
 ℮*www.philipsaunders.com/control.htm*.

Saunders, Philip, Jr. "Marketability Discounts and Risk in Transactions Prior to Initial Public Offerings," ℮*www.philipsaunders.com/marketability.htm*.

Savage, Terry. "Say 'I do' with a contingency plan in hand,"
 ℮*http://moneycentral.msn.com/articles/family/basics/6353.asp*.

Scaruffi.com. "Index of the World Countries by Gross National Product in Current Exchange Dollar," ℮*www.scaruffi.com/politics/gnp.html*.

Sheeler, Carl Lloyd. "Considerations in Valuing a Law Practice,"
 The Valuation Examiner, March/April 2001, pp. 6–9.

Sheeler, Ray. "Fairness Opinions and the Closely Held Business,"
 ℮*www.cbiz-onesource.com/valuationgroup/page.asp?pid=1526*.

Siebert, Mark C. "Risk Versus Reward in the Franchise Equation,"
 ℮*www.franchise1.com/articles/*.

Smeach, Les. "Does the 'Fair Market Value' Standard Provide for Equitable Distribution in a Marital Dispute?"
 ℮*www.schlabig.com/valuations/02_02.html*.

Smith, Susan K. "Prenuptial Agreements in Connecticut,"
 ℮*www.smith-lawfirm.com/div_pre-nups.htm*.

Spragins, Ellyn. "Ways and Means, Protecting Your Assets, Key-man Insurance Can Help Buffer a Company if It Loses a Star,"
 ℮*www.fortune.com/fortune/careers/articles/0,15114,367767,00.html*.

Stritof, Sheri and Bob Stritof. "For Love or Money, the Pros and Cons of Prenuptial Agreements," ℮*http://marriage.about.com/library/weekly/aa020801a.htm*.

Themediationgroup.com. "Pre and Postnuptial Agreements,"
 ℮*www.themediationgroup.com/pre_and_post_nuptial_agreements.htm*.

Trugman, Gary. "The Excess Earnings Method—Let the User Beware,"
 Valuation Trends, Winter 1999, ℮*www.trugmanvaluation.com/Archive/Winter1999.html*.

U.S. Patent Office, "Frequently Asked Questions about Patents,"
✎ www.uspto.gov/web/offices/pac/doc/general/index.html.

U.S. Treasury Department. "The Basics of Treasury Securities,"
✎ www.publicdebt.treas.gov/of/ofbasics.htm.

Valueinsights.com. "Axiology: The Science of Value,"
✎ www.valueinsights.com/axiology1.html.

Wall, Ginita. "Divorce and Taxes: Avoiding the Pitfalls," *Journal of Financial
Planning*, August 2002, pp 78–83.

Warsh, David. "Nobel-est in Economics: Three Americans Share Prize for
Corporate Finance Theories," *✎ www.boston.com/globe/search/
stories/nobel/1990.*

Willamette Management Associates, "ESOP Overview," Presented in
Durham, NC, August 6, 2002.

Yeager, Tim. *Introduction to Macroeconomics, ✎ www.econweb.com/
MacroWelcome/author.html.*

Sample
Correspondence

What to Expect

The following selections of sample correspondence include a typical engagement letter you would receive from a valuation professional and a typical client representation letter that you would have to sign. In addition, a sample document request checklist covers most of the information you will need to dig up, organize, and give to the valuator so he or she can complete the job. Of course, if you are doing your own valuation, you will want to consult these same records.

An Engagement Letter

July 31, 2003

Dr. Sally Pepper
Pepper Construction Company, Inc.
P.O. Box 1234
Durham, NC 27703

Dear Dr. Pepper:

This letter outlines our understanding of the terms and objectives of the valuation engagement.

We will perform a valuation of a 100% common equity interest in Pepper Construction Company, Inc. as of December 31, 2002. We plan to start the engagement on or about August 1, 2003, assuming receipt of the items listed in our Documents Request List by that time and (unless unforeseen problems are encountered) be completed by August 31, 2003.

The objective of our valuation will be to estimate the fair market value of a 100% common equity interest in Pepper Construction Company, Inc. The term "fair market value" is defined as follows:

The price at which the property would change hands between a willing buyer and a willing seller, neither being under a compulsion to buy or sell and both having reasonable knowledge of relevant facts.

Although our valuation is intended to estimate fair market value, we assume no responsibility for a seller's or buyer's inability to obtain a purchase contract at that price.

In performing our valuation, we will be relying on the accuracy and reliability of your historical financial statements, forecasts of future operations, or other financial data of your company. We will not audit, compile, or review your financial statements, forecasts, or other data, and we will not express an opinion or any form of assurance on them. At the conclusion of the engagement, we will ask you to sign a representation letter on the accuracy and reliability of the financial information used in the engagement. Our engagement cannot be relied on to disclose errors, fraud, or other illegal acts that may exist.

We will document the results of the engagement in a formal report. We understand that our valuation conclusion will be used for estate planning and insurance purposes, and that the distribution of the report is restricted to the internal use of the management of Pepper Construction Company, Inc. Accordingly, the report will not be distributed to outside parties to obtain credit or for any other purposes. If for any reason we are unable to complete the valuation engagement, we will not issue a report as a result of the engagement.

We have no responsibility to update our valuation report for events and circumstances that occur after the date of its issuance.

We estimate our fee for this service to be no greater than $10,000. If we encounter unusual circumstances that would require us to expand the scope of the engagement, we will discuss this with you before doing the additional work. Our fees will be rendered on a monthly basis and are payable upon receipt. Our valuation report will state that our fee is not contingent on the value determined by this engagement.

The fee estimate is for the valuation and valuation report and does not include any services that may be required defending our valuation report in litigation, including conferences, depositions, court appearances, and testimony. Fees for such services, if required, will be billed at our standard hourly rates.

We sincerely appreciate this opportunity to be of service to you. If you agree with the foregoing terms, please sign the copy of this letter in the space provided and return the letter to us.

Sincerely,

Heather Smith Linton, CPA, CVA
Linton & Associates, PA

Response:
This letter correctly sets forth the understanding of Pepper Construction Company, Inc.

Signature:...

Title:...

Date:...

A Client Representation Letter

Pepper Construction Company, Inc.
P.O. Box 1234
Durham, NC 27000

August 31, 2003

Heather Smith Linton, CPA, CVA
Linton & Associates, PA
P.O. Box 51220
Durham, NC 27717

Dear Ms. Linton:

In connection with your valuation of Pepper Construction Company, Inc. as of December 31, 2002, we represent to you that to the best of our knowledge and belief that:

1. We have made available to you all information requested and all information that we believe is relevant to your valuation. All significant matters of judgment have been determined or approved by us.
2. The financial statements furnished to you for the years ended December 31, 1998–2002, present the financial position of Pepper Construction Company, Inc. in conformity with Generally Accepted Accounting Principles consistently applied.
3. The income tax returns furnished to you for the years ended December 31, 1998–2002, are exact and complete copies of the returns filed with the Internal Revenue Service.
4. The Company has satisfactory title to all owned assets, and there are no liens or encumbrances on such assets nor has any asset been pledged, except as made known to you.
5. The Company has no commitments or contingent liabilities, including those arising from litigation, claims, and assessments, that are not disclosed in the financial statements identified above.

6. The Company does not have any (a) employment contracts with salaried employees, (b) stock option plans, or (c) stock redemption agreements with shareholders except to the extent indicated in written agreements furnished to you.

7. The Company is not currently negotiating the acquisition of new business interests or the disposition of existing segments or product lines.

8. The forecast of future cash flow earnings presents our assumptions and, to the best of our knowledge and belief, the Company's expected financial position, results of operations, and cash flows of the years ending December 31, 2003–2007, in conformity with the Generally Accepted Accounting Principles expected to be used by the Company during the forecast period, which are consistent with the principles that Pepper Construction Company, Inc. uses in preparing its historical financial statements. The financial forecast is based on our judgment, considering present circumstances, of the expected conditions and our expected course of action.

9. The valuation report will serve as a basis for estate planning and insurance coverage and accordingly will not be distributed to outside parties.

10. We have reviewed the preliminary draft of your valuation report, a copy of which is attached, and represent that the information about the Company presented therein is accurate and complete.

Signature:_____

Title:_____

Date:_____

A Checklist of Documents and Information

FINANCIAL STATEMENTS

___ Balance sheets, income statements, statements of cash flow, and statements of owners' equity for the last five fiscal years

___ Interim financial statements for the current year and the preceding year

___ Federal and state income tax returns for the last five years

___ Forecasts and projections for the next five years

OTHER FINANCIAL INFORMATION

___ List of cash accounts and cash equivalents

___ Aged accounts receivable summary

___ Aged accounts payable summary

___ List of marketable securities

___ List of prepaid expenses

___ Inventory summary and information on inventory accounting policies

___ Fixed asset and depreciation schedules

___ List of any items representing other significant asset balances

___ List of notes payable and other interest-bearing debt

___ List of any items representing other significant liability balances

___ Summary of leases and related lease terms for facilities, equipment, etc.

___ Details of any contingent liabilities

___ Analysis of accounts comprising major expense categories on the income statement

___ Schedule of officers' and directors' compensation and perquisites

___ Schedule of insurance in force including key-person, life, disability, casualty, liability, health

OTHER INFORMATION

___ List of shareholders or partners with the number of shares or units owned by each

___ List of subsidiaries or other businesses in which the company has an ownership interest. Please include their financial statements for the last five years.

___ History of the company including details of changes in ownership and recent offers to purchase

___ Description of the business and any business plans

___ Brochures, price lists, catalogs, or other product and company information

___ Organizational chart

___ Resumes of key personnel including age, position, education, experience, and compensation

___ Employee census including birth date, hire date, and compensation organized by functional grouping, e.g., administration, production, sales, marketing, etc.

___ Trade association memberships, relevant trade or government publications

___ List of competitors including location, size, and assessment of relative strength

___ List of the most significant customers and suppliers and the total amount of sales and purchases for each

___ List of intangible assets including patents, trademarks, copyrights, computer software, etc.

___ Details of transactions with related parties

___ Details of employee benefit plans

___ Copies of any value indicators such as appraisals or property tax assessments

___ Awards or commendations received by the company or employees

LEGAL DOCUMENTS

___ Articles of incorporation, bylaws, or other organizational documents and amendments

___ Buy-sell agreements, employment agreements, noncompete agreements, stock option agreements

___ Minutes of board of directors' meetings

___ Details of any litigation, including pending or threatened lawsuits

___ Reports or correspondence from regulatory agencies such as EPA, OSHA, IRS, EEOC

___ Franchise agreements

___ Attorney's invoices

Glossary of Terms

Glossary of Terms

This glossary covers the important terms you will need to know to maneuver in the business valuation field. More in-depth definitions and explanations are included in the body of the book where these terms are introduced.

adjusted net asset approach:
This is a valuation method that focuses on the balance sheet. You adjust the assets and liabilities to their fair market values, including intangible assets, and subtract the liabilities from the assets.

book value:
This is the net worth shown on a company's balance sheet, i.e., the historical net assets minus the net liabilities.

C corporation:
A regular corporation whose earnings are subject to double taxation. The corporate earnings are taxed at the entity level, and its shareholders are taxed individually when they receive corporate distributions such as dividends or liquidating distributions. Its shareholders have liability protection and different classes of stock.

Capital Asset Pricing Model (CAPM):
A model used to calculate the cost of capital (discount or capitalization rate) that is comprised of the risk-free rate and a risk premium that is proportionate to the systematic risk of the security or portfolio. The systematic risk, which cannot be diversified away, is represented by beta.

capitalization of earnings method:
A valuation method that capitalizes a single period measure of the economic income of a company to produce a value for the total company. You divide the earnings by the capitalization rate to arrive at the value.

capitalization rate:
The rate of interest used to convert one or a series of future payments into a single present value.

control premium:
An additional amount that a buyer would pay above the pro rata value of a business interest to gain a controlling interest in the company.

cost of capital:
The expected rate of return (discount or capitalization rate) that the market requires for a specific investment.

discounted cash flow method:
A valuation method that applies a discount rate to future projected cash flows and a terminal value to determine the present value of the company.

discount rate:
The interest rate used in the discounted cash flow method that represents the cost of capital to the company being valued.

EBITDA:
Earnings before interest, taxes, depreciation, and amortization.

ESOP:
Employee stock ownership plan is a qualified retirement plan that primarily invests in company stock, which makes the employees the indirect owners of the company.

excess earnings method:
A hybrid valuation method that capitalizes the earnings of a company that are in excess of a reasonable industry rate of return to determine the value of the intangible assets. The value of the intangibles is added to the value of the other adjusted net assets to calculate the value of the company as a whole.

fair value:
A proportional share of the total value of the company, not reduced by discounts. Fair value is usually the legal standard used in minority shareholder disputes.

fair market value:
The price at which a property would change hands between a hypothetical willing buyer and hypothetical willing seller, when neither is acting under compulsion and when both have reasonable knowledge of the relevant facts. Fair market value is the legal standard used for tax and many other valuation purposes.

GAAP:
An acronym for Generally Accepted Accounting Principles.

going concern value:
The value of all of the tangible and intangible assets of a business that is expected to continue operating into the future.

goodwill:
An intangible asset that results from the name, reputation, location, customer loyalty, standing in the community, etc. Goodwill represents the residual value of a company after all of the other assets have been valued or allocated a value.

gross national product (GNP):
It is the total dollar value of all the final goods and services produced in a one-year period. Economists use this number to determine the relative health of the economy.

initial public offering:
A corporation's first offering of stock to the public.

intangible assets:
Nonphysical assets such as patents, copyrights, trademarks, computer programs, franchises, mineral and gas rights, and goodwill that produce economic benefits for the owner.

intrinsic value:
The "true value" of a property. It represents what an investor or analyst thinks an investment is "really worth."

investment value:
The value of an investment to a particular investor. This is in contrast to the hypothetical buyers and sellers involved with fair market value.

lack of control discount:
Also known as a minority interest discount. An amount by which the pro rata value of an ownership share is reduced to reflect that the owner does not have control.

Limited Liability Company (LLC):
A form of business organization that is treated like a partnership for tax purposes and has limited liability protection for the owners similar to a corporation.

liquidation value:
The value of the assets of a company that will be sold individually and over a short period of time such as when a company is going out of business. The liquidation value is usually the lowest value for a company.

market approach:
A valuation approach that compares the subject company to similar businesses that have been sold. The difficulty is finding good comparison numbers for sales of closely held companies.

marketability:
The ability to quickly convert property to cash at the fair market value with little cost. Also known as liquidity.

minority interest discount:
Also known as the lack of control discount. An amount by which the pro rata value of an ownership share is reduced to reflect that the owner does not have control.

net book value:
Total assets minus total liabilities on a balance sheet.

premise of value:
The assumption about the type of value being determined in a business valuation. For example, going concern and liquidation value are premises of value.

rate of return:
The amount of income or loss recognized on a particular investment. You calculate the rate of return by dividing the income into the investment.

rule of thumb method:
A valuation method that uses the relationships between various factors to determine a value for a company. Usually you can find rules of thumb for various industries. For example, accounting firms are often valued at one-time gross revenues.

S corporation:
A corporation taxed under Subchapter S of the Internal Revenue Code. The income or loss of the corporation flows through to the shareholders and is taxed at a single level on their individual tax returns. The shareholders receive regular corporate liability protection and are considered employees of the corporation if they work in the business. S corporations have limits on number and type of shareholders and they cannot have two classes of stock.

standard of value:
The definition of the type of value you are calculating. Examples are fair market value, fair value, intrinsic value, and investment value. The standard of value can have a significant impact on the final value of the company.

tax basis:
The amount you pay for an asset, plus any additional costs of putting it into service, less depreciation. Gain or loss on the sale of property is calculated by subtracting the basis from the sales price.

USPAP:
An acronym for the Uniform Standards of Professional Appraisal Practice, which were issued in 1989 by the Appraisal Standards Board (ASB). Some, but not all, professional business valuation organizations are incorporating USPAP into their own standards. Critics contend that USPAP is more appropriate for real estate appraisals.

weighted average cost of capital (WACC):
The discount rate or cost of capital based on the proportionate share of the cost of debt and equity in the company's capital structure.

A

Accountant, 5

Accounting concepts, 202–204
Generally Accepted Accounting Principles, 135–137, 152, 153, 166, 176, 201

Accounting Principles Board (APB), 202

Accounts payable, 10, 23–24, 28, 206, 251–252

Accounts receivable, 10, 21–22, 28, 32, 131, 205, 208–209, 234–236, 251–252, 256

Acquisitions, mergers and, 48–49

Adjusted asset approach. *See also* Asset
accounting principles, 135–136
asset value reduction, 136
estimated earnings and rate of return, 150–156, 257, 304
example, 35–37, 141–146
in general, 4, 33, 134, 137–138, 140–141
income-based approach, 148–150
revisited, 166–169
types of assets, 134–135
using, 138–140

AICPA. *See* American Institute of Certified Public Accountants

Allee, Verna, 102

American Institute of Certified Public Accountants (AICPA), 6, 8, 135–136, 202, 344

American Society of Appraisers (ASA), 6, 7, 344

Annual Statement Studies, 262–263, 264

APB. *See* Accounting Principles Board

Appraisal Foundation, 6, 7

Appraisal Standards Board (ASB), 7

Appraiser Qualifications Board (AQB), 7

AQB. *See* Appraiser Qualifications Board

ASA. *See* American Society of Appraisers

ASB. *See* Appraisal Standards Board

Asset. *See also* Asset allocation; Earnings
asset division, 54
capital asset, 61–62
Capital Asset Pricing Model, 314–315
current asset, 249–251
discounted, 58
discussed, 204–205
fixed asset, 134, 211
intangible asset, 60–61, 76–78, 134, 164–168, 211
marked to market asset, 60–61
premise of value, 108
tax basis for, 59–61
valuation, 10–11, 34–35, 41, 60

Asset allocation, 61
depreciation and, 62–64
equitable distribution, 72

Attorney, 5–6, 57, 78, 89. *See also* Litigation

Axiology, 101

B

Balance sheet, 21–22, 28, 30–31, 134, 203–204, 212–213

Balanced Scorecard, 102–103

Banker, 5, 44

Bankruptcy, 97, 97–98, 98

Benchmarking, 247–248

Best practices, 247–248

BizStats.com, 255

Bogan, Chris, 247

Bonds, 212. *See also* Stocks
risk and, 127

Broker, 193–194

Business Reference Guide, The, 196

Business valuation
basic methods, 4
limiting conditions, 339
defined, 2
example
company overview, 17–18
economic trends, 19–20
financial statements examples, 20–27

qualitative analysis, 16–17
ratio analysis, 20–27
in general, 2–4, 10–12
history, 4–5
personnel for, 5–6
accountant, 5
attorney, 5–6
banker, 5
business broker, 5
professional organizations
costs to hire, 337–338
in general, 6–8
process/time frame expectations, 338–341
report interpretation, 341–342
selecting and comparing, 336–337, 344–345
service offerings, 332–336
purposes
financing, 118
in general, 112–113
litigation, 120–123, 333–334
partner or shareholder agreement, 117–118
purchase and sale transactions, 113–116, 333
taxes, 119, 333
uses, 8–9, 40–41
value
axiology and, 101–102
book value, 108–109, 134–135
defined, 100
equitable distribution value, 76
fair market value, 12, 55, 75–76, 104–106, 164
fair value, 76, 106
in general, 100–101, 103–104, 207–208, 227–228
going concern value, 76
intrinsic value, 13, 107–108
investment value, 12, 107
levels of, 120–121
market value, 105–106
premise of value, 108
present value, 177–178
readily ascertainable value, 93
standard of value, 12, 103–104, 109–110

STREETWISE® BOOKS

New for Fall 2003!

Low-Cost Marketing
$19.95 (CAN $31.95)
ISBN 1-58062-858-3

Business Valuation
$19.95 (CAN $31.95)
ISBN 1-58062-952-0

Also Available in the *Streetwise®* Series:

24 Hour MBA
$19.95 (CAN $29.95)
ISBN 1-58062-256-9

Achieving Wealth Through Franchising
$19.95 (CAN $29.95)
ISBN 1-58062-503-7

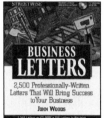

Business Letters with CD-ROM
$24.95 (CAN $37.95)
ISBN 1-58062-133-3

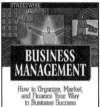

Business Management
$19.95 (CAN $29.95)
ISBN 1-58062-540-1

Complete Business Plan
$19.95 (CAN $29.95)
ISBN 1-55850-845-7

Complete Business Plan with Software
$29.95 (CAN $47.95)
ISBN 1-58062-798-6

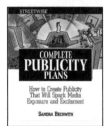

Complete Publicity Plans
$19.95 (CAN $29.95)
ISBN 1-58062-771-4

Customer-Focused Selling
$19.95 (CAN $29.95)
ISBN 1-55850-725-6

Direct Marketing
$19.95 (CAN $29.95)
ISBN 1-58062-439-1

Do-It-Yourself Advertising
$19.95 (CAN $29.95)
ISBN 1-55850-727-2

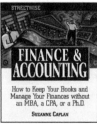

Finance & Accounting
$17.95 (CAN $27.95)
ISBN 1-58062-196-1

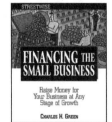

Financing the Small Business
$19.95 (CAN $29.95)
ISBN 1-58062-765-X

Get Your Business Online
$19.95 (CAN $28.95)
ISBN 1-58062-368-9

Hiring Top Performers
$17.95 (CAN $27.95)
ISBN 1-55850-684-5

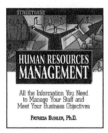

Human Resources Management
$19.95 (CAN $29.95)
ISBN 1-58062-699-8

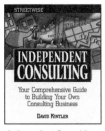

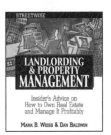
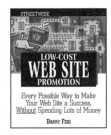
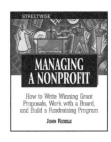

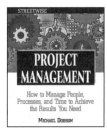
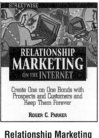
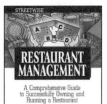

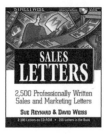
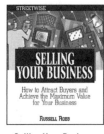

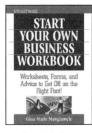
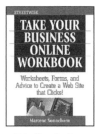